# unexpected

## Faith   Family   Flying

### in Papua New Guinea

# R I C H A R D   M A R P L E S

ISBN 978-1-64492-598-0 (paperback)
ISBN 978-1-64492-599-7 (digital)

Christian Faith Publishing, Inc.
832 Park Avenue
Meadville, PA 16335
www.christianfaithpublishing.com

Printed in the United States of America

*Jennifer*

*Sam, Matt, Nate*

*This is* our *story, but for you, words are not enough.*

*RLU*

*DLU*

# ACKNOWLEDGMENTS

THE STORIES THAT follow are entirely true, as I remember them.

For those of you that were there and remember them differently, I hope I have not offended you too deeply.

For my PNG brothers and sisters, my accounts of your culture are as I understand them, and where they are wrong, the errors are all mine. *Plis, lusim rong bilong mi.*

For the MAF missionaries that were uncles and aunts to my children, and brothers and sisters to Jennifer and me, thanks for being part of our story.

# CONTENTS

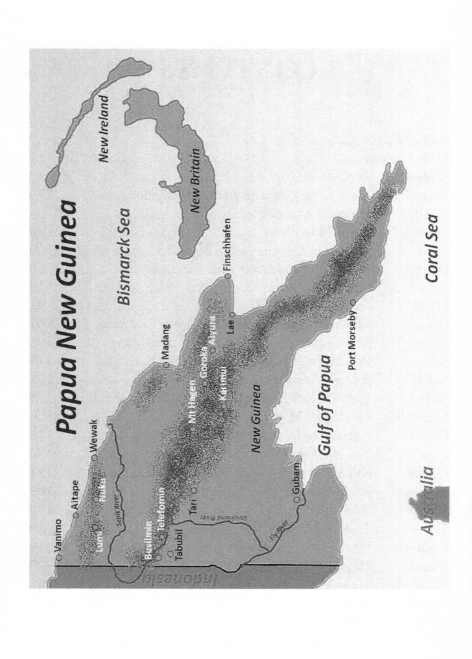

# PROLOGUE

I̲t̲ s̲t̲r̲e̲a̲k̲e̲d̲ a̲c̲r̲o̲s̲s̲ the night sky. It was more felt than seen. As if sprinting away from its own noise, attempting to capture its own silence, the apparition was long gone by the time it could be heard. Its tan colour, strangely referred to as "desert pink," blended in with the sand, a scant three hundred feet below. To the bug-eyed creatures confined inside the speeding specter, the sparse landscape was bathed in an eerie green glow. The craft gobbled up one kilometer of dunes every two seconds in a ride more akin to an old wooden roller coaster than a limousine on a newly paved road. Robotic controls jerked the machine around with no care for the comfort of the individuals inside. But then life trumps comfort every time. Lights appeared on the horizon: blindingly brilliant candles in the black night. Almost as soon as the radiance appeared, the aircraft was past it and gone—fires below the only evidence that it had even been there, the roar of engines lost in the scream of explosions. The two aviators inside the tactical jet fighter blinked tired, red-rimmed eyes behind the night-vision goggles that turned night into a green version of day. Tension slipped away as the plane climbed rapidly to a safe altitude far away from antiaircraft missiles and the men that sought to defend the dictator's realm. The fact that the weapons they had dropped had resulted in loss of life was left purposely buried in the subconscious, to be dredged up, analyzed, and accepted at a more appropriate time.

At age fourteen, this was my dream. At age twenty-four, it could have been my life. As a little boy growing up in England, all I ever wanted to do was fly. I flirted briefly with being a fireman, and fancifully a professional soccer player, but really all I wanted to do was fly fast air force jets. I was fascinated by World War II aircraft but wanted to fly the modern equivalents: Buccaneers, Lightnings,

Phantoms. As age advances, childhood memories devolve into a series of video bites. In one of those, I clearly remember my first view of a Tornado combat aircraft. I was in the kitchen at my friend Simon's house when the plane made a brief appearance on the TV news. This was the dragon I was determined to ride. Some fifteen years later, the first Gulf War erupted; and but for a change of life direction, that would have been me screaming over the dessert in the heart of a Middle Eastern night to unleash a load of bombs on a military airfield or scud missile launcher. Military pilots perform a vital sometimes dangerous duty in defense of our freedom, but for me, that was not to be my career because at age fourteen, the dream changed.

The summer after I turned fourteen, I attended a youth camp at Silver Lake Wesleyan Church Camp. I have little recollection of what we did. I am sure there was swimming and sports and chapel, but all I remember is one service. And not even the service itself, only the event and the questions. That day, I felt God calling me to be a mission pilot. Now there were two problems with that: Number one, there had been no audible voice, no herald angel, so how could I be sure that it was the voice of the Lord? Number two, I had absolutely no idea what a mission pilot did. I started to resolve the first of the problems by speaking with the camp speaker. The second, however, well, perhaps that is the essence of this story. I often tell people that if I knew then, when I was just fourteen, what I know now, I might have sought some other calling, something simpler and safer like underwater basket weaving. But the truth is, I wouldn't trade it for the world. They say that aviation is hours of boredom punctuated by moments of stark terror. Mission flying in Papua New Guinea has very little boredom, and while I didn't have any experiences that I would classify as terrifying, there certainly were moments of heightened awareness.

Those flashes of elevated adrenalin were often the result of the PNG factor: "expect the unexpected in the land of the unexpected." One of our PNG managers used to quote that anytime we had an unforeseen event. With a deep belly laugh, Poge would remind me, "Expect the unexpected in the land of the unexpected."

# INTRODUCTION

AVIATE, NAVIGATE, COMMUNICATE: the pilot's mantra and order of priorities. Fly first. Navigate second. Talk last. Just as early airplanes were imperfect, early air-to-air and air-to-ground wireless communications also lacked in perfection. Those primitive radio calls were plagued by weak signal strength and atmospheric disturbances, making straightforward messages unintelligible. The letters *B, D* and *G* can sound the same over a radio, as can *F* and *S*, and *M* and *N*. Consequently, letters were given words: *Bravo, Delta*, and *Golf* being unmistakable. The English vocabulary was reduced to some standard words and phrases applicable to the operation of aircraft. Even with improved equipment, the phonetic alphabet and standard phrases remain an integral part of aviation conversations.

My recollections of experiences with Mission Aviation Fellowship are not filed in my mind by date; they are organized according to place, aircraft, people, and event. So I share our story in true aviation fashion: twenty-six chapters for twenty-six phonetic alphabet letters; twenty-six chapters for twenty-six places, aircraft, people, or events.

# ALPHA

## -Aiyura *Gunshot*-

*TWANG!* SOUNDS LIKE the snapping of an elastic band. Possibly the noise created when checking the tension of a rope holding a couch in the bed of a pickup truck. It could also be the note created were I to try and play the guitar. *Twang!* It is also the concerning sound that overcomes the blast of two Pratt & Whitney Canada PT6 turboprop engines spinning three bladed propellers, and penetrates a pilot's noise-cancelling headset, when a 5.65 mm bullet passes through the 0.032 inch aluminum skin that comprises the body of a de Havilland Canada Twin Otter.

My high school years were undertaken at Trenton High School in Trenton, Ontario. I suspect that none of my English teachers remember me, but I certainly remember them. To this day, I can recite the copular verbs and at least the first four lines of Portia's speech in Shakespeare's play *The Merchant of Venice*. I do remember a couple of other things too. We visited the Stratford Festival Theater in Stratford, Ontario, to watch the play *Julius Caesar*. As I recall, there was a real live horse involved. I was probably supposed to remember points of a more literary nature. One thing that does stick in my mind from English class is *onomatopoeia*. I remember it because it is a cool word, like *hyperbole*. As my children grew up, I used to warn them against hyperbole when reporting on the antics of their siblings: "exaggeration for effect" was discouraged. *Onomatopoeia* is a word that sounds like what it is describing. Like *twang!* To be clear,

13

however, onomatopoeia was not the first thought in my mind when I registered the *twang!* caused by the high-velocity projectile fired from an AR-15 assault rifle meeting my airplane. In some countries where Mission Aviation Fellowship serves, a bullet intersecting the flight path may not be uncommon; but in Papua New Guinea, it most certainly falls into the category of unexpected. And in truth, it was so unexpected that is was not until much later that the reality of how close we had brushed with death became clear.

Aiyura, the scene of the incident, is located at the eastern edge of the Eastern Highlands Province, close to the border with Morobe Province. The boundary is defined by a significant escarpment where the road descends five thousand feet in little more than fifteen road kilometers through multiple turns and switchbacks. There are many significant risks to flying in Papua New Guinea, chief among them being the airstrips. But this would be due to surface condition, surrounding terrain, and associated weather, not gunfire. All areas of the PNG highlands have a deserved reputation for volatility, but this rarely impacts directly on MAF; we would only rarely be targeted. Having said that, just before our family arrived in PNG, and then again during our first year, Mission Aviation Fellowship was the victim of two armed hijacks, but both of those occurred in the Southern Highlands Province.

Aiyura is the home airstrip for SIL Aviation. Alternatively known as JAARS (originally Jungle Aviation and Radio Service), SIL Aviation is the flight department for Wycliffe Bible Translators, who in turn are alternatively known as Summer Institute of Linguistics. If that isn't confusing enough, where Aiyura is the airstrip, the home of SIL, known as the "center," is Ukarumpa. The uninitiated may be excused for any confusion since the airfield is just across the road from the center.

MAF PNG has a special partnership with SIL Aviation and also with Goroka-based New Tribes Mission Aviation (now Ethnos360 Aviation). In a country where reliable aviation information is hard to come by, sharing of intelligence is vital to a safe operation. Weather reports in particular are critical, and pilots can regularly be heard on the VHF communication radios passing their observations on conditions along with personal forecasts. "It's going off in a hurry," or "I think it will hold" are common phrases in the pilot's dialect—full of meaning for aviators, less so perhaps for those without wings. Notices to AirMen are a further vital area of data exchange. NOTAMs are a system for distributing information relating to safety of flight to and between pilots. In general, NOTAMs are managed by a government body. In PNG, perhaps because of the quantity of information and the very fluid nature of conditions, mission agencies maintain their own databases. These internal NOTAMs are shared in the cooperative spirit required as my brother's keeper. Overnight events at Duranmin several years ago demonstrate how conditions can change and just how critical this collaboration is. Equatorial jungles are not referred to as rainforests for no reason. Tropical rainstorms can drop incredible quantities of water in short periods of time, causing rivers to swell and flow with a mind of their own. Sitting in our house in an evening, the sound of the rain coming was like being on the receiving end of the charge of a thousand horses; I clearly understand the expression "rolling thunder." When the rain would reach the house, the pounding on the tin roof made conversation impossible even from just across the room. It was just that kind of rain in Duranmin that caused the swollen river to depart its banks and carve a new path, slicing off nearly a third of the runway.

The best aspect of the relationships with SIL Aviation and NTMA were the friends. Papua New Guinea is part of a poorly defined region of the south pacific identified as Melanesia. It is debatable which countries comprise Melanesia. Perhaps this is because the identity of Melanesians is not based in geography; instead, it is linguistic and cultural. Whereas Westerners will base decisions on finance, expediency, and efficiency, Melanesians base their choices in the first instance on how it will impact relationships. The creation of a bond, a connection, is the fundamental foundation for accomplishing anything. Although on the surface Westerners may be different, I do wonder if under our veneer, we also work more effectively when there is a friendship. The trust born out of mutual respect and friendship leads to accomplishment of great things.

Our first encounter with NTMA occurred during our first year in PNG while we were based in the north coast town of Wewak. I was the only MAF pilot based in Wewak, flying a Cessna 206 serving more than thirty airstrips scattered over an area of some twenty-eight thousand square kilometers. Wewak airport is not really huge, but the runway is properly paved and long enough for the single-aisle-size passenger jets. The airport hails back to World War II, with water-filled bomb craters still in evidence on the north side of the field. The original airport, from before the war, was located just a couple miles east. The MAF housing compound lies at the western end of what used to be the Wirui runway, although only those who know can see evidence of its existence. In the early years, MAF flew from the Wirui runway. Pilots could walk out the door of their house and jump in their plane. That might have been an advantage back then, but once operations moved down the road to Boram, that plus disappeared. We were left with houses located near a swamp, close to the ocean, but not close enough and beside a dusty road. People talk about watching paint dry, but in that house, we could see mould and mildew grow on the walls. By contrast, the New Tribes Mission housing compound was located on Kreer Heights. Not that the houses were significantly higher than ours, but the elevation gave them access to breeze of which we could only dream. At Boram airport, NTMA were our next-door neighbours. As I prepared my brown-and-yellow striped 206 for flight each morning, Brent and Dave would be doing the same with their red-trimmed version of the same plane. We would compare flight plans and weather reports. I always liked to know where my closest help might be should I encounter some difficulty.

There really aren't that many aircraft in PNG, and there were many days when the only aircraft in our area were MAF and NTMA. I think that is what made it all the more amazing the day Brent and I found ourselves heading for exactly the same piece of sky. He was flying west to east, and I was transiting south to north. We chatted on the radio and realized that we were going to cross paths. As we compared location, speed, and altitude in more detail, it became evident that if we weren't careful, we would be seeing the whites of each other's eyes. Caution being the better part of valour, Brent climbed a couple hundred feet, and I dropped a couple hundred. Good thing because in the end, we passed over the same banana tree at exactly the same time. Could have been uncomfortably close.

Dave and Carla's kids were close in age to ours, and we grew to really appreciate spending time with them. But all too soon, our year in Wewak was over. We moved up the coast to Vanimo, and they moved to the highlands. Dave and I would randomly meet at an airstrip every few months and catch up on family gossip. When we moved to Goroka ourselves a few years later, it was great to be able to reestablish our friendship. They became our best friends outside of MAF, with our boys in particular connecting with their sons, sharing birthday parties and motor-bike adventures. Later on, Dave became chief pilot of NTMA while I was chief pilot of MAF. Our friendship was a great basis for cooperation in leadership.

Our other great friends in NTMA were Bobby and Rhesa. Bobby started out as an aircraft maintenance engineer but, as often happens in missions, was eventually "press-ganged" into leadership as the head of NTMA PNG. We enjoyed many evenings in their home with their daughters and highly energetic mini-poodle cross. Bobby was just one of those guys that you could call on for anything. Whether it be to change a tire on the boys' motorbike or have one of their engineers have a look at a problem with our plane, Bobby was always there.

With MAF aircraft maintenance based in Mount Hagen, thirty minutes flight up the Wahgi Valley, rectification of an airworthiness defect in our Goroka region was always a challenge. Fortunately, our relationships with NTMA and SIL Aviation allowed us to call on them for assistance. The Marawaka Valley is prone to some interesting local winds that can result in crazy turbulence. Sendeni in particular is cool. With windsocks located at the threshold and halfway up the runway, it is not uncommon to see them indicating winds from different directions. One of our aircraft, caught in a sudden downdraft well beyond committal point, resulted in a hard landing that saw both the left main wheel and the nose wheel depart the aircraft. Thankfully, there were no serious injuries; but the aircraft, of course, was of no further value as a means of transportation. As chief pilot at the time, it fell to me to organize the initial response. It was a no-brainer to grab the phone and call my helicopter pilot friend at SIL Aviation. MAF does not operate helicopters, so we are reliant on others when we have need of a chopper. Thanks to Bev, I was on site just a couple hours after the accident.

Bev was part of our extended mission family for practically the whole of our PNG experience. We first met Bev when he stayed with us in Vanimo, not long after we relocated there. Whereas MAF positions pilot families in several locations, SIL Aviation has all their assets based in Aiyura / Ukarumpa. This is simply a reflection of different philosophies in which there is no right or wrong. Up to that point, I had very little interaction with SIL Aviation, but Bev just called our house saying he would be in town overnight and was looking for a place to stay. I was smart enough to know that I needed all the friends I could get while flying in Papua New Guinea, and inviting Bev to stay with us was possibly one of life's greatest investments. Over the years, Bev stayed with us several times, each visit a real encouragement to us. I think the craziest was when he called late one evening about a MEDEVAC: a MEDical EVACuation. In the mission aviation world, a MEDEVAC is usually interpreted as involving an aircraft. In this case, however, it was a firmly ground-bound affair. A PNG employee of SIL needed to get to the Goroka hospital with minimal delay. Night flying in PNG is just not a thing, so this would be a two-hour drive from Ukarumpa to Goroka. Driving the highlands highway is not an adventure to be undertaken lightly at any time, let alone at night, so Bev was hoping to make the return in daylight. A bed and breakfast at hotel Chez Marples was in order.

During my stint as chief pilot of MAF PNG, one of the things that I thoroughly enjoyed was the opportunity to meet with the leaders of SIL Aviation and NTMA at mission aviation conferences. It was very useful to get together and share notes and ideas. It was a joy to work with Dave, Jonathan, and Chris from SIL alongside our friends from NTMA. With mission resources seeming to be on the decline, my dream was for us to be able to find ways to share resources on a footing that was more established than friends helping friends. I was hopeful that we could establish systems that would withstand the transitory nature of mission leadership. I felt that we were on the cusp of something great, but time overtook us, and those holding leadership positions changed before we could institute anything concrete.

On the day of the *twang!* the unexpected events moved at a pace that no level of cooperation could have controlled. The Marawaka is a dead-end valley named for the river that furrows the center of its depths. Where it breaks out of the mountain trough, the Marawaka flows at little more than sea level, surrounded by mountains rising up to 6,900 feet. Over the 29 kilometers upstream to its headwaters, the peaks climb rapidly through 8,600 feet, 10,700 feet, 11,100 feet, topping at 11,400 at the end of the valley. The communities of the Marawaka Valley, like the majority of isolated villages in PNG, are subsistence farmers. The Marawaka people do have one advantage: coffee. They grow phenomenal quantities of the most amazing-tasting coffee. The towering escarpments negate the building of roads, and the Marawaka is not a navigable river. Consequently, options for the sand-coloured beans in their fifty-kilogram bags to make it out of the valley to the factory are exactly one: airplane.

The Boikoa community sits halfway along the valley. The airstrip is 510 meters long with an attention-grabbing 13 percent slope and a cool bend at the top end. The people work the steep slopes, harvesting the coffee cherries by hand, husking them in manual mills, carrying them to the airstrip on unbelievably strong shoulders. On coffee run days, all the seats are removed from the Otter. Besides giving more room to move around and load the aircraft, the weight savings permit an additional eighty kilograms of payload. Of the twenty passenger seats normally installed, the last row of three seats is permanently installed. Often there are passengers that also want to travel, so the seats in row 7 still allow limited capacity to accommodate them. On the day of the *twang!* there were three passengers looking to get to Aiyura. Expecting several runs between Boikoa and Aiyura, we elected to leave them for a later flight. As it turns out, that was one of the best decisions I have ever made.

The flight from Boikoa to Aiyura is little more than twenty minutes. On breaking out of the Marawaka Valley, the route cuts across the Imani and Lamari river valleys before a quick S-turn through the Aiyura south gap provides a clear run into Aiyura. Under normal conditions, unimpeded by cloud, fog, or rain, the aircraft can fly straight onto the downwind leg for landing runway one four.

At airstrips where there is no air traffic controller, pilots fly a standard pattern when preparing for landing. This "circuit" involves flying parallel to but in the opposite direction to the runway. A turn left or right as applicable places the aircraft at ninety degrees to the runway. A further ninety-degree turn, at the right moment, aligns the aircraft with the runway. Circuits are by convention flown with all turns left. At Aiyura, hills to the east of the runway prevent a left circuit. At Aiyura, the downwind leg places the aircraft to the west of the runway, with the community of Ukarumpa sandwiched between the flight path and the runway. It is a requirement to keep some distance away from the community for noise abatement. An Otter flying overhead the high school, elementary school, and Bible translators is quite disrupting. The turn onto base leg is where the adventure begins. The Schindler hills are exactly where the aircraft needs to fly, and as the aircraft descends for landing, the hill rises up to meet it. In fact, when properly positioned, the pilot should be able to glance out the left window and be eye to eye with birds in the trees. Schindler's Hill is named after Professor Schindler, who moved to PNG in retirement and then started a primary school, located on Schindler's Hill, that continues on decades after his death. It was right then, with attention focused on the landing process, that we heard *twang!*

Immediate assumption was that a cargo strap securing the twenty-seven bags of coffee had let go. Now having never experienced that phenomenon in many years of flying, it is strange that my first thought would be cargo strap failure. A quick check of the coffee revealed nothing amiss. Landing was completed without further incident or interruption. It was then that the fun began. We were met by some of our SIL Aviation pilot friends with news. Ukarumpa is located at the intersection of three different tribal groups. Although related, like most families, they don't always agree. Unlike most families, in PNG, family disputes often turn vicious. Unbeknownst to us, the communities in the vicinity of the airstrip had erupted in tribal violence, with as many three separate and unrelated fights going on at once. Traditionally, tribal wars in PNG have been fought with bows and bush knives (machetes). In recent times, guns have become more prevalent, and on that day, high-powered assault rifles were among the weapons of choice. It seems that an escaped prisoner was among the instigators. Up on Schindler's Hill, close to the airstrip, he took aim as we approached to land and pulled the trigger. The bullet passed through the rear cabin door and exited out the roof.

On the ground at the airstrip, we heard detail of what was going on, and the source of the *twang!* was lost in what seemed a larger problem. It was clear that there were conflicts all around the airstrip, and continued operations into Aiyura were not advisable. One of my closest friends in SILA indicated that he didn't think we were in any danger of being directly involved in the clash. On reflection, that statement is rather humorous, considering that we already had two bullet holes in our plane. I am sure people wonder how we could not have discovered bullet holes. A high-velocity bullet travelling through thin aluminum acts like a drill boring a very small clean hole. The exit hole in the roof was invisible. The entry hole in the door was camouflaged on the outside by a paint stripe and on the inside by a piece of metal trim.

Considering the uncertainty and volatility of the situation, the decision was made to cease operations into Aiyura for the day at least. Following contact with our team back at home base in Goroka, plan B called for us to return to Goroka fifteen minutes to the east, then fly to Negabo twenty-two minutes southwest. It was on arrival at Negabo that our normal in-transit walk-around revealed the puncture wounds. The cause of the *twang!* was now glaringly clear. And how close we had come to tragedy was equally apparent.

Passenger aircraft of all sizes have interior trim, similar to a car that hides all sorts of interior workings: wires, pipes, cables. Removing the plastic that covers the ceiling of the aircraft reveals the main structure of the aircraft. The projectile had threaded a needle-thin path between a couple of longerons, which are the bones of the aircraft, narrowly missing two cables that connect the flight controls to moveable surfaces on the tail of the aircraft. The bullet was just millimeters from parting those cables and denying us the ability to control the aircraft from going up—or down. Further contemplation led to the conclusion that we had been protected from harm in multiple ways. Less than a single degree down in the aim of the rifle would have seen the metal slug impact a fuel tank in the belly of the aircraft with potential movie-like results. A similar move to the left would have seen Mrs. Marples' little boy with an additional and unwanted hole in his body. Furthermore, we gave thanks that we had chosen to not carry any passengers from Boikoa to Aiyura.

Have you ever watched people in window seats in airplanes when the aircraft is landing? Most passengers are contorting their bodies to get a good view of the scenery. The Otter is no different. In the last row, row 7, to see anything at all, people have to lean forward to see out of the little windows. Should we have had passengers on board, one would certainly have been seated on the left side of the aircraft where the bullet passed through. That person would certainly have been leaning forward to look out the window. The bullet would have entered through the aircraft door and passed through the passenger's head before exiting through the roof of the aircraft.

In many ways, just another unexpected event in the land of the unexpected. Unexpected that we would be shot at in the first place. Unexpected that the bullet completely missed anything vital, including the pilots. Not unexpected that God was with us.

# BRAVO

## ~Just a Little Talk with Jesus in Busilmin~

BUSILMIN. IF YOU can imagine the end of the world, Busilmin is it.

While the artists and philosophers of Renaissance Europe were busy with painting and literature, great adventurers were sailing seas and discovering lands previously unknown to fifteenth- and sixteenth-century Europe. Marco Polo, John Cabot, Christopher Columbus, Vasco da Gama, Francis Drake. Prior to these explorers, conventional wisdom held that the earth was flat, that the world had an end. If that were true, that the world has an end, then the last stop before falling off the edge would be Busilmin.

Busilmin brings the definition of isolated to life. The headwaters of the Sepik River are hidden beyond Feramin; but if you float downstream many miles from where it becomes a real river, transiting the impressive Sepik Gorge, passing the mouths of both the Eliptamin and Miyanmin valleys, you will eventually arrive at the point where the tiny Din River empties into the Sepik. Tracking back upstream, the valley narrows perceptibly, dramatically. With the near-vertical slopes climbing ever higher, the sun touches the valley floor for but a few fleeting hours each day. As the stream peters out to a needle-thin line of pale blue on the map, this is Busilmin. Not that there is anything to see. The intense tangle of the jungle conceals any signs of habitation from view.

It is this isolation, this remoteness, that defines existence in the depths of the rainforest. Death is life. Life is death. Survival is the bridge. Even in the most inaccessible parts, by law, pilots must record the names of each and every person that is travelling on an aircraft. As we say in our predeparture passenger briefings, "in the unlikely event of an unscheduled landing," there must be evidence of who was onboard the airplane. This is a real concern for pilots in developing countries. Ask a mother the name of her infant, and the response is often a bewildered expression. A head count after boarding often reveals a discrepancy between the manifest and reality. In many cases, this inconsistency is the result of "undeclared infants." Mothers won't name their children until they reach two; not that most people in PNG have any idea when they were born or even how old they are. So a child will be named when it appears reasonable to believe that it will survive. This attitude is the practical outcome of an infant mortality rate approaching 4 percent, higher yet under the rainforest canopy. Eight times higher than countries classified as developed. No wonder that mothers strive to maintain an emotional detachment, for without a name, the infant does not count as a person.

For a person raised in the West, this is just one of many discrepancies relating to value of life that need to be understood and accepted. For missionaries, the correct balance of respect for culture with the heart of God can be a real challenge. It is a simple matter to confuse what we think is correct with what the word of God says. Death rituals are a clear example of this dilemma. In Papua New Guinea tradition, a body must be returned to the deceased's home village for burial. This is usually accomplished with a dedicated flight called a charter. I clearly remember my first "body charter."

Just a few weeks after my instructor released me to solo operations in the lowlands area referred to as "the Sepik," I was tasked to fly my Cessna 206 to Lumi to transport the body of a young woman who had passed away. The Sepik is a vast area of flatland between the central and coastal ranges. After flowing past Busilmin, the Sepik River continues a tortuous path down through the mountains and out into the lowlands, crossing and recrossing the border with Indonesia. It then winds several hundred kilometers collecting innumerable rivers before emptying into the Pacific east of the coastal town of Wewak. Lumi hugs the coastal mountains at the northern border of the Sepik plain.

Powered by a single piston engine, the Cessna 206 was built by the Wichita, Kansas–based company started by and named after Clyde Cessna. The original 206 came off the production line in 1964. By the time I was captain, my ride was the turbo charged G model: a "much newer" machine built in the late '70s. MAF applied a multitude of modifications to the basic aircraft to increase its utility for operations at higher altitudes and on unprepared runways. Larger tires allow the aircraft to operate off soft surfaces. The Robertson STOL (short TAKEOFF LANDING) kit improves low-speed performance enabling the aircraft to take off and land in shorter distances. Modified seat belts improve survivability. The baggage is carried in small area behind the last row of seats that steps up six inches from the aircraft floor onto a shelf. A cargo pod attached to the belly increases baggage capacity to a realistic amount. The aircraft was designed as a six-seat aircraft, but another conversion to MAF aircraft provides seat belts for eight passengers. For many years, law in Papua New Guinea allowed small children to share a seat belt. It was this provision that enabled me on one occasion to exceed eight passengers on board. I landed at a location where I was presented with a passenger list containing eleven names for my diminutive aircraft. I took the opportunity to express to our man on the ground that I didn't think this would work. The unexpected answer was that the passengers were all one family. A rapid assessment of the clan revealed mom, dad, teenage son, four small children, two very small children, and two infants. With our extra seat belts and the ability for small kids to share, we flew away with twelve people in our six-seat aircraft.

On arrival at Lumi to collect the body and grieving relatives, I was surprised to discover that the deceased was in a black body bag. I am not entirely sure what I expected, but a body bag was certainly not on the list. And the surprises continued, for the number of people that wished to accompany the body, when accounting for the physical space that a body takes up, exceeded the capacity of the aircraft. Or so I thought. As I sought to explain the problem in my relatively new Melanesian Tok Pisin language, people replied with many "helpful" suggestions. My Western upbringing did rebel at the proposal to place the body bag in the cargo pod. The loading door on the side of the pod measures twenty-six centimeters high and sixty-nine centimeters long. To get a body bag through the door would have required Houdini-like contortions for which I was not prepared. The final compromise involved removing the last row of seats, placing the body bag on the floor of the aircraft, with head facing forward, and then...bending the knees to get the legs up onto the shelf in the rear baggage area.

Strangely enough, that experience was not to be my most bizarre encounter with PNG bodies and burial customs. Several years after the body-bag incident, now flying the larger Twin Otter aircraft, I was called on to return the body of a young man to his home village of Warasai. He was possibly in his late teens, a student at school in the village of Nuku. Many young people must leave home if they wish to attend high school. This is certainly true for high school, but even for some in elementary school. The student had become ill. Death followed quite quickly and suddenly. The availability of a body bag is extremely remote, and in remote communities, there is unlikely to even be rough coffin. In Nuku, for this young man, there was an old tablecloth in a blue checked pattern and a roll of plastic. Wrapped up exactly as you would picture a mummy, even the significantly larger cargo holds of the Otter would not have accepted the body. All we could do was remove some seats and lay him on the floor of the passenger compartment. We need to secure the body and so ran a couple of straps over the swathed package. By that time, I had seen a lot of things over the years, but I vividly recall the body being wound so tight that facial features, in particular the nose, were unmistakable.

While that may have been the most interesting body package, it tends to be funeral custom events that hold place in my memory. Western funerals are inclined to be reserved, quiet affairs where raw emotion is expected to be kept in check. By contrast, PNG funerals are very charged and emotionally unguarded. Biblical descriptions of people expressing sorrow in sackcloth and ashes are right at home in the land of the unexpected. People will literally cover themselves in mud to indicate that they are in mourning. Arriving at an airstrip with a body, it would not be uncommon to see ladies crawling to the aircraft on hands and knees. Once, I was even daubed in mud by the grieving as I sat in the cockpit. But most striking expression of grief in PNG is the incredibly loud, harsh, crude wailing. After all these years, I remain a little unclear of how this plays out. I have flown groups of people who sit silently in the aircraft, looking out the windows, pointing things out to each other, who then transform before my eyes as we approach their village. They break out into a moaning, almost howling clamour that penetrates past the noise of the engines and through the noise-cancelling headset. It seems almost counterfeit for some. I wonder if, in fact, it is actually a genuinely supportive gesture that we could learn from: a sympathetic discordant din that allows the closest ones, those who are feeling the loss most deeply, to thoroughly express their sorrow through heartbreaking cry without shame.

Cultural norms sometimes defy our own logic. There was a very old man that had been released from the provincial hospital in Vanimo, basically to go home and die as there was nothing more to be done for him. I say very old, but I find in PNG, it is all but impossible to estimate age. Male life expectancy is early sixties, so the patient could have been anywhere between forty and seventy. Those living in the most isolated parts of New Guinea lead the hardest of lives. As subsistence farmers living in wet conditions with poor shelter and minimal health care, early death is almost a given. Hospital in PNG is nothing like hospital in Canada: there is no food service, no changing of the bed, or cleaning of washrooms. A patient is expected to have a *wantok*, a close relative, with them to meet all those basic needs. This person is referred to as the guardian. And so it was that our passenger manifest comprised not just the old man but his younger caregiver and a few other healthy relatives returning to their home in Gubil, some fifty minutes flight time to the south.

Halfway through the flight, just crossing the Sepik River, I received word from Ludmer, our cabin attendant, that the man had passed away, right there on the plane. My initial response was to ask Ludmer if he thought the patient was dead or dead-dead. Melanesian

Tok Pisin is a language created to enable the eight hundred plus language groups of Papua New Guinea to communicate with one another for trade and business. As such, the language is in many respects challenged when it comes to depth of vocabulary. *Dai* or *indai* are the words for "death." But these are alternatively used to indicate unconsciousness, a coma, or even just serious illness. An announcement of *mama bilong mi indai* does not actually mean that a person's mother is dead. To indicate that a person has truly passed on from this life, one must say *dai pinis*, directly translated, "finished dying." Ludmer reported that all indications were pointing to the likelihood that the old man had indeed finished dying and was now dead-dead. Unexpected. Since the purpose of the flight was to take the man home to die, there did not seem any valid reason to return to Vanimo, so we continued on and reported by radio a change of passengers on board to flight service: now one less living plus one body. The death on the aircraft is, however, not the most astonishing aspect of this tale. That little shocker was to come after landing.

Gubil is probably in the top five airstrips in terms of difficulty on the approach, but on that day, we completed the landing with no further dramas. After shutting down the engines, we opened the passenger door for people to disembark. First out was the guardian, and a more sorrowful-looking bearer of bad news I have never seen. It may be that he was genuinely upset, or it may be that he knew what was coming. As the word rapidly spread, older ladies from the small community sprang out from the assembled group and proceeded to hit the hapless young man. More unexpected was that he just took the hits, and further that no one jumped to his defence. From my perspective, the situation deteriorated even more as sticks appeared. I even observed women going home, only to return with what I can only imagine was their favourite "beating" stick. In a culture where women are certainly not equal, it was quite astounding to view a throng of women striking a man while all the other men just stood back.

In need of understanding, I questioned Ludmer, a PNG man from Nuku area. He told me that this custom was not one practiced in his area but that he understood the dynamics. The young man, the guardian, the one entrusted with the older man's care, was in trouble for failing to advise the community of the man's death. He was not being held responsible for the death. He was simply accountable for neglecting to tell them. In my mind, of course, this was completely unfair; after all, the man had been alive when we took off. Through no fault of the guardian, death also had boarded the aircraft and seized the man en route. How was that young man possibly supposed to have passed the message? Apparently, Western logic does not apply. This was custom. These were the rules. Everyone knew it. Everyone accepted it. Even the man taking the hits.

However, my most marvelous encounter with funeral customs took place at the ends of the earth: Busilmin. There are many place-names that culminate in the suffix *min*: Feramin, Telefomin, Tifalmin, Eliptamin, Myanmin. *Min* is the local language word meaning "people." So Busilmin is simply where the Busil people call home. We departed from the gold-mining town of Tabubil located just 40 kilometers south-southeast of Busilmin. On the map, departure and destination look really close. In this case, looks are an illusion. Theoretically, it is just a short 3,500 feet climb from Tabubil at 1,600 feet to Busilmin at 5,100 feet. Theoretically. The most direct route passes between Mount Akrir at 8,583 feet and Mount Aiyang, whose summit sits at 10,909 feet. In the clearest of weather, the aircraft must climb to at least 10,000 feet in less than 17 kilometers. If flown precisely and at maximum performance, a Twin Otter can just make it. Unfortunately, the biggest is yet to come. In the next 15 kilometers, the aircraft must continue to climb in order to avoid the 12,595 foot peak of Mount Scorpion. Of course, this is only possible if the weather is cooperative. When the peaks of Akrir, Aiyang, and Scorpion are obscured, the alternate route to Busilmin gives passengers the distinct impression that their pilots are lost. Picture drawing a counterclockwise circle. Instead of turning northwest on departure, the secondary course starts with flight to the east up the "chute," followed by a turn to the north through the "low point." Crossing over the "crocodile tail," the pilot alters track northwest through the "Sepik Gorge." For the next several minutes, the pilot keeps a sharp look out the left window looking for a clear path through to Busilmin. If the long way is required, a road to Busilmin is often not found until it appears southwest of the aircraft. Total distance flown will be about 125 kilometers.

Regardless of the route flown, the terrain dictates that the aircraft invariably arrives over Busilmin three thousand to four thousand feet above the elevation of the runway. This is way too high since an aircraft is usually positioned one thousand feet above the runway in preparation for landing and consequently requires a spiral descent to achieve the correct altitude.

And that is how we arrived on the day in question. With the valley identified and the runway in sight, I was surprised that the rear of the aircraft remained eerily silent. By now the wailing should have commenced and be impinging on my concentration. Around one turn. A second. A third. Still no signs of mourning from the passengers in back. I turned around to check that all was as it should be. Passengers were seated with seat belts securely fastened. The casket also remained strapped to the floor. Although people looked sad, there was not the sense of complete devastation and hopelessness that I associate with the discordant weeping.

As we got established on crosswind, all remained quiet, and focus now needed to be solely on flying the aircraft. From this point on, our plane would be flying very close to terrain. The left wing tip seemed to be dangerously close to the trees, clinging to life on the sheer slopes. Any closer and we would be in real strife; any further away, and we would be incapable of configuring correctly for landing. With the runway out of view behind us, we reduced power on the engines to decrease speed towards that required for landing. We extended the first stage of flap. Flaps are a part of the wing that are used for takeoff and landing. Flaps extend out and down to the back of the wing, effectively changing the shape of the wing to improve the ability of the aircraft to fly safely at slower speeds. As the mountains ahead filled the windshield, we executed a right turn, lowered more flaps, and flew yet slower, remaining within breathing distance of the ridges. Because Busilmin airstrip is trapped in its own separate valley, it remains hidden from view until quite late, forcing us to mark progress by reference from one geographical feature to the next. Finally, we caught sight of the strip of grass that is the airfield. A sharp turn aligned us for landing. But this is Busilmin. This is the end of the earth.

For pilots, Busilmin airstrip is not friendly. It is five hundred meters long with an 11 percent slope and a bend in the last quarter. It's like trying to land inside a giant rain gutter. The closer to the runway the aircraft gets, the closer and higher the mountains get to the right and to the left. With over a kilometer to go till touchdown, there is nowhere left to go but straight ahead. Committed to land. Any deviation from runway heading from this point on involves a nasty meeting with a rock wall.

Through all of this, the passengers made none of the vocal expressions to which I had become accustomed when operating a "body charter." Touchdown was the usual adventure: ordinary for the pilots, somewhere between pulse elevating and terrifying for everyone else. Even that failed to elicit an expression from our guests. Busilmin has no parking bay. Aircraft just sort of turn at the top of the runway, coming to a stop on a part that is hopefully reasonably level. Just ahead, there is a river that is hidden from view. Securely setting the parking brake is highly recommended.

Befitting its reputation as the end of the earth, the crowd at Busilmin that day was small—and quiet. Very quiet. Although the passengers had been quiet, I still expected the villagers to demonstrate anguish in traditional fashion. The volume is usually sufficient to overcome engine noise, which of itself is substantial. Not this day. As is my custom, I concentrated my gaze out of the left window as the propellers slowed towards stop. Primarily to ensure that no one was approaching the aircraft and so in danger of a nasty collision with the still-turning propellers, my attention was drawn to five men standing on a small hummock a short distance from the aircraft. I cracked open my door and heard a sound that I thought I would never hear anywhere in PNG, let alone in this isolated community the world has forgotten.

PNG music is not like Western music. Western music has a predictable rhythm and cadence. Even the most tone-deaf individual can tell you whether a song feels complete, whether the next note should be a bit higher or a bit lower, whether a song "sounds right." Papua New Guinea is a challenge for a classically trained musician; nothing makes musical sense. When a song feels like it should end, it keeps going. When it feels like it should keep going, everyone shuts up and sits down. For Westerners, it also feels a bit screechy. Of course, this is all from a biased viewpoint. Nevertheless, perfect four-part male harmony was far from what I anticipated hearing as the door opened. The expected eardrum-assaulting barrage of hopeless wailing was absent. Instead, as the passenger door was opened and the coffin gently lifted down, the body of the deceased was welcomed home with such beautiful harmony as you have ever heard.

> I once was lost in sin but Jesus took me in
> And then a little light from heaven filled my soul
> He bathed my heart in love and wrote my name above
> And just a little talk with my Jesus made me whole
> (Now let us) have a little talk with Jesus (let us) tell him all about our troubles
> (He will) hear our faintest cry (and we will) answer by and by
> (Now when you) feel a little prayer wheel turning
> (Then you'll) know a little fire is burning
> (You will) find a little talk with Jesus makes it right
> (Rosie Wallace, Sony/ATV Music Publishing LLC)

Surprised. Astounded. Amazed. Gobsmacked, as Australians might say. And yet overwhelmed and overjoyed. Thankful to be witness to this phenomenal expression of an isolated community utterly transformed by the power of the Gospel of Jesus Christ. Early missionaries have been accused of confusing conversion by Christ with conversion to Western social values. This was something totally different. When any of us meet the living God, we are confronted with our weakness. We are challenged to become more like the Christ of the Bible. We are transformed from an existence played out in hopelessness and fear of death, to lives lived in anticipation and trust. The transformation I was observer to that day was not about a change of music style or language. It was not about betrayal of culture in exchange for the missionary's personal desires. It was about a believer's earthly remains being welcomed back to his temporal home by other believers who lived in expectation of a reunion in a heavenly home. The singing was in celebration of a life lived for God. It wasn't a performance: this was Busilmin, the end of the earth. There was no one there to see. I was humbled to be a quiet bystander and witness to the fruit of the labour of someone who had gone before. I will certainly never know who brought the story of transformation through Christ to this tiny community, but God was there. The words of Jesus were fulfilled that day in my presence: "You will be my witnesses to the ends of the earth" (Acts 1:8, NIV).

# CHARLIE

## ~Crocodiles *on Board*~

TALES OF PILOTS and jungle creatures abound. It would be a minority of mission pilots that don't have an animal anecdote. In Papua New Guinea, dogs and cats are regular passengers. Day-old chicks travel in the thousands. Pigs are relatively common, sheep and goats on more rare occasions. Many types of birds have travelled over the years, but there are complications with birds. Crocodiles, however, necessitate a special level of care.

Unlike Africa or South America, Papua New Guinea is devoid of a wealth of large creatures. There are no monkeys or big cats; no elephants, antelope, or wildebeest. This is one aspect of the dietary challenges for the people of PNG. The lack of wild game results in a protein-weak diet. Many of the groups that MAF partners with seek to redress this imbalance through a variety of community-development projects. For those that live on rivers, fish are an option. And some of these are of kinds unlikely to be encountered in the average Western grocery store. During one visit to the village of Yabru for a celebration marking the opening of the airstrip, we were treated to fire-roasted "bolt cutters." For those squeamish about small bones in your white fish, then bolt cutter is not the fish for you. Bolt cutters are a vegetarian piranha, but not the small, little creatures of folklore. The bolt cutter is about the size of a chicken but with a vicious set of teeth.

A few riverside communities turned fish into an income source. While we lived in Vanimo, MAF served the very isolated community of Magleri. The hot, sticky, sultry air I am certain contributed to the quality of fish that we would carry from Magleri to other communities remote from river access. The Magleris would catch hundreds of fish, smoke them, bag them, then wait for MAF to transport them. With no industrial process to help, it takes a lot of time to prepare thirteen cubic meters of fish for transport. Thirteen cubic meters is about the capacity of the de Havilland Twin Otter when configured for cargo only. By the time the aircraft arrived, the fish had a very distinct odour. By the time the bags were loaded, secured, and the doors were closed, we were overcome with flies—flies that would already have laid eggs in the rich incubation source of a dead fish. Back at base, aircraft cleaning was required to remove lots of unmentionable remains.

More sustainable schemes entail the transport of live animals into isolated communities. Some villages with an appropriate climate, including sufficient rain, create fish ponds. Passengers can be seen boarding with plastic bags of fish heading home to stock the pond. There have been times when the pet-store-style clear plastic bag has been replaced with a bucket. In countries where the niceties of air travel are less understood, it creates an interesting dilemma. With the airstrips generally rough, pails of water sloshing about are not really desirable as either checked bags or hand luggage. Usually, confirmation of a lid and reduction in water level is sufficient for the crew to be happy in furthering community development. Sheep and goats have also been tried in the jungle. Seemingly relatively simple to look after, goats in particular seem self-sufficient in their apparent willingness to eat practically anything. They tend not to cause too much trouble in the aircraft as long as they are properly restrained. Sustainability is an obstacle for all these programs. The seed animals obviously have to live long enough to reproduce.

My first couple years as a Twin Otter pilot were flown predominantly in a crew pairing with Ruben. He is a Papua New Guinean from whom I learned tremendous amounts not just about flying safely in PNG but also about PNG culture, traditions, and thought processes. MAF has a few locations where pilot families live where there are no stores. Planning ahead is a necessary skill as shopping trips only occur at six-week intervals. The difficulty is that the people of PNG, even town dwellers, do not plan far ahead. As subsistence farmers, they will plant; but with a year-round growing season and rapidly maturing plants, sowing does not have a deadline. When shopping ourselves, we often wondered what was going on behind the eyes of those who watched us with keen interest. In town, people will buy what they need for the day. Part of the reason for this is that they probably do not have a fridge, but it is really about the mind-set: why think ahead if, when I am hungry, I go outside and pull a coconut from the palm? My friend Ruben told me he could never be based in one of our remote locations because he could not possibly think far enough ahead to buy sufficient food to last six weeks. And that is the issue with fish, sheep, and goat projects: it takes too long. The animals are eaten long before the project becomes sustainable.

Pigs seem to do slightly better. Perhaps that is because they are one of the very few animals that do run wild in the jungle. PNG pigs are not the cute little pink things that showed up in your child's book of sounds animals make. These creatures are more like feral boars covered in coarse brown hair and not afraid to defend or attack when provoked. That being said, any attempt to transfer one of these beasts must be undertaken with appropriate precautions. Traditionally, live pigs are secured to a pole: forelegs lashed together, hind legs likewise. Then a sturdy branch passed through with more vines to hold the animal secure. For air transport, this method is not recommended.

Many of life's hardest lessons are learned through pain or negative experience. In the past, MAF has flown some pigs of epic proportions. Unfortunately, some of those have ended with a pilot having a story to match. Live animals are limited to thirty kilograms, which for a PNG pig is actually not very large. Even the cute little piglets are a handful when not properly packaged. Animals need to have a crate that will allow the animal to stand and lie down. Then there is the matter of the, uh, mess. I have never come across a potty-trained pig, and even family pet dogs are likely to lose control when feeling scared. Of course, this standard is what the pilot is looking for so as to avoid exciting tales. Nonpilots, of course, don't necessarily get this.

It is a legal, moral, and common-sense requirement to deliver a passenger briefing prior to departure. There are, of course, the standard things like seat belts, emergency exits, and prohibition against smoking. There are plenty of urban myths, or in this case, I suppose rural myths about passenger-briefing failures. In PNG, there are plenty of stories about passengers leaving the aircraft following an accident without releasing their seat belts. The people are gone, but the seat belt is still secured, as if the person was never there. I can, however, vouch for this possibility having found seat belts still connected after *normal* landings. There was a person in the seat when we took off; I myself fastened the seat belt. Somehow the passenger slipped out of the restraint without releasing it. There is a rhythm to a good briefing. It is normal to have to project over conversation, but it is a strange sensation to have that patter interrupted by the surreptitious mew of a kitten or muffled squawk of a bird. Most Papua New Guineans, men included, carry a hand-woven bag called a *bilum*: like a woman's purse, a receptacle for everything one might need. Bilums come in all shapes and sizes, and one must be extremely careful when helping passengers with their baggage. Several pilots have welcomed embarrassment when helping a lady with her bilum, moving to load it into the baggage compartment only to discover a baby inside. Food, clothes, babies—they all fit. But inside the plane, in small bilums, kittens, birds, and even small piglets are counted as stowaways. And stowaways are not welcome. So the briefing is paused, and the negotiation begins. Of course, it isn't really a negotiation as the creature must go. Birds flying around the cockpit, kitties skittering under rudder pedals, pigs hurtling around like pin balls—events all designed to elevate a pilot's blood pressure.

Providentially, my personal experience with escaped animals is limited to puppies loose in the rear baggage locker. I probably should have known better actually. Years ago, before our children were born, before MAF and PNG, we acquired two cats. Although we came by them as a set, they were very different, not siblings. Spitfire was a lilac point Siamese cross. Mugsy was simply a DSH: domestic shorthair, cat speak for mutt. Slightly cross-eyed, Spitfire was everything you can imagine in terms of attitude from a Siamese named Spitfire. Mugsy was perhaps also what her name implies. Friends would always inquire if Mugsy was "with kitty."

The twosome came with one-cat carrier. We were rather poor in those days, so when we went on holidays, the babies had to travel with us; we couldn't afford a kennel. Never having had a pet as a child, all my cat-wrangling wisdom could be written on the head of a pin. So I elected to separate the step-siblings into the commercial cat carrier and a homemade one. I found a cat-sized box and cut a hole in it, into which I placed a grill: a cookie cooling rack that we still have. I failed to account for Mugsy's desire to be with Spitfire and what motivation can do when merged with cat claws. Mugsy freed herself from the box. Subsequently, the two travelled together. Even when Spitfire, prone to motion sickness, vomited on Mugsy's head, she was still happier to be in the same carrier. So when presented with two puppies for travel on my plane, I should have known better, but I still allowed them to travel in cardboard boxes. No real surprise then when I cracked open the door on the rear baggage compartment and found cute little puppy eyes staring down at me. Happily, the puppy had not found the need to relieve himself.

Not all of my creature adventures involved domestic animals. There is a wide variety of insect life in PNG, it being very much like National Geographic in real life: stick bugs, leaf bugs, huge centipedes, large cockroaches, praying mantis. There is also a great assortment of moths, which are a favourite of gecko lizards. The geckos that inhabited our house in abundance measured from barely a centimeter in length to about five centimeters from nose to tail. They can fit into any crack or crevice, appearing when least expected. This is a problem when flying.

The Cessna 206 single-engine airplane has the aircraft equivalent of automobile four-sixty air-conditioning. For those not familiar, four-sixty air-con is standard equipment on most cars: open the front and back windows of the car, drive at sixty miles per hour. The majority of single-engine aircraft have small inlet holes in the leading edge of the wing. Maybe three centimeters in diameter, the openings led by a pipe through the wings to outlets in the cabin. For the pilot, this vent supplies air just in front of his left temple. Once the plane starts moving, cooling begins. The faster the plane travels, the higher the level of air-con. The downside would be the potential for more than air to access the cockpit through the air vent. Normally, there is a screen to stop unwanted airborne particles. Pesky little geckos, however, liking small spaces, can access the vent from the inside and hide there, until air moving at two hundred kilometers per hour overwhelms its small sticky feet and blows it out into the cockpit—and straight down the pilot's shirt.

When an airplane takes off, the normal process is to accelerate until there is sufficient airflow over the tail control surfaces to allow the pilot to raise the nose of the aircraft, lifting the front wheel off the ground. This is called rotation. A little more speed, and the main wheels lift off, and the aircraft is flying. Large passenger aircraft must have sufficient runway to accelerate to takeoff speed and still have enough pavement to abort the takeoff and stop without running off the end of the hard surface. This is a simple explanation of accelerate-stop distance. Typical MAF runways do not meet accelerate-stop requirements. For MAF pilots, for the majority of our runways, by the time rotation occurs, there is not enough runway left to stop safely. Instead, pilots nominate a safe-abort point. Where there is a nonmechanical problem prior to the safe-abort point, the pilot can safely bring the aircraft to stop before the banana trees. For any problem after that point, if the aircraft can fly, the pilot must continue the takeoff. I was taking off at one of those limited-length runways. I had just raised the nose wheel when the tiny gecko flew out of the vent, smacked into my chest, and disappeared down my shirt. No decision though. I had to keep going and ignore the wriggly on my tummy. Fortunately, geckos aren't poisonous and don't bite.

Unfortunately, snakes and spiders do bite. I don't like snakes. I haven't liked snakes since I was four years old. We were taking a walk in the Kielder Forest while on a family holiday in Northumberland, England. I was playing that game that little kids like: running ahead of the pack, hiding in the trees, then jumping out to scare everyone. That backfired big time. Safely hidden around a corner and in some bushes, it was all quiet. Except for the hissing. As I glanced down, a seeming hair's breadth from my ankle, curled up and unamused, was a dark snake with a diamond zigzag pattern. I had managed to just about plant my foot on a specimen of England's sole poisonous snake. As far as I can recall, the only snake I have had on the aircraft was one I knowingly carried. Why someone would want a green tree python as a pet is beyond me.

Along with snakes, spiders also feature in some of the best pilot stories. The Twin Otter has an area under the cockpit floor called the hydraulics bay, so named because that is where the hydraulic oil pump and other associated bits are located. The hydraulic system on the Otter powers the brakes, flaps, and steering. There are access doors on either side of the aircraft that are opened every morning by the pilot to check the hydraulic system for leaks. It is a dark hole. To properly check all the systems that are under the cockpit floor, the pilot must actually stick his head into that hole. Spiders like dark spaces. Tales abound of pilots coming eye to eye with spiders: hairy spiders, hairy spiders the size of your hand. Fortunately, this type of story is not in my repertoire; else, I might feel for spiders as I feel for snakes.

Birds are more common passengers. At least they were prior to the big outbreak of bird flu. As the epidemic spread, the transport of birds by air in PNG was prohibited. The exception was commercially produced day-old chicks. Basically, hatcheries provide boxes of freshly hatched chicks to be shipped all over the country. Isolated communities will purchase several boxes and raise the chicks to maturity as a source of protein. From a pilot's perspective, day-old chicks are easy to transport but incessantly noisy. They travel in boxes of fifty and chatter constantly. Multiply that by ten, fifteen, twenty boxes, and the din can cause insanity. Back in the "old days," the variety of avian travelers was somewhat broader. Alongside mature chickens, although much more rare, ducks also travelled. Varieties of small parrots regularly stowed away in bilums. More exotic and larger by far are the guria birds: Victoria crowned pigeons. The origin of the Tok Pisin name for this pigeon is unclear since a *guria* is also an earthquake. The guria bird outstrips all other pigeons growing to three quarters of a meter at maturity. It is an indefinable blue colour;

almost slate gray yet definitely blue, with a large crest adorning its head. Slightly disturbing, however, are the deep-red eyes. Where you and I have a coloured iris surrounded by white, the guria has only red. Yet pride of place in PNG culture would go to the cassowary.

The cassowary is a large flightless bird in the size and style category of the emu and ostrich, but infinitely more dangerous. While inherently predatory, the cassowary is well able to defend itself by virtue of what can only be described as an immense talon on the middle of each of its three-toed feet. In conflicts between cassowaries and people, the human often fares poorly, as borne out by medevacs we have flown. The cassowary is covered with black feathers that give way to a blue-skinned neck, rising to the head, which is crowned with a helmet-like structure running the length of the skull. Adult birds are far too large to transport either safely or humanely. Only infants can really be carried unharmed. Papua New Guineans create woven baskets for the carriage of cassowaries, and really small specimens can be seen in what amounts to a woven purse. In a culture still transitioning to monetary systems, other items are invested with value and employed to represent wealth. In the coastal regions, kina shells are used for this purpose; hence, the name for PNG currency: kina. Cassowaries are also valued and used where significant worth must be transferred. Chief function would be in the paying of bride price. Bride price is one cultural custom that is often misunderstood. While it is certainly true that a woman's place in PNG society is below man's, bride price is really not about this. It is not about a woman being bought as a possession. In times past, marriage would most likely have occurred within the extended family, and bride price allowed for the reallocation of wealth within the family, keeping all members on a more even financial plane.

The one bird that is rarely seen at all and almost never on our aircraft is the signature bird of paradise. There are several species of these shy birds, but all are characterized by phenomenal plumage. Actually quite small, these birds have tail feathers like individual branches measuring well in excess of the bird's body length. The mating dances are naturally exotic, but since the birds are shy, very few people are privileged to observe this dance in person.

Joining with the guria, cassowary, and bird of paradise as PNG unique creatures are the cuscus and tenkile. A cat-sized creature in the possum family, to me, the cuscus looks like a child's stuffed toy. The innocent-looking eyes are framed by a face that is plastic in appearance. They are astonishingly docile. I once had a passenger on the aircraft apparently wearing a fur hat. It turned out to be a cuscus curled up and comfortable on the man's head. By contrast, the tree kangaroo is less docile and significantly larger. Smaller than the more well-known and stereotypical Australian kangaroo, tree kangaroos grow to the size of a small child. The tenkile is a specific type of tree kangaroo whose natural habitat is limited to a very small area surrounding the village of Lumi located in the Torricelli Mountains in the northwest corner of Papua New Guinea. Hunted to near extinction, a conservation program has been in effect since the turn of the century. MAF has flown members of the program for many years. I also had the privilege of carrying some of these amazing creatures from Wewak to Lumi as part of a plan to reintroduce and strengthen the tenkile population. We were careful to have these energetic creatures travel in cargo compartments. Live kangaroos—no matter the size, free, and bouncing around in the passenger cabin—is the stuff nightmares are made of.

Tales of PNG animals in aircraft would be incomplete without a crocodile narrative. In some parts of the world, crocodiles are cultivated from juvenile through to full-sized maturity. Most people would probably not consider the crocodile as a "domestic" farm animal, yet the process is reasonably efficient. One of the major farms in PNG is purportedly operated by a commercial chicken producer. The remnants from the chicken harvest are utilized to raise the crocodiles. In turn, the skin of the crocodile becomes shoes and belts, and the meat becomes, well, meat. One of our friends once fed me coq au vin, which was later revealed to be croc au vin. The old cliché "tastes just like chicken" turns out to be true in this case, perhaps a bit more wild in flavor. Perhaps the crocodile diet might also have something to do with the croc au vin taste. The young crocs are usually captured in the wild while still quite small, transported to the farm, then grown for harvest. "Quite small" in this case works out to about forty-five to sixty centimeters from nasty teeth through to reptilian tail. The adventure began early in our first year while based in Wewak on the north coast of Papua New Guinea.

Our family ended up in Wewak as the only MAF pilot family. It is preferable that a new family be paired at a location with a family that has been with MAF and at the particular base for at least a little while. In our case, this just wasn't possible; so although I was properly trained in terms of flying into all the airstrips, some of that additional nice-to-know information was missed. Information like the people at Ambunti regularly send live crocodiles to Wewak to meet the Air Niugini flight to Lae. Information like the real meaning of the classic line "the other pilot used to"; that would probably have been useful information. Ambunti airstrip falls into the "easy" category as far as airstrip difficulty is concerned and, as a regular port of call, was a place that I had already been to on many occasions even in our short time in the area. I landed the Cessna 206, taxied into the parking bay, let the temperatures and pressures stabilize, then pulled the fuel mixture control to shut down the engine. I was met as usual by our MAF agent. At most airstrips, there is a local Papua New Guinean that helps out by preparing the passenger and cargo manifest. On that day, the manifest said "crocodiles." As the new pilot, without all the prior knowledge I really needed, I was immediately at the disadvantage. However, knowing that there was no way a crocodile could access the cabin from the cargo pod attached to the belly of the aircraft, I agreed to take however many crocs could be accommodated in that compartment. And that is when the negotiations notched up into high gear.

"Narapela pailot i bin amamas long karim ol insait wantaim em yet." The other pilot was happy to carry them in the cabin with him. Yes, well, "dispela pailot i fret long karim pukpuk klostu, ol i gat draipela nil long kaikaim mi." This pilot is afraid to carry crocodiles that close to me; they have big teeth and will bite me.

The conversation went back and forth for a while. In typical PNG fashion, they asked, and I answered—three times. Unless the same answer is given three times, it could be that the answer might change. My fear prevailed over their insistence, and so we loaded six crocodile boxes into the pod, and off I went to Wewak incident free. It did give me a cool story to share with the family that night around the dinner table. Some days later, I was back in Ambunti as before this was the last stop of the day on the way back to Wewak. Also as before, I was met by the agent with the manifest. Asking what we had for the plane, I was told forty-eight crocodiles! Imagine my surprise. Flashback to the previous conversation regarding dangerous reptiles: had I not been clear? Was this another case of *traim tasol* (give it a go) with the new pilot? Back in the present, a deep breath, a quick prayer for wisdom, what I hoped was a disarming chuckle: "But last time I only took six because that's all that will fit in the pod." Now it was their turn to laugh. Not a disarming chuckle but a serious hoot at the naivety of the pilot: "No, pilot, last time you took fifty-one." It seems that I had indeed carried six boxes on the previous flight, except each box held eight animals. Each box was divided into four segments, and into each segment went two crocodiles, tail to tail. Mouths were theoretically banded shut. The hunters went on to tell me on the last flight they had tried to cheat and put three crocodiles in three slots instead of the normal two. Apparently, things had not gone so well, so we were back to packing the creatures in the way the cartons were intended. Doors shut, passengers briefed, engine started and pre-takeoff checks complete, launch for another uneventful flight to Wewak. Again, lest you think the story ends there, I shall continue with part 3.

I have no anecdotes of fighting it out with an oversized lizard in a space the size of a compact car over the tropical rainforest. When our family moved on from Wewak, the pilot that replaced me continued to carry crocodiles out of Ambunti with no in-flight dramas. However, one afternoon, he was late landing in Wewak, and the Air Niugini jet had already departed for Lae. The crocodiles were required to experience an unplanned overnight stay in the MAF Wewak aircraft hangar. Arriving next morning, the staff was surprised to discover one box slightly open and one crocodile missing! The croc that had achieved freedom was never recaptured. Rightfully or not, I have always felt that the escape of that crocodile is my vindication for refusing to carry live crocodiles with me in the passenger cabin. Oh, Papua New Guinea, expect the unexpected.

Pumping fuel by hand into the Twin Otter.

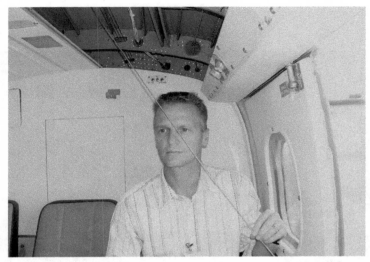

The path of the bullet shot at us in Aiyura, Eastern Highlands province.

A Tenkile - tree kangaroo.

On the ground at Busilmin airstrip, Sandaun province.

# DELTA

"Where?"

"Down there."

"Where?"

"Right there."

"Where?"

"Right there, where the strip of green is."

"It all looks green."

"No, the light bit over there."

"You mean there?"

"Yes, right there."

"But that's not enough room! It's on the side of a mountain! It is the side of a mountain!"

I think that is about how the conversation went between Jennifer and Karl as we headed into Dusin with our three little children for a week of bush orientation. I had flown as observer on a few flights in Papua New Guinea, but this was the first for Jennifer. Because of this, I offered for Jennifer to sit in front for a better view while I handled the kids in the back. Jennifer had flown with me a couple times in Canada, but that was while I was still training ten years earlier. In truth, Jennifer is not a big fan of flying in small planes. However, this aligns her with at least 90 percent of the wives of MAF pilots; most of them are not comfortable flying in small planes. Maybe they have heard too many pilot stories.

I remember the first time I took Jennifer for a flight in a Cessna 172 training aircraft. It was her first flight in any plane where there is seemingly nothing between you and the ground. In comparison to a passenger jet, there is much less noise dampening, much less temperature insulation, much better visibility. All those aspects combine to deliver a ride where a person feels and fully experiences every motion. On return from that first ride, Jennifer had to pry her cramped fingers from the bottom of the seat onto which she had been holding tenaciously. Her hands remained in a claw-like grasp for the next twenty minutes until circulation recovered sufficiently to permit a return to normal range of motion. Jennifer's second flight with me was much better—from her viewpoint. It was in a Cessna 180 "tail dragger." Most people are familiar with large aircraft where there are wheels under the body/wings and then under the nose of the aircraft. This configuration did not become the norm until the 1950s. Prior to that, most aircraft had wheels under the body/wing; but instead of a nose wheel, there was a wheel under the tail instead, giving rise to the moniker "tail dragger" as the tail appears to drag along the ground. In the earliest of planes, there wasn't even a wheel under the tail; it was simply a skid, such that the tail really did drag during ground operations. The Cessna 180, with only two people on board, has a significant excess of power, so it really jumps into the air on takeoff. Jennifer found that ride much more enjoyable; little did she know that even as the pilot, I felt that I was just barely holding on to a wild beast by the tail.

Mission Aviation Fellowship families new to Papua New Guinea undertake a period of orientation. There are some seemingly simple things like obtaining a driver's license and a bank account. It can actually take several trips to the correct office to actually walk away with a license. A common problem is, no film for the camera! The most important part of orientation, the part that makes everyday life possible, is learning the language and gaining an initial understanding of the culture. In a country with less than eight million people, but more than eight hundred distinct languages, communication is a huge challenge. Melanesian Tok Pisin developed as a business language to enable these diverse groups to speak with one another, primarily for the purposes of work or business. The history of the language is somewhat muddy, but it contains words derived from several European languages combined with Melanesian grammar. Our language course spanned nine days. Today it is stretched to twelve days, but even at that, after those few days, there really is nothing more to teach. There is limited vocabulary and limited tenses. Context is everything, so the only way to learn more is to practice. Having taken five years of high school French and not feeling anything like fluent after that, I approached language learning with some trepidation. I determined, however, that I would not be beaten and, after some prayer, ventured outside the razor-wire-topped fence of our housing compound to see what sort of trouble I could get into.

Papua New Guineans are very relational, so finding someone to talk to in Tok Pisin is very easy. While you may get many laughs at poor pronunciation, bad grammar and errors in what you are attempting to say, it is all good-natured. Perseverance makes a huge difference. Those that persist gain acceptance. For a language with such few words, it is decidedly easy to make a blunder. Mine was in our early stages of language classes. Jennifer was doing much better than me, getting answers right; and so I, joking, called her a "keener." For us, of course, that would mean a student who is motivated and progressing. Unfortunately, the lady teaching us understood me to say "kina." Kina is PNG currency. It is also slang for "tu kina meri," which translated directly would mean "two-dollar woman." A now very red-faced teacher had to explain to us that I had just called my dear wife a prostitute!

Using Tok Pisin to explain biblical things is also a challenge. Many English words are represented in Tok Pisin by a complete phrase, thus the Tok Pisin Buk Baibel is almost twice the size of the English Bible. There are some theological terms that take just a couple words in Tok Pisin. *Kotim bel* is the phrase meaning to be "convicted," as in feeling convicted in one's heart of sin. So *kotim*, as in "taken to court," and *bel* for "heart." Regrettably for Jennifer, replacing the letter *o* with the letter *u* makes a substantial difference. In preparing her testimony in Tok Pisin, Jennifer indicated that the Holy Spirit had "kutim bel" rather than "kotim bel." Once the language teacher recovered from uncontrollable laughter and picked herself up off the floor, we learned that "kutim bel" is a caesarean section. So it would seem that instead of the Spirit convicting Jennifer, the Spirit had given her a caesarean section.

Culture shock is something that people are warned about yet can still take us by surprise. We all subconsciously assume that everyone else is just like us, especially those that look like us. In truth, we had more culture shock going to Australia than we had going to Papua New Guinea. However, even after seventeen years in the country, I still feel that there is so much that we do not understand. They say that every culture is like an onion: layers upon layers. We tend not to see this in our own culture, but it is there. So during our orientation process, we really only get to see the first layer, but hopefully also grasp that there are so many more layers. As part of this cultural introduction process and also to help with language acquisition, families are sent to a remote location, a village with an airstrip served by Mission Aviation Fellowship. Our family undertook this bush orientation at Dusin. Compared to some other mission groups, MAF bush orientation is a bit wimpy. Other groups send their missionaries into the jungle to build their own house and live in it for a month. We find that for our purposes, a week is sufficient; and for our family, we felt every day of it. Our children were just five, three, and less than one, so it was quite the adventure.

There is nothing quite like the feeling of watching the airplane depart and realizing that you are now on your own, in a village from which there is no escape, with people that you do not understand. It is a very lonely feeling. We were fortunate in that our accommodation for the week was the house of a missionary that was no longer in Dusin. While the house was Western in style and much better appointed than the homes of the PNG folk, nevertheless, there were still a few challenges. There is neither electricity nor water supply in Dusin. The house had a rainwater tank, such that any rain landing on the roof flowed into the gutters and down into a big tank. Note that water for a tap or toilet requires pressure. The water from the rain tank had to be transferred to a smaller header tank on the roof of the house. By a wobble pump. Twice a day. Something like two hundred strokes of the pump to fill the tank. Cooking was by propane on a regular-type stove, but the real test was the fridge. It was a kerosene fridge which operates on quite a different set of thermodynamics than a normal electric Western fridge. Once we got it lit, it seemed to cool things down, but not really to the temperatures I expected. As the week progressed, the fridge became room temperature, the freezer became fridge temperature, and Jennifer's meal plans evolved to use up all perishable items as soon as possible while leaving sufficient nonperishable to last till the plane came. This left us praying ardently for good weather, airworthy aircraft, and a healthy pilot for the day we were to be retrieved. It wasn't until later that I learned the trick of kerosene fridges: they need to be rotated regularly. By rotated, I mean flipped upside down and left to sit that way for a while. Obviously advisable to remove all food and extinguish the flame first. Apparently something about recirculating the coolant.

Aside from the daily water transfer and ongoing battle with the fridge, we tried to accomplish what we were there for: to practice our Tok Pisin and learn a bit more about life for people in the isolated communities of Papua New Guinea. PNG society is quite separated as far as men and women are concerned, each with clear societal roles. So while Matt hung out with me, Jennifer would take Samantha and baby Nate and go be with the women of the village as they sat around and chatted while they did their chores. It was a source of significant frustration for Jennifer that most of the women just seemed to giggle in response to almost anything she said. Admittedly, our Tok Pisin was far from fluent, but we felt it should have been at least somewhat understandable. Sometime after our return from bush orientation, this came up in conversation. It seems that many ladies in Dusin only speak their local language; they do not understand Tok Pisin! So their nervous chuckles were simply embarrassment because they understood not a word of what Jennifer was saying!

Departing our main base located in Mount Hagen in the Western Highlands Province, aircraft turn north crossing the Wahgi Valley to jump the Sepik Wahgi Divide mountains through the Tremaearne Gap into the Jimi Valley. In good weather, this is easy. When the cloud is built up on the ridges, the process requires somewhat more care. Aircraft transiting the Tremearne West Gap require at least seven thousand feet of altitude. The spur valley on the north side of the gap takes a wicked left-hand turn just after crossing over the gap, so being able to see through before committing is essential. En route to Dusin, aircraft skip across the Jimi Valley, named for the river that runs through it, and then look for a molehill bump sprouting from the valley floor. This pimple marks the entrance to the Dusin valley, buried in the southern edge of the Bismarck Range. The valley is shaped a bit like a capital *L* rotated ninety degrees clockwise. Aircraft enter the valley along the short arm, with the airstrip located at the apex, oriented to point straight down the long arm of the *L*.

Dusin is a mostly grass runway just 450 meters in length with a slightly stepped slope averaging 8.2 percent. The only flat bit is the parking bay, and even at that pilots are cautioned to enter the parking bay at right angles since when the surface is even just a little bit damp, aircraft are prone to slide sideways. The parking bay is inconveniently halfway up the strip, and with it being so short, aircraft invariably travel past it on landing. The means that the pilot has to make a very cautious turn in the narrow confines of the strip width and then taxi down the hill to the parking bay. Much trickier than perhaps it sounds. Dusin is located on a spur ridge 5,800 feet above sea level, with the surrounding mountains rising to 8,000 feet on almost all sides. The valley floor is just 3,200 feet above sea level. This makes it very difficult for the pilot to judge his height when approaching to land as the runway appears to float halfway up the mountainside. With about half a kilometer to touch down, there is no turning around. An attempt to go around past this point will see the aircraft having an unpleasant encounter with a prominent chunk of granite just to the left of the runway threshold.

I believe my first encounter with Dusin was early on in my training in what is referred to as the observer phase. A new pilot will tag along on an operational flight to observe how things work, listen to the communication radio chatter, and start to get an appreciation for the complicated interaction of weather, terrain, and operational needs. I was riding along on a Twin Otter flight, filling the role of cabin attendant/load master. The flight was planned from Mount

Hagen to Dusin, then Simbai with a final leg back to Mount Hagen. Dusin to Simbai is just eighteen kilometers. The alignment of the runways, terrain, and flight paths dictate that takeoff from Dusin requires no turn to head towards Simbai. It is wheels off, straight ahead for the Simbai Gap; and just four minutes from departure, the airplane is in the circuit for landing at Simbai. The Twin Otter is a twin-engine twenty-passenger-seat aircraft that is operated with two pilots. In the four minutes between Dusin and Simbai, the crew must complete the following tasks: after takeoff checklist, VHF departure radio call, HF departure radio call, crew briefing for landing, descent checklist. The first time I observed the dance, it seemed an impossible goal. Once I had flown the Otter and gained some experience, I learned that four minutes even allows time for a spot of lunch on the way!

After flying as captain on the Twin Otter for a few years, I became a training captain and began to introduce pilots to this amazing machine, both as captain and as first officer. When I first learned to fly, I swore that I would never be a flight instructor; turns out my first job in aviation was just that. I worked for seven years primarily as a flight instructor teaching pilots from no experience at all right through to more advanced training on multiengine aircraft. When I moved into the training role on the Twin Otter, I leaned heavily on the experience I gained in those early years. My initial aversion to becoming a trainer may have been the result of knowing the mistakes I made while a student. The thought of basically being along for the ride while rapidly approaching the earth at one hundred kilometers per hour in a machine controlled by someone who doesn't really know what they are doing does not fill one with joy. Just like driving a car, people only learn to fly by doing. A flight instructor must balance this need of the student to try with his own desire for self-preservation. I clearly remember my first noteworthy adventure as a flight instructor.

Pilots in general and students in particular are prone to one, or a combination of, a handful of dangerous attitudes. Professional pilots have learned to recognize and overcome their own shortcomings; student pilots, not yet. And new flight instructors do not necessarily have the experience to recognize these in their students. When picking up a student who has been taught by another instructor, it can be difficult to separate competency from overconfidence. I was in the very early days of my first job when I was assigned to review spin recoveries with a student who was partway through the training for his private pilot license. An aerodynamic spin occurs when yaw is present at the point of a wing stall. For the nonaviators, this is a bad thing: the airplane is pointed toward the ground and approaching it at rather a tremendous rate. The view through the windshield is all ground, which is whirling around at a dizzying pace. This is a situation to be avoided at all costs. However, should one occur inadvertently, it is prudent to know how to rectify the situation. Hence, pilots are trained in recognition and recovery from spins. The process for recovery is quite simple: full opposite rudder, power to idle, ailerons neutral, control column forward. When the rotation stops, ease out of the dive and add power as required to recover lost altitude and speed.

There are two small glitches in this system which I knew and, unfortunately, assumed my student knew. When asked about the recovery process, he was quite confident, but I failed to recognize the glitch. Many aircraft flight manuals indicate that the control column should be moved "briskly" forward. *Briskly*, I discovered, is a word whose meaning is open to interpretation. Many training aircraft are built with a degree of stability such that moving the control column "briskly" forward is neither required nor, in fact, desirable. So my student and I departed the aerodrome, climbed to safe altitude, and conducted all of our safety checks. We then entered a spin from which I commanded the student to recover. That was where it all came to pieces: the student interpreted "briskly" as jam the control column all the way forward with vehemence and passion. I immediately found myself hanging from the shoulder harness with accumulated dust and debris freed from its hiding places floating around my ears. In our tiny training aircraft, the student's actions had placed us into an inverted spin: no fun at all. I am fairly sure that my call of "I have control"—meaning I was taking over the driving—was less professional in tone and emotion than I would have liked. Survive, we did; much wiser, I became.

Over the years, I have landed on many airstrips where conditions were less than ideal even for a mission pilot. Some of these resulted in what is politely referred to as "loss of directional control": think black ice in a car. In an aircraft with multiple engines, there is the advantage of being able to steer with asymmetric thrust. If there is more power on the engine on one wing than the engine on the opposite side, the aircraft won't go straight. In an aircraft already not travelling in the right direction, two wrongs do make a right: the power imbalance, correctly applied, forces the obstinate beast to comply with the pilot's wishes. On occasion, the time this can take— to regain control—is frighteningly close to the time available prior to impact with an immovable object. And sometimes, regardless of the pilot's best efforts, the plane just does its own thing.

Arou is an airstrip in the Southern Highlands that should possibly never have been opened for operations. Its proximity in both distance and elevation to the nearby river made it a prime candidate for flooding and just general dampness. Dampness equals slippery. I landed there one day as copilot, flying with a new captain. It was my turn to land, and perhaps as the more experienced pilot, it was a good thing.; for at touchdown, the Twin Otter commenced a graceful pirouette as it travelled straight down the middle of the runway. My hands and feet did a rather impressive dance over the controls and engine power levers in a vain attempt to bring the brute to heal. But we just kept going around, completing a complete and perfect 180-degree rotation, all the while perfectly maintaining the center line of the runway. With the aircraft now moving backward, the propellers trying to pull us forward, we came to a stop just about where we intended to park the aircraft, almost like it was intended. Almost like doing a handbrake turn to slide into a parking spot in busy shopping mall. A trick I have no intention of repeating either accidentally or on purpose.

In general, aircraft will have directional control issues when, just like a car, one wheel loses traction. That is basically what happened the day I flew into Dusin on a training flight with Richie. This was

Richie's first operational training day in the Twin Otter. He had been an MAF pilot in Papua New Guinea for a few years already, flying the single-engine piston aircraft. He was now transitioning onto the Otter. We fly the Twin Otter with two pilots, and the normal progression for a pilot new to the type is to gain some experience in the first-officer (co-pilot) role before training in the captain role. Training starts with some ground school. This is classroom instruction where the trainee is taught— hopefully learns—about aircraft systems and operational procedures, together with how the two pilots work as a crew, sharing the responsibilities in a clearly defined manner designed to avoid communication breakdowns. Ground school takes about eight days, by the end of which most students are pretty glassy-eyed. Instruction in the airplane commences with a couple of dedicated training flights. During this endorsement phase, the trainee pilot practices all normal and abnormal manoeuvres and procedures. Once considered competent, the second stage begins. LOFT (line-oriented flight training) is intended to teach the pilot how to operate the aircraft in service. Endorsement and LOFT are conducted only with a pilot approved as a training captain on the aircraft. Our flight into Dusin was Richie's first LOFT operation. Richie had been to Dusin before, so he was familiar with its peculiarities. In MAF rules, pilots new to a type are not allowed to be in control of the aircraft for landing and taking off at our most challenging strips. So for this landing, I was the driver.

The day was clear with no indications that we would experience anything above a normal level of adventure. The approach to land was a pretty good demonstration to my new co-pilot; even the landing was reasonable. Abeam the parking bay, it all went to custard: that means not good. We encountered a soft and slippery bit. More accurately, the left main wheel encountered a soft and slippery bit. With the left main hindered and the right main unbound, the aircraft executed a very rapid left gyration, presenting us with an exceedingly up close and personal view of the hillside that marks the southern boundary of the airstrip. The Twin Otter is just shy of sixteen meters in length. Dusin airstrip, ditch to ditch, is about twenty-five meters wide. On the completion of our surprising change in direction, and still moving at fifty-five kilometers per hour, there remained about seven meters between the nose wheel and the drainage ditch; seven meters between us and an awful lot of paperwork.

This is why I love the Twin Otter. Like most aircraft of its size, it is graced with a system of reverse thrust. The propellers normally push air backward to make the plane move forward. In reverse thrust, the pilot is able to control the angle of the propeller blade such that air is pushed forward to help stop the aircraft's forward motion. In a Twin Otter, maximum reverse thrust is rarely needed or used. Maximum reverse thrust is highly effective. Experience at Dusin suggests that it can slow an Otter from fifty-five to zero in six meters. The view out front was impressive: the man-high kunai grass blown completely flat. Happily, the remainder of Richie's LOFT was somewhat more pedestrian. Just another unexpected escapade in the land of the unexpected.

# ECHO

ELIPTAMIN IS A small community nestled in the middle of the Bismarck range slightly more than seventy kilometers from the Indonesian border. The Eliptamin River valley itself stretches just seventeen kilometers from the dead end in the east to the intersection with the Sepik River to the west. The village and its airstrip are located at the extreme eastern end. Like a great many highlands airstrips, Eliptamin poses challenges for the untrained. Located at 4,500 feet above sea level, the runway measures 574 meters by 26 meters and slopes up at 8 percent (the top is 46 meters higher in elevation than the arrival threshold). Pilots are cautioned about soft surface off centerline, tailwinds for landing, turbulence in the afternoon, and most critically, visual illusions due to rising terrain.

During their training for a flying license, pilots are usually taught to land at airports where the runway is flat, and the terrain leading to it and away from it are also essentially flat. Pilots learn to judge their three-dimensional descent path to the runway using a combination of observations, including the peripheral sensation of the ground getting closer to the aircraft. Where the terrain does not cooperate, pilots need to actively ignore this peripheral sensation and rely on other cues together with aircraft instrumentation to produce a safe arrival. At Eliptamin, the final approach course, when the aircraft is aligned with the runway, is flown over the deepest part of the valley where the river wends its way towards the Sepik. The pilot experiences the sensation of being very high on approach; the ground is much farther below the aircraft than the pilot has learned to expect from his training. For a pilot who doesn't actively compensate, his aircraft will end up being dangerously low as he reaches the runway. In extreme cases, a pilot can actually be flying below the height of the runway yet be convinced he is higher than the strip!

At Eliptamin, the issues actually start much earlier. A good pilot will start his approach to a bush airstrip by flying overhead the field to assess runway conditions. In isolated communities, runway state is reviewed with the acronym Wind LASSO. "Wind" means to check the speed and direction of the wind, including gusts. Aircraft prefer to land into wind as this decreases landing distance. However, for strips like Eliptamin, where the prevailing local wind will often be straight up the valley, pilots regularly need to land with a tailwind. LASSO, interpreted, becomes "Length, Altitude, Surface, Slope, and Obstructions." Length, Altitude, and Slope are where the pilot compares his expectations with what he is seeing. In poor weather, more than one pilot has been saved the embarrassment of landing at the wrong airstrip by following procedure and noting that the strip out the window does not match the description in the pilot's Route and Aerodrome Guide. Close observation and assessment of Surface and Obstructions are very important in remote-area operations. The pilot must evaluate grass length and possible "surface contamination": water, animals, soccer field? Dogs, chickens, pigs, goats, and people are all impairments to landing. Where clear terrain is in short supply, it is not uncommon for the runway to serve dual purpose as a soccer or rugby field. This is especially true around Easter when communities often have big celebrations. Goalposts must be removed before the plane can land! At one location, we couldn't land because the runway was being used as a drying platform for coffee beans. While the beans would not have significantly affected our aircraft, the entire crop would have been redistributed back into the jungle. *Obstructions* refer to items that might affect the landing and takeoff paths. In the jungle, trees can grow at a phenomenal rate, rapidly obscuring the approach path.

Having completed the inspection and deciding that there is nothing new that would preclude a safe landing, the pilot continues to fly perpendicular to the runway to establish his path on the downwind leg. Right here is where people new to PNG flying start to exhibit significant nervousness: the windscreen fills with mountainside and individual leaves take on clarity before the pilot can turn onto the downwind leg. The pilot then aims directly for a mountain and makes sure he is sufficiently low to clear the approaching ridge with little room to spare. Now into a tight bowl, it is power back, speed decreasing, flaps out, left turn, and push the nose down heading for the next ridge. A tight left turn into the center of the valley positions the airplane on final approach. Very soon, the aircraft must be established on the correct flight path at the correct speed. The point of no return, a small creek snaking right to left a few hundred meters before the runway threshold, marks the committal point: if the aircraft is not stable before that point, the pilot must conduct a missed approach. Once the little stream is in the theoretical rear-view mirror, the plane must land: going around is no longer an option as it will result in an unfavourable meeting with the mountain behind the strip.

In true PNG fashion, Eliptamin is just a few kilometers from its neighbours. Telefomin, Miyanmin, Gubil, and Duranmin are just few kilometers away: a few minutes by plane, days of rugged terrain on foot. A hop over the ridge to the south, through the Eliptamin road gap, puts one in the wide Telefomin valley; in fact, practically on top of Telefomin airstrip, which is hard up against the backside of that ridge. The two airstrips are little more than eleven kilometers apart as the aircraft flies. Over the ridge to the north and at sixteen kilometers distance lies the Miyanmin valley. Hidden in this valley are both the Myanmin and Gubil airstrips, both holding their own share of stories. Getting there, however, is less than simple as the ridge towers 3,900 feet above the Eliptamin runway. A straight-line flight time of five minutes is nearly doubled due to the need to make an orbiting climb before the plane can actually make any en route progress. Flying the Twin Otter to its very maximum performance can reduce the impact of this climb, but any error in judgment will negate any gains as the pilot will need to turn away from the mountain to make an additional terrain-clearing orbit.

Unfortunately, the Eliptamins relate most directly with the people of Blackwara and Duranmin, unfortunately because the flights to those communities are fraught with challenge. Duranmin is twenty-five kilometers east-northeast over the ridge that marks the end of the Eliptamin valley. Duranmin is buried deep in the bottom of a tight twisting valley that is often obscured by cloud. Duranmin is the runway that lost a third of its length in torrential overnight rain. The approach to Duranmin is at the ultimate end of non-standard. The pilot must execute some serious terrain flying, hugging the terrain close to the right wing tip before effecting a tight left turn to find the opposite side of the valley. Although now on final approach, the runway is not yet in sight due to the meandering nature of this slender valley. The pilot must trust his training and knowledge of the environment and keep the aircraft on its descending profile, dauntingly handy to the trees. At seemingly the last moment, a final bend to the left reveals the airstrip. To land or not to land must be settled immediately as the missed approach path follows the river to the right and requires a maximum-performance climb.

And then there is Blackwara. The circuit area at Blackwara is rather benign in comparison to Duranmin and Eliptamin, but the runway itself has caused many pilots to feel the frustration of a bogged aircraft. Being located very close to the river, the water table hovers not far below the runway surface. A rise in the river level results in a hidden erosion of runway strength. Route and Aerodrome Guide cautions regarding a "soft and draggy surface when wet" must be considered. Hard experience has resulted in an MAF prohibition on landing our larger, heavier aircraft after significant rain. There is no aircraft parking bay at Blackwara, so after landing, the aircraft pulls up at the side of the runway, maybe two-thirds of the total length from the landing threshold. Stopping in four hundred meters can be a challenge if wind gusts grab the aircraft late on approach. If the aircraft passes by the parking area, there is a great temptation to make a slight right then left turn to return to the parking bay. This is an ill-advised manoeuvre as the right side of the runway just up from the parking bay is very soft. The wary pilot will continue to the end of the runway where the surface is firmer for an aircraft to turn around. An attempted turn prior to the runway end can end in a bogged aircraft.

People talk about that "sinking feeling." In an aircraft on a PNG airstrip, that sinking feeling is the precursor to some significant effort. The pilot will need to engage the community to manually pull the aircraft out of its muddy ruts and back onto relatively solid ground. Blackwara is a relatively new airstrip, not in existence when our family first landed in Papua New Guinea. Western missionaries never ventured to Blackwara, but that doesn't mean it is an unreached people group: their relatives to the north in Eliptamin have taken on the responsibility for the spiritual salvation of their extended family.

It is interesting to see how other cultures celebrate—or not—what we consider to be normal holidays, predominantly Christmas and Easter. I would suggest that in Canada, at least, Christmas is far bigger than Easter, and perhaps not just outside the church. Certainly, the commercial aspects of Christmas far exceed those of Easter. The push for Christmas sales begins at the start of November and seems to continue well into January. This trend seems in part to be reflected in the Western church where Christmas banquets are often held by the end of November. Christmas carols are often sung from the first Sunday in Advent, four weeks before Christmas. But for Easter, except for those that remember Palm Sunday, events are limited to one weekend with perhaps a special service on Good Friday. Papua New Guinea is quite the opposite.

As Christmas approaches, shops do make an attempt to decorate, and they do play Christmas songs. I have always wanted to ask, but been too restrained to do so, what exactly goes though the mind of a Papua New Guinean when they hear the song "I'm dreaming of a white Christmas"? With no concept of snow and where Caucasians are referred to as "white skins," I often wonder if PNG people think the song is "I'm dreaming of a white [people] Christmas." One of the big struggles missionaries have had and continue to have in the presentation of the Gospel is the false link between spiritual blessing and physical blessing. This can also be seen on television in Canada, but in PNG, this is called *kago cult* (cargo cult). There is a subconscious connection between Jesus and things since the missionaries arrive bringing Jesus and carrying possessions. So although there is an increasing trend towards the accumulation of "stuff," Christmas is still nothing like in Canada; the buying of presents would be the exception.

While the lead up to Christmas is muted, churches do celebrate the season with services on Christmas Eve and Christmas Day. During our days living in Vanimo, we became quite involved in our little bush church, to the point where I was asked to be the speaker at the Christmas Eve candlelight service. Putting aside the wisdom of having a candlelight service in a building with a grass roof, it also was strange to celebrate Christmas in the tropics where it is perpetually summer. My parents were visiting with us. I was the planned speaker, and so I was supposed to have a short flying day on that Christmas Eve. Our final landing was at Green River, a half-hour flight time south of Vanimo. Green River is a very uncomplicated airstrip, so we anticipated no issues, until we loaded the plane for departure and the left engine failed to start, wouldn't even turn over. The starter was totally dead.

Now, the Twin Otter may be a mighty machine, but even it won't get airborne on one engine. Our smaller aircraft have piston engines, but the Otter is powered by two turbo props. A turbo prop is a jet engine that turns a propeller. Lots of science in that, but the key bit is that you can't "bump-start" (also called "push-start") a jet engine. For those who are real drivers and are competent with a standard transmission, you are probably aware that should the starter fail, you can start the engine of a manual-transmission car by pushing it forward then engaging the clutch while it is moving. A similar thing is possible with piston-powered airplanes: it is called "hand swinging," and it is not for the weak of strength or courage. The engine switches and fuel system must be set for the engine to run, the aircraft must be suitably restrained, and then the pilot steps in front of the aircraft, reaches out, and takes a firm grasp of a propeller blade by hooking his fingers over the top of the blade, preferably above his head for leverage. Giving a mighty downward push, with full body behind it, one hopes the engine will come to life. Should the engine roar, the propeller will immediately start rotating at something in the order of one thousand revolutions per minute. For a propeller with three blades, this means a blade will slice through the air, where the pilot's fingers were, fifty times per second! So the main thing when hand swinging is to be sure that you arrange for your body to move away from the aircraft immediately after pulling on the propeller. But since the Otter is not powered by a piston engine, this was not an option.

One can theoretically start a jet engine by blowing lots of air through the front end, but this won't work for the Otter, even if we had a source of high-speed air. So for us, dead starter equaled dead engine. Now in my entire time in PNG, I was only ever stuck out in the bush overnight once; this would have been my first, and what a rotten time for it to happen. After major discussions with my copilot Yong Kim and with the chief pilot and with the chief engineer, I climbed up on the wing to have a little peek just to make sure that all those wires were still attached. With the wing sitting three meters off the ground, climbing up on top of an Otter without a ladder is no mean feat, and getting down would certainly bring out the health and safety people. With time running out, we elected to give it one more go—and wahoo! The engine roared to life. We made it back home in time for me to rapidly shower off the day's excitement and run out the door for church. A couple days after Christmas, we made the trek to our maintenance base in Mount Hagen to change out the starter motor. Seems that it had contracted an aversion to operating when hot.

Easter in New Guinea is much more an event. Most denominations view this time as the most significant ministry occasion of the entire year. Youth camps are huge for some churches with young people travelling many hours to attend. Many congregations also plan large outreach events over the long weekend, evangelistic crusades to remote areas involving the assistance of Mission Aviation Fellowship. Involving numerous people, these are no small events, usually requiring the use of the Twin Otter as the largest aircraft available. Sound systems, electricity generators, multiple guitars both acoustic and electric, and even entire drum sets are involved, not to mention food for the team. Many of these launch from more "major" centers, but for the people of the Eliptamin valley, this is not considered an impediment. So we landed at Elips to load up for the roughly sixteen-minute flight to Blackwara.

Now, organizing this sort of mixed load requires some planning, experience, negotiating, and a generous dose of wisdom. Especially wisdom. At most of the airstrips, MAF has an agent who works on commission and has been trained to prepare the load manifest. However, for flights such as this, it is not uncommon for there to be somewhat more to load than has been declared to the agent. Getting a good look at everything that people want to send and then reweighing while loading is a prudent strategy. People are more used to being limited by space than by weight. In town, the public transportation vehicles (PMVs) stack up till there is no more room; personal space is not a consideration. So when it comes to the airplane, the pilot often needs to conduct a little tutorial: "Mak bilong balus I pulap. Sapos yumi putim sampela mo insait long balus strong bilong en no inap winim na bai yupela lukim balus kisim bagarap." The aircraft is full up to its maximum weight. If we put more inside, then the plane will not be strong enough to take off, and you will see the aircraft crash.

MAF pilots become adept at maximizing space, making sure that the baggage compartments are full up with weight when they are full up by space. The other factor to consider is balance. Like trying to find equilibrium for a teeter-totter, an aircraft in flight must have even weight distribution: too heavy at the front end or at the back spells disaster. Cargo in excess of that which will fit in the baggage compartments needs to join the passengers inside, and sometimes there just isn't enough space. This is where the negotiations begin as everyone has to be in agreement whether the people or the things are the priority. The drums, sound system, guitars all must go. "What about the massive bilums filled with taro and pumpkin? Can some stay back? Surely there is food in Blackwara." I personally hope that some of those large string bilums (woven bags) will be selected as excess to needs. The things are totally unwieldy and weigh ridiculous amounts. Lifting over thirty-five kilograms to shoulder height to make it into the airplane is rather a challenge. Of course, having seen many pilots try this, many locals see this as a great source of entertainment.

An apparently frail lady will walk up to the airplane with the bag strap slung around her forehead and the load on her back and drop it on the ground for the pilot to take care of. Novice pilots always get caught: little old lady, how heavy can this really be? So the pilot grabs it, expecting an easy lift and ends up pulling himself face-first into the ground as he discovers, to his chagrin, that the bilum is rather more dense than anticipated. The knowledgeable pilot will plan his attack: plant his legs, grip with both hands, bend the knees, then with a swift motion (utilizing generated momentum) sling the offending article up and into the airplane. Passengers on, briefings complete, engines started, checklists and radio calls complete—we are ready to launch this outreach.

An uneventful takeoff was followed by a climb down the valley to gain height. If the mental math is correct and the pilot ekes best performance from the aircraft and the weather is cooperative, then a right turn after a couple miles back towards the Eliptamin bowl will see the aircraft achieve sufficient altitude to clear the ridge that separates Eliptamin from Miyanmin. The most direct route from Elips to Blackwara threads a needle between Mount Stolle to the west and Fiamolu Mountain to the east. Respectively, these mountains soar to 9,200 feet and 10,000 feet above sea level. If the weather is good, then the pilot can navigate visually at 10,000 feet. If the weather is less than ideal such that the peaks are hidden in cloud, then the aircraft must be flown at an altitude that is known with certainty to clear the rocks with room to spare; in this case, 12,300 feet is necessary. Descent into Blackwara must be delayed until clear of Fiamolu Mountain and visual with the rest of the terrain. This does not occur until eighteen kilometers from Blackwara. For passenger comfort, descent rate is limited to no greater than one thousand feet per minute. With Blackwara elevation being sea level, the aircraft needs to lose at least nine thousand feet from minimum cruise altitude down to circuit altitude of one thousand feet—nine minutes, during which the aircraft eats up twenty-five kilometers. Even in a simple world, this would mean a circling descent for passengers and crew. But this is New Guinea, so things are rarely simple.

A 2,600 foot ridge blocks the direct route just five kilometers from Blackwara. Pilots seek to descend down into the tiny Alibai River which hooks up with the only slightly larger Niar River. It is the Niar River that bends around the final ridge, right turn followed by left. If the pilot remains focused and flies with precision, holding airspeed and refusing deviations in descent rate, then the aircraft will arrive exactly on target for the downwind leg into Blackwara. Any divergence from the ideal, and everyone gets to experience one more doughnut in the sky. The pilot cannot afford to be anything less than self-critical: too high at the start will undoubtedly result in too high at the end of the process. Being just 10 feet too high over the threshold can result in a 50-meter addition to the landing distance; and when the runway is only 574 meters long to begin with, well, you get the picture.

The flight to Blackwara that day and the subsequent landing were actually all very unremarkable. There was no cloud to manoeuvre around, no aircraft bogged to the axles in wet, soggy mud. What there was, however, was a warm and traditional PNG welcome. The outreach team and pilots were each adorned with a lei of tropical flowers. More memorable for me, and something that was unique, was the gift of a headdress made from cockatoo feathers. The cockatoo is a type of parrot that, in PNG, is generally white all over with a large head crest and a playful personality.

After Easter, we revisited Blackwara for the return trip to Eliptamin. The aircraft-loading drama was repeated, complicated by the gifts with which the team was loaded down. The vision of Mission Aviation Fellowship is to partner with others for the spiritual and physical transformation of isolated communities. It was a real and unexpected treat to be part of this passing of transformation from one isolated community to another.

# FOXTROT

## ~Flour Balls *and Other Kids' Escapades~*

FLOUR BALLS. SORT of like a plain doughnut, only not. A combination of flour, water, sugar, and baking powder rolled into an orb the size of a pool ball and deep-fried. They don't do much for me, but for my friend Ruben, there is nothing quite like flour balls with a cup of tea. Indeed, most Papua New Guineans delight in a snack of flour balls. And included in "most Papua New Guineans" are our two boys. As they became old enough to be released solo on the unsuspecting population of the town of Goroka, Matt and Nate enjoyed the short walk to the little gas station/store across from the MAF office to pick up a few flour balls. At just a few cents a bag, it is one of the things they miss intently. That and Bu.

Now, Bu was the source of some discussion in our house. I should, of course, indicate that Bu is a drink: a PNG version of an energy drink. To my tongue, the deep-red liquid is rather sickly sweet. As a father, the bigger worry is the heritage of Bu. In PNG, a large portion of the population are addicted to the chewing of buai. In combination with lime and mustard sticks, the chewing of betel nut can produce a mild euphoric effect similar to ingesting significant amounts of caffeine. The lime is not the lime you are thinking of, and the mustard stick isn't mustard. The lime is ground, powdered coral: pure calcium hydroxide. Not the green citrus fruit. The mustard stick is like a green bean, only nothing like a green bean. The betel nut itself is hidden in a husk the shape of a lemon but about the size of a small plum. Once out of the husk, the exposed kernel, the chewing bit, is equivalent in size to an average strawberry. In contrast to the mild buzz, the blend of nut, mustard stick, and lime side effects include mouth cancer. But for nonchewers, there is another rather disgusting consequence: buai mouth.

Although no ingredients are red, when blended by chewing, the mixture turns blood-orange red. Teeth and lips become stained. It is rather startling to approach a person on the street that looks "normal," until they break into a large grin, revealing a mouth in this very unsettling colour. Fortunately, PNG does not have a voodoo culture, for that merged with buai mouth could be disturbing. Worse than that even is the excessive amount of saliva generated by the chewing, which is summarily ejected from the mouth, usually just onto the ground. The red splats on the ground are rather unsightly, such that towns now have signs: "Lukautim taun bilong yumi, tambu tru long spet buai" (keep our town clean; spitting of betel nut is forbidden). In the PMVs, driver/operators also ban the spitting, but not the chewing, of buai. Passengers then must collect this surplus, often in an empty Coke bottle. Not very pleasant at all. Even more interesting is to watch a driver's door open at ninety kilometers per hour to witness a liquid stream in this bright pomegranate shade ejected into the vehicle slipstream.

While the carcinogenic effects tend to be ignored, there is more than one way in which buai can be dangerous to your health. We have conducted significant numbers of medevacs (MEDical EVACuations) for a wide array of health issues, including buai-related injury. Betel nut grows on trees, some of such stature that harvesting requires a monkey climb, made more hazardous by the need to carry a machete to lop the nut bunches off the main branch. One poor fellow buried his bush knife into the trunk so as to have both hands free for the next stage of the ascent. Regrettably, the strength of his blow was insufficient to securely lodge the knife in the tree, and it let go at an inopportune moment, plummeting to the ground. It carved a path between the man's body and trunk, where the space for the passage of the offending weapon was inadequate. The tree, being of sterner material than the gardener's abdomen, the path of least resistance went in favour of the stomach, where the machete literally carved a path. I was happy that by the time we arrived on scene to transport the man to hospital, someone had conducted first aid and returned the man's insides back to his inside. As far as I know, the unfortunate harvester made a full recovery.

Bu drink doesn't actually contain any betel nut, so in the end, this dad caved and allowed his kids to partake in limited quantities, encouraging them to "drink responsibly," as appropriate for any other energy drink. Of less concern are the meat pies. As you may have gathered, fast food in PNG is not the same as in Canada. Although I have seen T-shirts from Dairy Queen and McDonalds, these types of establishments are not to be found in PNG. Their place in society is taken by the kai bar. On the menu are such delicacies as deep-fried chicken feet and lamb flaps. From my perspective, chicken feet are little more than overdone skinny pretzels, and lamb flaps are great if you like a little meat with your fat, but flavour is on the tongue of the taster. Also available are flour balls and meat pies. The meat pies are probably a leftover from the days of Australian administration, and so long as you aren't squeamish about the possible lineage of the contents, they do taste good.

While the boys enjoy the contents of the can, they tell me that there is additional entertainment to be found with the can once it is empty. Funny, but it's a bit like when they were toddlers, and the box was as much fun as the present it held. But to fully appreciate the Bu bomb, you need to hear about Kea (kay-ah) and the river and up-track. And before Kea and the river and up-track, perhaps a little background on the difference between risk management for kids in PNG and in Canada. As my children like to remind me, I am not as young as I used to be, and I think perhaps I grew up in a different time. A time when running around on the back roads on our bikes was acceptable. A time when we could take those bikes, pretending they were powered, and whip back and forth through the "lake" under the train bridge. A time when we could play unsupervised in Farmer Gray's field at the end of our little cul-de-sac. Climbing the tree with the "six-foot drop," building and rebuilding the tree house. Perhaps those were simpler and less-dangerous times for young children. Fortunately for our boys at least, to extent, for them, those times still exist in PNG. There were at least four things that Matt and Nate enjoyed in their teenage years: soccer, Kea, up-track, and "Lillie."

"Lillie" was a Honda 125XL, bored out by a previous owner to be a 175. Fairly ancient itself, the bike was good for one rider but struggled with two. That never stopped the guys from trying, however. Flat tires, starting issues, and the repair of fenders and headlights were all part of the joy of owning this treasured toy. Ownership was a partnership between the three of us, although I never learned to ride. And being of limited intelligence when it comes to two-wheeled vehicles, it was a very good thing that I had friends who were competent bike mechanics. Not street legal, the boys drove "Lillie" around the New Tribes Mission facility and up-track.

The NTM facility was built on the side of a hill that continued to rise outside the back fence. At the top of the rise stood an electricity transmission tower, no longer used for that purpose yet ideal for slinging hammocks. The tower was actually in the middle of a cow field. Not those sandy brown Jerseys with the eyes that suck you into believing they are cute and cuddly. Not the stereotypical black-and-white Holsteins. More like Brahma cows. The ones that you might equate with India: large with generous horns. It was a great place to ride bikes with friends. There are, of course, plenty of untold stories of jumps that failed to play out according to script, encounters with the cows, one involving a pedal bike and a rope! Groups of boys would venture up-track on a weekend for an overnight stay under, hopefully, the stars. Firewood and various canned foods would be hauled up to the tower, usually a bit of kerosene to aid with the ignition and a bush knife to split the wood. And therein lies the craziest story. The story of how Matt cut his hand with a machete and was sewed up by his friend.

Medical care in New Guinea is somewhat different than in Canada; expectations are perhaps less, and we as parents certainly took care of much more ourselves than we might have living in Canada. Like the time Matt ran into our clothesline and split his head open just beside his left eyebrow. I think that stitches might have been recommended, but where we were living at the time, it seemed more prudent to employ a couple of butterfly closures, kiss him on the head, and send him off again. A book titled *Where There Is No Doctor* was our constant companion in those early years. Later on, we were privileged to live where another mission had a clinic which we were able to access. So Matt and a couple friends were off on an up-track adventure. It was after midnight, and the boys were chopping wood for their fire. The timber was being somewhat stubborn, and the bush knife had lodged in the end of the stick. Matt picked it up with his right hand on the handle to slam the knife-stick combination on the ground and held the stick with his left. Just prior to impact, the wood released the machete such that when the stick hit the ground, the knife shifted slightly to the left; and instead of cleaving the wood, it carved into Matt's hand. There is very little ambient light in the bush of PNG, so the boys inspected the wound by flashlight and tried to stem the tide with what little supplies they had at their disposal. It soon became apparent that additional resources were going to be needed. As it so happens, one of the friends with Matt was the son of a medical professional. The decision was reached that perhaps waking up the dad was the best course of action.

Down the track in the dark, hoping that all the cows were asleep, a covert knock on the bedroom door. "Uh, Dad, we've got a little problem." Amazingly, the blade had sliced between thumb and forefinger, narrowly missing both tendons, so it was a simple flesh wound. Difficult to say how this would have turned out if the tendons had been cut, probably not much differently; but as it was, stitches was still the obvious requirement. Off to the clinic. Clean up some blood so the depth of the problem could be ascertained, then followed by a little freezing. On graduation, the friend had aspirations to join the medical profession himself, so after a couple stitches were in, the friend had a turn, successfully completing a couple sutures, leaving it to the professional to finish the job. Matt fully recovered with a scar and a cool story to go with it. We knew none of this until the phone rang at 2:00 a.m. By then it was all said and done, but in the land of the unexpected, that's what we expect.

Up-track was not the only source of adventure; there was the river. The river is the Asaro River. It commences at the top end of the Goroka valley, wending its way southward along the edge of the mountains till it meets up with the Bena River, becoming the Tua River, into which eventually runs the Wahgi River. The waterway gradually increases in size and volume as it weaves its meandering course. People of all ages and ethnic backgrounds enjoy tubing along its twists. A truck tire inner tube is an ideal mode of transport for the river run, but care is required especially during wet season when the ride can rival any attraction to be found at a major theme park. Launching invariably presents the greatest hazard.

On one occasion, I went with the kids and some friends when the river was at the height of its ferocity. Stepping into the water and endeavouring to settle into my tube, which was rather more child size than man size, I was flipped head over heels and washed downstream in a swirling maelstrom of bumps and crashes over submerged boulders, which left me with visible memories for an extensive period of time. Try as I might, my feet refused to find purchase in the overwhelming current, and I was mildly concerned that I may just be committed to white water body surfing for the next several kilometers. Fortunately, I was washed into a calmer—relatively calmer, that is—spot where I could finally stand up. Reversing my situation in the tube allowed me to stay afloat, but riding face-first is somewhat higher risk than travelling sitting in the tube. The diameter of the tube precluded that orientation, so face-first it was with an eagle eye for those hidden obstacles reaching for my now trailing legs. Now imagine experiencing all of that in the dark.

They say that boys have a limited understanding of physical consequences—fear of death—until they are about twenty-five. They say that at that age, a "risk-aversion" hormone is released, and the young man is suddenly aware of his own mortality. I have no idea if the science backs up that theory, but personal observation does. When we lived on the north coast, there was a waterfall we could hike to that had delightful vistas and a great little pool. We had lots of fun there with our young kids. Three of my favourite photos are of me with each of our children battling the waterfall. The water streamed down a rock face into the pool that was only deep in the very center, a deep well that sunk into the pool yet only a very few meters across. To jump off the escarpment maybe five meters above required the intrepid adventure seeker to launch out at least that far, over the sloping face to find the tiny target. On one occasion, we took some visitors with us to enjoy our hidden spot. Those of us who had passed that key age and apparently received our dose of fear hormone, there was no way we were going to stalk death by attempting that leap. With so many ways for it all to go wrong, not least of which was missing the target, the attraction of climbing to the top of the falls was severely limited. Not so much for those with fewer years under their belt.

So the prospect, the very concept of attempting a tube trip down the river in the dark would no more penetrate my consciousness than sticking my head in the mouth of a crocodile. Yet for Matt and his buddy, this seemed like not just great fun but a brilliant idea. Armed with nothing more than a brace of inner tubes and two theoretically waterproof flashlights, the valiant duo sallied forth into the night. It is my theology that guardian angels were about that evening, for no sooner had the pair set sail than one flashlight disappeared into the depths of the river. Not to be dissuaded, the boys completed their adventure and returned home with no one the wiser. I suspect, however, that there was an appreciation of having got away with something, for it was some months before the complete story surfaced at the family dinner table.

And there is Kea. I think this is best understood by indicating that "what happens in Kea stays in Kea." The trip to Kea requires a twenty-minute walk along the highlands highway. Of itself, this is sufficient danger for many. Many drivers consider road rules and speed limits to be of an advisory more than binding in nature; and with many potholes and decaying pavement edges, the concept of a "right" side and "wrong" side of the road is also somewhat flexible. Having survived that part of the trek, it is then another hour and a half through the jungle in search of the oasis called Kea Falls. The track passes through the village that owns the falls. Unlike Canada, the vast majority of PNG land is owned by individuals and families.

At any given airstrip, it is possible to look upwards to a mountain and enquire to whom it belongs. The answer is probably convoluted and would be in the order of, "Left of the second banana tree is Joe's, right of that but below the bi rock is Bob's, and everything else is mine." So to enjoy Kea Falls, visitors must have permission. As it has been a regular adventure spot for many years for mission kids, the village graciously allows the teens to pass through. Unexpectedly, this spot in the bush is actually safe for mixed groups, so this is one place that girls can also enjoy the astounding PNG countryside. Similarly to up-track, although limited to daylight hours, the kids sling hammocks to laze away the day, boil water to cook packages of instant Maggi noodles, and goof around in the water. And oh yeah, one more thing: Bu bombs.

I hesitate to recount this, so I think we will put it in the category of "I have heard that." Similar to "I have a friend with a problem." When delivering our briefings for passengers on our aircraft, in addition to operation of seat belts and location of emergency equipment, we advise the public that smoking is prohibited, as is the carriage of "gas masis." It was probably not until "my friend" told me of the inherent entertainment value that I realized why we collect and remove the "gas masis": cigarette lighters. The cheapest versions are liable to explode when striking a hard surface with passion or when heated. I am told that a cheap plastic lighter inserted in an empty Bu can, which is then subsequently half filled with kerosene and placed in a fire, results in a rather dramatic event. Do not try this at home! Especially when there is a fire ban on. PNG doesn't have fire bans; even in dry season, forest fires just do not happen. I have watched walls of flames gobbling up the jungle grass over an entire hill side, only to stop and burn out for no clearly obvious reason. But as Nate tells me, "Hey, Dad, at least it's not drugs."

And in that, he is correct. Not one of our three children would trade their PNG upbringing for the world. The experiences they had, while foreign in many aspects to their peers in Canada, forged both memories and character. Their appreciation for culture and diversity has been enhanced by their childhood on the other side of the world, maturing as people in a country maturing as a nation. Surrounded by adoptive aunts and uncles from around the globe, and free from the possibly stifling societal expectations and pressures for children in the West, our three youngsters lived the stories from which adventure tales arise. We were far from clear what to expect when we took our tiny tots away from family and friends to this intimidating land. I suppose we did anticipate that, in some way, there were things we were "giving up." And while we did experience robberies and tropical illnesses, and we did miss out on extended family Christmases, our kids were in no way deprived. We gained far more than we lost, and perhaps that is the most unexpected thing of all.

# GOLF

## -Gubam *Cake and Sauce*-

"AND DOUGHBOY OVER there is building the Hoover Dam!"

I always enjoyed our family dinner table. Well, almost always. It was good at the end of the day to gather round our table for supper and share stories of the day. When Sam, Matt, and Nate were young, we used to play "guess where dad went today." However, kids being kids, not all dinners were wreathed in smiles and laughter. There were times where inappropriate attitudes and behaviours were expressed that required some fatherly admonition. Sometimes this disagreement between parent and child centered on food: likes, or more probably, dislikes. I believe on that day, two of our three little darlings were in trouble for some misdemeanor, and perhaps my day had been overly taxing. Regardless, I was on a roll with disseminating parental reprimands and figured if I was scolding two, then I might just as well do a preemptive strike on number three. At that time, the target of my vexation was in the habit of separating his food: meat from potatoes from vegetables. Only on this day, he had deemed it best to build up a mound of potatoes to hold back the tide of gravy. All I could think of by way of reproach was the "Hoover Dam" outburst.

We did our best to teach our kids to eat all types of foods, but I guess it is natural that we all have something that we would prefer not to eat. As parents, we attempted to at least have our young ones express their preferences in a polite manner. When they were slow to clear their plates, it was clear that, despite protestations to the contrary, they actually did not like what had been served. "Really, Mom, I'm not that hungry" was rarely believed. But in truth, I have my own limits. One evening we had visitors over who kindly brought dessert. Jennifer served me a whopping big slice of a delightfully prepared sweet. Unfortunately, crème brûlée turns my stomach. Politeness, however, dictated that I force it down. Great gulps of coffee contributed to my success, but once the visitors had departed, I explained to my dear wife that crème brûlée was high on my list of "no-eat" foods. Cooked chocolate pudding also sits high on that list, so it is only fair that my children be permitted foods that they just will not eat. Onions and peppers are not favourites, for one. Anything breakfast is a problem for another. It is a challenge when there is a child that doesn't like toast, cereal, or oatmeal, and you live in a country where breakfast options are severely limited. For the third child, it was "pudding." To this day, we are all unclear exactly what it was he objected to. What we did know, however, was that there was one particular dessert that he would eat, but only if we called it "cake and sauce."

Cake and sauce was a dessert made in two parts but baked as one. The cake mix went into the glass baking dish first, followed by the sauce on top. In the oven for forty-five minutes, the two components exchanged places with the cake rising to float on top of the sauce that had sunk to the bottom. Out of the oven, the cake had a nice crusty shell. The spoon would break the surface and sink into the moist cake below. Further pressure, and the spoon plunged through into the gooey sauce below. Now imagine landing an airplane on that!

Once our children began to abandon us for university back in Canada, our Saturday mornings, and sometimes Sunday mornings too before or after church, were given over to attempted voice communication with them. I do not describe these as phone calls as that would give entirely the wrong impression of how we were attempting to chat. The cost of a single phone call would have required me to sell the family farm, plus possibly a leg, a kidney, and three toes. So Skype became our best friend. For those who may not be familiar, Skype is a computer program that allows voice communication between computers, or between a computer and regular phone. Much cheaper than attempting phone to phone, it is unfortunately dependent on a stable and sufficiently fast internet connection. When we first arrived in Papua New Guinea, this form of conversation was barely possible since internet was still in its infancy even really in Canada. The other factor that contributed stress to this chat quest was the time difference. Samantha was either thirteen or fourteen hours behind us, depending on the time of year, and Matt was sixteen or seventeen hours behind. Matching their schedules to ours made reliable internet a really big deal for us. But of course, this is the developing world, so nothing should be taken for granted. Computer and internet modem required power, so not only did we need the internet to work but also the electricity. We bought a new computer battery to remove that factor from the equation and a UPS (uninterruptible power supply) for the modem. Yet for a period of time, internet connectivity became a problem at our house. This was eventually resolved by the purchase of yet another piece of equipment: an antenna mounted high on the roof with line of sight direct to the internet transmitter. This acquisition was still in the future that Saturday in March, so we had transferred the entire process to the airport office where we were able to establish an acceptable internet connection.

In the middle of chatting with Matt, we received word that one of MAF PNG's Cessna Caravans had "found" a soft spot on the runway, and the propeller had gone through the dirt, causing some damage. The Cessna Caravan looks like a Cessna C206 on steroids. Powered by the same engine as the Twin Otter, the Caravan flown in Papua New Guinea at the time of this incident was an example of the original design, equipped with nine passenger seats. Dubbed the "short Caravan" in comparison to the extended-body Grand Caravan, one of our managers alternatively called it the "baby Caravan." The aircraft had flown thirty minutes southwest from its home base in Kawito in the isolated Western Province to Gubam primarily to pick up a medevac patient. The older man, suffering from pneumonia and huddling close to the fire for warmth, had fallen into the fire and received some significant burns. It may seem strange to note a single province as isolated in a country that defines the word, yet even though it is the largest by landmass, the Western Province is arguably the least developed. The patient wasn't actually from Gubam but from the neighbouring village of Bimadiben.

As the plane flies, the two communities are fifteen kilometers apart. Fortunately, the ground is relatively flat in this southern lowlands area. Unfortunately, it is subject to swollen rivers and extensive patches of marsh. Since the runway at his home village of Bimadiben was unusable due to long grass, the man had been carried through the jungle to meet the plane at Gubam. It may not seem that long grass should stop an airplane from flying, except that is exactly what it does. When grass gets too long, it impedes the acceleration to the point that an aircraft literally cannot achieve sufficient speed to take off in the runway length available.

The Caravan had come to grief at the very end of the runway. In PNG terms, the 690 meters of runway would be considered quite long. The lack of significant downslope to aid in acceleration and a surface that seems to hold tightly to the wheels dictate that pilots avail themselves of every possible meter. Together with air in the tanks and altitude above the aircraft, runway behind the plane is one thing of no use to a pilot. The parking bay at Gubam is very close to the southern end of the runway, so the pilot taxied the airplane the short distance back to the very start of the airstrip. It may seem unlucky that the nose of the aircraft broke through the grassy surface and sank deeply into the mud. It is far better to have this kind of incident at taxi speed. Finding a soft spot at takeoff speed will see the aircraft on its back and the pilot hanging from his straps, if not much worse. So in hindsight, the sequence of events was probably good.

In light of the visible damage, it was fairly obvious that the Caravan would require significant attention before taking to the air again, so the stranded pilot had carefully checked the rest of the airstrip to see if it was safe for another aircraft to land. This type of event is not unheard of. Construction of a bush airstrip is an inexact science and a massive undertaking when limited to manual labour. Giant tree stumps may simply be buried. Hiding as a ticking time bomb, over the years, the wood rots away, leaving a veiled void: a tiger trap into which an unsuspecting aircraft can drop. The airstrip appeared to be firm and strong, and with one of our aircraft having just landed on it, we were all confident that the problem was isolated and that surface would support another aircraft. The weather was less than ideal on the Saturday, and the distances involved suggested that a whole day be set aside for the rescue. So after some discussion, it was decided that myself and fellow Canadian pilot Jason would fly to Gubam in the Twin Otter the following day to assess the damage to the Caravan, pick up the pilot, and complete the medevac.

Sunday dawned with clear skies, which was a rarity during that season. We were airborne by 7:20 a.m. First stop was just twenty-seven minutes to the west at our engineering base in Mount Hagen, where we picked up some aircraft maintenance engineers and equipment, and also topped off the fuel tanks. The Twin Otter may be a great "off-road vehicle," but an efficient long distance cruiser it is not. Winds were howling at ninety kilometers per hour at ten thousand feet as we tracked along to the southwest. Arriving overhead Gubam at just before 10:00 a.m., we had a good look at the situation. Unlike most airstrips in the highlands which are very steep and necessitate landing in one direction and taking off in the other, Gubam is like a "normal" runway in that we can land and take off in either direction. With our Caravan "parked" at the southern end, we had to decide which direction was the best for our own landing: over the Caravan, or heading towards the Caravan. Approaching over the disabled aircraft potentially reduced the LDA (landing distance available). Heading towards the aircraft once the wheels were down on the ground invited a disaster should we fail to stop in the LDA. In the end, the wind decided the issue for us as it was too strong to do anything other than land over top of the disabled aircraft.

We roared in over the immobilized plane to an approach and touchdown that were uneventful. Initially uneventful, that is. As we slowed down on the runway, we could feel a certain sluggishness to the surface. This was not unexpected as the middle of the strip is known to be what we refer to as "draggy." We were easily slowed to a fast walking pace by the midpoint of the runway, yet caution was still extremely advisable, so I hesitated to try and turn around at the midpoint of the runway, electing instead to wait till a bit farther along where it would hopefully "feel" a bit better. Having flown the Twin Otter for well over fourteen years, I was well attuned to the personality nuances of this machine. I could sense when things were not quite right, when the plane was being tempted to give up a little speed when in flight or slide a little when on the ground. What happened next was something unprecedented in my experience. Without any warning, the nose wheel abruptly "disappeared," and all I could see out the front window was grass! It all happened so fast, much faster than the reading of this description. I felt the aircraft catch and the nose start to bog. I added power, hopeful of powering through this assumed soft spot. The speed of events meant that barely had I added power when, unbidden, my hands were reducing the power again as my subconscious signaled that we were not getting out of this quickly. The Otter had come to rest on its nose with the nose wheel hidden in the ground to a depth of ninety-three centimeters. From the outside, it appeared that the aircraft had no wheel under its nose baggage; it was completely hidden from sight, swallowed whole by the earth. As we were moving very slowly at the time, there were no injuries; and, in fact, the aircraft remained in flyable condition with damage limited to a few wrinkles in the skin under the nose. The engines, slung under the high wings, provided sufficient ground clearance for the propellers even with the nose buried to the hilt.

With the assistance of the men, women, and children of Gubam, we were able to raise the Otter back to a level plain. That makes the arduous process sound rather uncomplicated. Normally, when an aircraft nose wheel is bogged, we load a few bodies in the back of the aircraft to try and tilt it backwards while two gangs pull on long straps secured to the robust legs to which the main wheels are attached. In this case, those very wheels had furrowed their own trenches. The lone spade for the entire community made an appearance for us to smooth out the tracks and hopefully provide a reasonable path along which the accumulated manpower could reverse the aircraft. The situation was more tenuous than first appreciated. Even as we enacted our strategy, the main wheels were observed to sink farther into the weak subsurface. As strain was put on the straps, the aircraft seemed to pivot, driving the left wheel even farther under.

A few rough-hewn boards appeared, and after much effort, the aircraft was recovered onto those planks, which provided snow-shoe-like support for the three wheels on which our aircraft perched. The exertion required to raise the aircraft from the bog deterred me from any attempt to taxi the aircraft clear of the runway. There was no way I was going to drive our four-tonne three-million-dollar basically undamaged aircraft over a now-known-to-be-questionable surface. In the midst of this, I placed a call to the chief pilot to share with him our unbelievable story and strongly advised him that the next aircraft to visit Gubam should be of the rotary-winged species (a helicopter).

The weather we had negotiated on the run into Gubam, together with the time of day, dictated that we were going to have the opportunity to sample the hospitality of the Gubam community. This was to be just the second time in all my PNG flying that I was to be stuck overnight. The weather continued its uncooperative trend such that it was not one but two nights that we all bedded down in Gubam. Our three days in Gubam were an insight into how the "other half" live. If Busilmin is the end of the earth, then Gubam is conceivably at the other end. Besides the incongruity of a cell phone tower in the middle of the village, there is little evidence of the twenty-first century in this little village of less than five hundred people. Gracious hospitality was extended to us during our stay, and yet we were far from the lap of luxury. Fed and kept dry from the significant rain, my old bones were pleased for the comfort of a real bed by the time we departed Gubam. We spent our nights sleeping on a split bamboo floor—not even remotely smooth.

On our first evening, I approached dinner with an amount of trepidation. Sak sak and taro are staples of PNG diet. Sak sak is the processed pulp from inside the trunk of the sago palm while sago is a rather bland root vegetable. Both are essentially pure starch with very little taste to excite the Western palate. My low expectations were replaced with a very tasty cassava (like potato) and greens cooked in genuine fresh-off-the-tree coconut milk. It is perhaps best not to ask the origin of the greens as they could be edible leaves of just about anything from the jungle floor. A steady diet of the same stew over the next three days did have some interesting side effects on my lower GI tract. Having gratefully and thankfully consumed dinner, the sun went down; and with little else to do, we retired to our "beds."

A local pastor had sacrificed for us, vacating his family from his three-room elevated house such that our merry band would have a place to lay our heads. We were provided with mosquito nets under which we were protected from the hoards of evening marauding mosquitos that no doubt carried doses of malaria and possibly even dengue fever. Malaria can be treated reasonably effectively with medicine, but for dengue, the only treatment is time—lots and lots of time. However, the airborne creatures bothered me less than the four-legged kind. In the middle of the night, I sensed a rustling nearby and cracked an eye in time to observe a black ghost whistle by just inches from my face. Unclear whether I had observed a large rat or a small cat, I actively convinced myself it had been a kitten, attempted to find a spot where the bamboo contoured to my back, fluffed up my bag now doubling as a pillow, and pretended to go back to sleep.

Shelter, water, fire, signal are priorities for those involved in aircraft accidents in remote regions, but stories of those unfortunate enough to be stranded for long periods recount that boredom is one of the biggest enemies to survival. I have to say that even our three short days in Gubam confirmed that to me. It did, however, provide us with lots of time to investigate what was going on with this airstrip—which brings us back to cake and sauce. As we walked up and down, left and right, doing our best to cover the entire seventeen thousand square meters, it appeared at first that nothing was amiss: exactly as the first pilot had reported. We acquired the single spade that we had used previously to extricate the aircraft and dug a few test holes. The initial five to thirteen centimeters was a firm crust, giving the appearance of a surface sufficiently strong to bear the weight of our aircraft: a crust very much like our representative cake. However, this shell concealed a lower layer that was extremely soft, exactly like the sauce that was hidden by our cake. Once through that surface crust, we discovered that it was possible to push a long stick straight into the ground to a depth in excess of one meter. Push the stick with just a couple fingers: no hammer, no pounding, no leaning, no effort whatsoever. These conditions made it extremely dangerous to attempt a takeoff. As an aircraft gathers speed along the runway and as it rides over the surface undulations, the shock absorber that connects the nose wheel to the fuselage rides up and down, soaking up at least some of the bumps. As the weight ebbs and flows on that nose wheel, so would the pressure on that unpredictable runway skin. The odds of the aircraft burying its nose a second time escalate to heights that would make a Las Vegas bookie squeal like a girl. To attempt a takeoff in these conditions was out of the question.

It was rather obvious that the runway was floating like the cover on a backyard pool. With the few tools to hand the community immediately bent backs to the task of digging out the drains. As fast as they shifted mud, the trench filled with water. Dug to a depth of at least a meter, water leaked out from under the airstrip, into the ditch, and away. At least it tried to go away. Unfortunately, the water table was so high due to an extensive rainy season that the water just sort of sat in the drains.

The inclement weather that had caused the high water levels continued to conspire against us over the next couple days, and it was not until Tuesday afternoon that a helicopter from Wycliffe Bible Translators/JAARS was able to reach us. Between the medevac, a few other stranded passengers, aircraft engineers, and pilots, there were twelve of us to move out of Gubam. The chopper transferred the patient to a nearby strip where another MAF aircraft flew him the one-hour journey to a hospital in Kiunga. After two more shuttles to that airstrip, myself, Jason, and engineer Tim were the last to depart our temporary home. In PNG unexpected fashion, there was, of course, one last twist.

By the time the helicopter lifted off to transfer us to the MAF base at Kawito late on Tuesday afternoon, the weather had closed in again, with a band of rain blocking our path across the Fly River. As our pilot Johannes searched for a way through the rain showers that obscured our path, I had visions of another night "out bush" at Wasua or Lewada. It was with a great sense of relief that the storm abated, and we spied a path between the now dissipating bands of precipitation that took us to MAF Base Kawito. While not exactly home, it was a whole lot closer in creature comforts than we had enjoyed in Gubam. A veritable feast awaited our merry band and, of more interest to me, a bed with a mattress! The following morning, we boarded a Twin Otter and headed home, for real this time.

As they pondered two aircraft stranded in their village, these folks reminded us that besides Mission Aviation Fellowship, there is no one else. Without MAF, their isolation becomes complete. For MAF, the challenge was now to decide how to get our aircraft out of Gubam. Given a reasonable runway, the Twin Otter could fly out under its own power. The Caravan was going to need at the very least a new propeller. Detailed inspection had revealed that the blades were no longer securely attached. So with both planes marooned, and likely to remain that way for some time due to the dubious runway strength, thoughts turned to alternative solutions. Due to the wealth of natural resources with which Papua New Guinea is blessed, there are significant mining operations, all of which require significant levels of helicopter support. Some of that rotary-wing assistance is in the form of brawny Russian-built helicopters: machines capable of lifting the three tons of empty Twin Otter out of Gubam, but at a price. We then sourced some matting similar in concept to that used by the military in PNG during World War II as they turned jungle into runways. Laid down on top of a weak surface, this matting provides the necessary reinforcement to keep the aircraft out of trouble. The amazing Otter would only demand about 150 meters of this material for a safe takeoff roll; by the end of which, in its empty condition, it would easily fly away.

By the time we had collected sufficient pieces from the manufacturer, the conditions at Gubam had stabilized with a sufficiently long period of dry weather to encourage us that a safe takeoff was now possible. This was not just some optimistic guess. We had done some more scientific strength assessments before our first departure from Gubam; and during some follow-up helicopter visits to the site to repair the Caravan, repeat analysis showed that the surface was improved, at least until the next period of rain. Improved adequately to risk two takeoffs: one Otter and one Caravan.

*Risk* is an interesting word and provides the postscript to this story. *Risk* is a word with which MAF pilots are intimately familiar. It is the assessment of the probability of something bad happening weighed against the reward earned if everything turns out well. Every takeoff at our challenging airstrips has an element of risk: the potential for things to go very badly. We accept a level of risk that others would not in order that we might reach the isolated with physical and spiritual transformation in the name of Christ. There is always the possibility that something bad will happen, but we mitigate the risk, minimize the potential for incident through training, procedures, meticulous calculations, and patience. And of course, always expecting the unexpected.

The Eliptamin Crusade team at Blackwara airstrip.

Matt riding Lily, the boys' motorbike.

Mike Foxtrot Bravo with the nosewheel buried
at Gubam, Western province.

Traditional highlands celebration dress at the Goroka cultural show.

# HOTEL

## ~Hagen: *The Wild West~*

FOR THE MAJORITY of travelers to Papua New Guinea, the airline gateway is the capital city of Port Moresby. Port Moresby is referred to by most simply as Moresby, but we have another name for it: *the other PNG*. And so although we passed through Moresby on our initial arrival, our real introduction to Papua New Guinea was the highlands city of Mount Hagen. For the last three months, our family had been in Ballarat, Australia, experiencing—enduring, perhaps—MAF orientation. In truth, we felt far more culture shock in Australia than we ever felt in PNG, but that is a story for another time. So we journeyed north from Melbourne to Cairns in Far North Queensland—still Australia. After an overnight stay, we were up way too early for our flight to Papua New Guinea. Having successfully negotiated customs and immigration with our three little ones and multiple suitcases, we proceeded to the domestic terminal. We were pleased to have been met by our MAF PNG Moresby office manager as the trek from international to domestic, then domestic itself, is nothing short of a zoo for those who don't have the luxury of being comfortable with the culture. The flight to our eventual destination of Mount Hagen, capital of the Western Highlands province, passed through Wewak, which four months later was to be our first real PNG home. The seating arrangements for five on the Fokker F28 Fellowship meant that we had an additional seatmate.

I was riding herd on Sam and Matt while Jennifer was holding on to Nate, who was still shy of six months old. At this point, it is important to understand the affinity PNG ladies have for young blonde Caucasian children. It's as if the kids are magnets that draw in the ladies. Back then, the sight of little white children in PNG was quite rare, so Jennifer's neighbor couldn't help but engage in conversation. On hearing that we were heading to Mount Hagen to live, the lady's reaction was perhaps not the level of encouragement Jennifer was hoping for: "Oh, that's the Wild West!" A slight segue is important at this juncture to explain that *white man* is a descriptive term in Papua New Guinea with no racism attached or intended.

By the time our aircraft landed in Mount Hagen, like Moresby clipped to simply *Hagen*, it was late in the afternoon. If we thought that Morseby domestic terminal had been a zoo, then Hagen was pure bedlam. We eventually learned how to negotiate the chaos with comfort, but that afternoon, we were again relieved to be met by a few white missionary faces floating in a sea of dark-brown faces with broad buai smiles. Hagen is the third city of PNG, distant in population from Moresby and Lae at just thirty thousand. That first night, we were fairly convinced that we had indeed arrived in the Wild West. The house we were assigned for the duration of our orientation period in Hagen was a semi in the Tarangau area. The other half was the home of MAF PNG's most senior Papua New Guinean manager, for whom we became extremely thankful in the following days. The two semis were separate from other MAF houses in Hagen and contained within their own razor-wire-topped steel fence. Arriving at the house in the dark, we were unaware that we were living opposite the local bar. During the night, some patrons became involved in an altercation that culminated in loud voices in a language in which we were not yet conversant, accompanied by some collisions with our metal gate. The following morning, our neighbor Kos explained the events of the previous night with the assurance that we were quite safe. We were further comforted by the knowledge that *tarangau* is the Tok Pisin word for "eagle." With Isaiah 40:31 being part of our missionary story, this eagle reference seemed to be further assurance that we were where God wanted us to be, even if our entry to this new culture was daunting in the extreme.

Our first couple months in Hagen were spent coming to grips with language and culture, although it was to be several years before we felt truly competent in either of those areas. We learned much about the ebb and flow of life in our new home from simple tasks such as the acquisition of driver licenses and opening of a bank account. There was learning to drive and shopping and security.

*Driving,* "narakain olgeta." A totally different something. It starts, of course, with the fact that driving is on the left-hand side and continues with the secondary detail that all vehicles are standard transmission. For our coworkers from Australia and the UK, neither of these are truly problematic, whereas for the majority of Canadians, both are skills to be mastered. Having noted that driving is on the left, I must acknowledge that evidence to the contrary can be found in abundance. I clearly remember one trip from the airport to town early in our time in Hagen. The route follows the highlands highway. I was sitting towards the rear of a fifteen-seat van, which type is to be found in abundance with many used for public transportation. We were legally on the left, following another similar vehicle. On the opposite side of the road were three further vans, all heading in the same direction as us! We were being overtaken by three vehicles, each one hard on the bumper of the next, on a two-lane poorly paved twisting road. It is hard to actually follow the rules since it is tough to know the rules.

When Samantha reached the age at which most teens learn to drive, we decided to bite the bullet and obtain a PNG driver's permit for her. To enable us to instruct her accurately, Jennifer visited the Department of Motor Vehicles to purchase a "rules of the road." Unclear of the correct title, Jennifer struggled to communicate what it was she was seeking. Initially, the lady offered Jennifer a road map. In the end, Sam got a license on the basis of her Canadian learner's permit. Later, we discovered that MAF had secured a copy that was jealously guarded and only loaned out on pain of death.

What we learned in those first weeks, we passed on to our three children as each one took their turn learning to drive: the true meaning of defensive driving. With the PNG optimistic mind-set, potholes are merely a chance for energetic driving, speed limits become suggestions, and road rules are advisory only. Of course, with very few lines painted on the road, it is tricky to align the vehicle. Best practice is to assume that every other driver will most certainly do the unexpected. When a truck overtakes, expect to be cut off. When approaching a blind corner, better yet a blind corner on blind hill, anticipate that there will be an oncoming van in your lane. If there is a pedestrian on either side, be prepared for the person to cross the road at a time of least convenience, to you.

While adjusting to the intricacies and subtleties of PNG ground transport, we were also engaged with the intimidating prospect of feeding our little family. When moving to another country, there is one major hurdle at the grocery store: back home is irrelevant. It doesn't matter what it costs back home. Equally it doesn't matter what is available back home. We were now in New Guinea and planning on staying there for a long time, so it was imperative that we gain an appreciation for the new rules by which we would be playing. Brands are not the same. Availability varies. Price comparison is meaningless.

Grocery shelves in Hagen were stocked with a variety of products but with very few recognizable brands. Some items were produced locally, but imports were from Australia, New Zealand, Indonesia, and Malaysia. Breakfast cereal was available, but at a price that encouraged us to find alternative breakfast foods. Breakfast muffins, English muffins, bagels, and freezer waffles were all unheard of. Fortunately, Jennifer is comfortable in the kitchen, so she quickly adjusted to the baking of all those delicious breakfast options—totally from scratch. Those early excursions to the shops took lots of time as it was necessary to scrutinize each and every shelf for something that would fulfill the role of a brand we used in Canada. Things like canned corn were pretty simple, but with the language barrier, it was almost impossible to explain what we were looking for and end up with the correct product. We had learned this lesson while undergoing our orientation in Australia. We had gone to the store seeking shortening for a pie crust. Asking for Crisco received a blank stare by way of reply. Following a long explanation to a store clerk involving some description of what it looked like and what it was used for, we were directed to a fridge where we found something the size and shape of a block of butter but the colour of shortening. Unclear why the shortening was in the fridge but attributing its rock-hard consistency to its temperature, we departed for home reasonably confident we had triumphed. We left the block on the kitchen counter to soften, a fruitless exercise as it happened. While Copha, the product we had bought, is technically a shortening, it is made from coconut oil and will never soften at room temperature.

We also learned that that there is a very different art to purchasing. In Canada, if one is willing to exercise patience, there is very little need to purchase anything at full price; it will almost certainly be available at a reduced price in the near future. In PNG, it seems that it is quite the opposite. If there is something that you want, and may want regularly, then when you see it, buy out the store—now! It may well vanish from the shelf and not reappear for months. Cheese was one particular item that needed stockpiling, especially if it was seen at a respectable price. And best not to be too squeamish about a bit of mould or weevils. They say that the length of missionary experience can be determined by the weevil taste. New missionaries will throw out the rice, pasta, flour, or whatever the bugs have selected as their residence and restaurant. Those missionaries who have established themselves will scoop out the grains that are wriggling and continue on with dinner preparation. The old hands? They are excited for the extra protein! On one occasion, it was just the boys at home: me, Matt, and Nate. I was making my classic chicken and pasta dish with whatever spices I could pull out of the freezer. On cooking the pasta, there were definitely a few small insects attempting the backstroke. We had a men's consultation, fished out the obvious ones, and my mutual consent agreed that any black spots we saw when the dish was complete would be accepted as specks of spice. Nobody died, so it must have been all good.

During our time in New Guinea, we always employed some help in the house, probably just two three half days a week. Some people may think that this is inappropriate for missionaries whereas, in fact, is was a combination of expected behaviour and necessity.

There was a level of cultural expectation that we would contribute to the local economy by employing ladies to help us around the house and men to keep the constantly growing garden at abeyance. The style of building and the level of dust dictated a minimum twice-weekly clean of the house. Help in this area was appreciated, considering that keeping up with the scratch baking was an all-day affair one day a week. For example, to make a batch of bagels involved mixing the yeast dough, letting it rise for twenty minutes, shaping the dough into bagels, letting it rise again for twenty minutes, dipping them in boiling sugar water for about forty seconds on each side, baking for twenty minutes, cooling for a couple hours, then packaging and freezing. With limited lunch options, bake day also included sausage rolls, pizza buns, savoury muffins, and pizza pockets. And let's not forget cookies and cake.

The easiest way to understand our grocery dilemma may be to reflect on our first time back in Canada. We were going to be staying with our best friend, and despite my assurances that his fridge would already be full in anticipation of our arrival, Jennifer refused to arrive empty-handed. Just a quick stop at No Frills, she said. Only a few moments, she assured me. A simple in and out for a handful of purchases, she promised. So there she left me, flying solo with our three little children trapped together in the minivan in the middle of a parking lot. "Won't be long," I promised them. "Mom's just running in and right out." I am sure that was Jennifer's honest intention till faced with the quandary of choice. Now, you may think that a store called No Frills will have less selection than full-service grocery outlet, and that may be true; but in comparison to PNG stores, the options are multitude. In PNG, the choice was often distilled to available or not. So there was Jennifer, overwhelmed by six choices of cereal, more than one kind of bread, options for margarine, frozen juice, or bottled or canned. Convinced that she had succumbed to some evil lurking in aisle 12, I was preparing a search mission when Jennifer staggered from the store loaded down with a solitary bag. "What happened?" I gently inquired. "Did the card not work? Did you get lost?" From behind a glassy stare, all she could muster was, "Too much choice, too much choice." An exaggeration, you might think, but, in fact, not so much.

It was the cost of items that caused the greatest consternation. We returned from our first grocery expedition with about three bags' worth that was supposed to last for a week! Aside from the challenge of actually finding types of food, how could we possibly afford those prices? Everything was so much more expensive than back home, and then we went to the market.

In towns in PNG, there is always a town market. In fact, even in some more remote centers, there will be a market. The PNG people are traditionally subsistence farmers. With little in the way of wild game and no means of refrigeration, the garden is the main source of food. Fortunately, PNG has what is essentially a year-round growing season. There are some fruits, like mangoes, for which there is a clear season, but everything else is pretty much available all the time for the same price. For the sellers, it is a way to generate an income. For the buyers, it is a way to eat traditionally at a reasonable price. For missionaries, it is the welcome antidote to the sticker shock of the grocery store. Potatoes, broccoli, carrots, onions, lettuce, tomatoes, cucumber, peppers, pineapple, sugar fruit, and bananas sufficient for a week for less than fifteen dollars.

But as with many things in PNG, the market is not for the faint of heart. The market itself is okay; it is the getting in that is a drama. Parking is a challenge, the entrance is jammed, and pickpockets abound. But once inside, the vendors, predominantly ladies, are delightful. Happy to help with selections and packing of our market bilums, for us, they were also a ready source of security intelligence. Many was the time Jennifer was advised to leave: "O misus, man nogat I stap nabaut na hevi bai kamap. Moa beta u pinis haraip na go." Interpreted, "Missus, there are some bad people around, so you had best finish your shopping quick and leave." Even in a town like Mount Hagen, the regular merchants at the market knew who we were even if we didn't know them. Quietly appreciative of what we were doing to help out their country, they would aid us, often providing a gift of an extra sugar fruit of banana to our little kids. The market is not particularly clean, pigs sometimes rummaging through piles of composting leaves, and the produce is not the uniform shape and colour demanded by the North American consumer. And yet the flavours are so superior. Bananas in Canada taste like cardboard in comparison. Carrots are sweet. Pineapple is rich. Mangoes are to die for.

With the help of those friends experienced in the ways of Papua New Guinea, we managed to come to terms with grocery shopping. Language was another test for us. Melanesian Tok Pisin used as a common language in PNG is actually relatively simple with limited vocabulary and tenses. In some countries where MAF serves, it can take months to acquire a reasonable level language competence, some language courses alone lasting six months. Ours lasted nine days. After that, there was nothing left to teach. All we could do was practice. I had studied French all through high school and was, I suppose, expected to be fluent, but I certainly never felt confident. So it was with trepidation that I ventured outside our fence to find some locals with whom to practice my newfound linguistic skills.

Fortunately, Papua New Guineans love to help people learn their language—at least one of their languages, that is. In Hagen, there is sufficient English around that when my Tok Pisin failed, we could get back on track with a bit of English. I found that I could not be too sensitive to criticism since my errors were met with laughter, followed by correction. Asking my ad hoc helpers to talk more slowly, I implored them to "tok isi," which did not help because on the loud street, asking them to speak more quietly was the opposite of what I needed. Understanding and communicating that what I wanted was for them to talk more slowly, a request to "tok isi isi" gained me what I needed.

Sunday rolled around, and armed with our limited Tok Pisin, we ventured out to church to sink or swim. We did our best to be anonymous by sitting close to the back, but did rather stand out in the crowd. I clearly recall standing up for the first song; I felt like everyone else had reached their zenith while I was still unfolding my knees. Not a tall man, I still seemed to be much taller than anyone else in the congregation. The service progressed, and if we caught every third word, then we thought we were doing well. Tok Pisin may be relatively straightforward, yet when spoken at speed and with local inflections and slang, it still takes time to catch on. We were happy just sitting there, taking it in, working hard to follow, until we became mindful that the leader was talking not just about us but to us. Some mild confusion and embarrassment on our part, a little English from the leader, and a few kind chuckles from the worshippers, and all was good. Perseverance on the street, at work, and at church saw gradual improvement in our ability to communicate effectively such that, a few years later, I was comfortable to preach in Tok Pisin as I would in English, with limited notes.

In a country with seven million people and over eight hundred languages, I remain surprised how regional Tok Pisin is. After five years or so living on the north coast, I was on a trip into Hagen with my parents, who had come all the way to PNG to visit with us. We stopped in to see a Bible college where I entered into conversation in Tok Pisin with a Papua New Guinean professor. After a while, he asked me where I was from in PNG. Replying that we were living in Vanimo, he expressed the view that he could tell by my accent and expressions that we were from the Sepik provinces.

Following the interruptions of our first night in Hagen, we gradually became accustomed to the risks of living in this strange land. It was rather bizarre to come to the conclusion that we lived a schizophrenic life: boarding the plane in Canada, we would consider ourselves lower middle class; descending the plane in Morseby, observers would consider us lower upper class. And that, in part, was what made us targets for the more nefarious characters that are part of every culture. Many people knew our purpose in PNG and quietly kept us safe, but the thieves and pickpockets that occasionally passed through saw only possibilities. We had a few compound break-ins, attempted holdups at knifepoint and gunpoint, and for a period, our car was accessed more times than I care to remember; but even in that, strangers cared for us.

Years on from our Hagen introduction, we had moved to the town of Goroka. One Saturday, as was my custom, I went to the market. As I completed my purchases, a man whom I have no recollection of seeing before approached me and informed me that

I really needed to get to my car. As I left the market area to return to the car, two more men completed the story: someone had tried to steal our spare tire, but "the crowd" had apprehended him. On turning my gaze to the car, it was clear something was afoot: a good two hundred people were crushed around our vehicle.

It seems that two guys had forced a window, then removed the tire from the car; but in the process, some passers-by had intervened and were holding one of the men, along with our tire. At this stage of my narrative, it is best to interject a little education on New Guinea justice. When "the people" get involved (read: take matters into their own hands), justice can be swift and, from my perspective, even brutal. The suspect had been fairly roughed up and was bleeding from a number of cuts on his face. There was a policeman there, and he, along with the rest of the crowd, wanted to know if "mi laik kotim em, or mari mari" (take him to court or have mercy and let him go).

In PNG, it can, on occasion, pay to be a bit of an actor and certainly to indicate that you know how the system works. So we "danced" a little on what I wanted to do. There were a few interested parties who thought I should let him go, and in an apparent effort to encourage me in that direction, they hit our suspect a couple more times, drawing blood (one of the strikes splashed blood on my face). And so the moral dilemma with which we were faced many times over the years: have him arrested and sent to jail, or release him due to punishment already received? Is it appropriate to let the man receive corporal punishment without due process, or should I have spoken out against this? Ethics and morality. Right and wrong. Culture. This is perhaps one of the most challenging aspects of missionary life. As Christians, right and wrong is fairly obvious, or is it? This land of the unexpected is a different world than the one we came from, a land in which each day we had to be prepared for unexpected opportunities to be Christ to those He came to save.

# INDIA

## -Immanuel Jude: *From Stone Age to Computer Age*-

WE CHOSE NAMES for our children very carefully. *Samantha Christine* means "one who listens" and "follower of Christ." Our second born and first son is called *Matthew Thomas*. We chose *Thomas* as that is my middle name. For his first name, we were undecided between *Benjamin* and *Matthew*, so we asked our best friend to decide for us, and *Matthew* he became. This has been a very wise choice as our *Matthew* is very much a "gift of God." For our youngest, the choice was rather simple: *Nathaniel Christopher*. His name ties our little trio together as his names are the same as his older siblings. *Nathaniel*, like *Matthew*, means "gift of God"; and *Christopher*, like *Christine*, means "follower of Christ." Additionally, *Nathaniel* is the first name of the second MAF pilot and first to give his life for the Gospel. In Papua New Guinea, the naming of children carries some significance. Some people choose to name their children after their favourite MAF pilot. One lady we knew had named her children Rod White and Don Harvey, both former pilots. Many parents elect to give their offspring Christian first names. Perhaps this is a result of the significant numbers of missionaries that have ministered in PNG over the last century. There are quite a few Davids, a significant number of men named John, and for ladies, Esther and Bathsheba. Considering the Bible story, I don't think I would choose Bathsheba as a name for my daughter. And though it is quite biblical, Immanuel Jude was never in the mix of options for our boys.

I met Immanuel Jude during our first year in PNG while based in the town of Wewak on the north coast. Immanuel was responsible for preparing the flight manifest, loading the cargo, refueling the aircraft, and boarding the passengers. Except for pilots and senior management, most of the roles in PNG—and, in fact, in the majority of MAF operations in developing nations around the world—are undertaken by citizens of those same countries. Accounting, aircraft engineering, maintenance of buildings and vehicles, human resources, and aircraft ground support are all accomplished by Papua New Guineans. However, it is quite a challenge to bring local people into the cockpit. Pilot training is expensive no matter where it is undertaken, and for a person in a developing country, it is even harder. In PNG, the idea that "it takes a village to raise a child" is literally true. The extended family selects the most promising candidate and pours resources into him or her. Assuming that the representative achieves success, there is a responsibility to "climb the ladder" and reinvest in the community back home. If the child grows up to be a pilot, there is an expectation that he will constantly look for better, higher-paying jobs such that the village's return on investment is increased. This is a terrible and immense pressure for a young person to withstand.

While the pilot is quite literally at the pointy end of the process, it takes a lot more than a pilot, a plane, and some fuel to bring transformation to isolated communities. A programmer collects all the requests for service and forms them into an efficient plan for the pilot. On the day of the flight, the passengers arrive at the terminal, just as if they were getting on a major airline, with some minor differences: the traffic officer (TO) being responsible for somewhat more than the check-in staff. All passengers are weighed; the law of averages in passenger body weights doesn't work with very small numbers. Cargo is also weighed. The traffic officer verifies that the combined total is less than the magic number provided by the pilot as the maximum allowable payload weight. The TO then loads the cargo in the aircraft, adds fuel as necessary, and even conducts the passenger briefing. Immanuel Jude was quietly efficient at this job. When I worked with him in Wewak, Immanuel was twenty-seven years old. He did not know that Caucasian people existed until he was seven.

Of the nearly eight million population of Papua New Guinea, I estimate that about 75 percent are not just rural; they are isolated rural and, for the most part, still living by traditional means. The people are subsistence farmers. Trees are cut down and burned. Root vegetables planted among the rotting brush. Houses in these remote communities are framed with tree branches, woven bamboo for floors and walls, kunai grass for the thatched roof. During our first few years in PNG, it was still very common to meet people at jungle airstrips clothed in traditional attire. For women, this might be a grass skirt, just a grass skirt. During the years we lived in Vanimo on the north coast, our PNG church sent missionaries into the jungle along the border to minister to communities that time had passed by. These villages had no airstrip, no connection to the outside world.

I remember clearly the report of the missionaries on their return to the church after several months away. Even as Papua New Guineans in a poor church, they were shocked at the poverty of the folks they had encountered. "They have nothing," was the report. "No pots, no clothes, the women just wear grass skirts." The young man wanted to be sure we understood, so he held up an example of the skirt. It was strands of long grass hung from another piece of grass that formed a waist tie. But there was more daylight through that skirt than grass. The threads were little more than wisps at one-centimeter intervals. Traditional dress for men is no more modest in Western eyes. As if it were yesterday, I recall one of my first flights into Mamusi. Among others, there was an older man dressed to kill for his trip into the town of Mount Hagen. Probably not the most appropriate phrase to describe a PNG man, as, on occasion, they actually do "dress to kill"—literally. However, this man wore a blazer and a loincloth! Stuffed in the back of the loincloth waist band, in traditional style, "as gras." *As* is the Tok Pisin word for "backside," *gras* meaning "grass."

For this particular gentleman, I was concerned that he would turn into a medevac en route since his "as gras" was more like half a tree, branches and all. More disturbing for some would be the prevalence of "Telefomin trousers" in the western part of the country. With the exception of cultural shows, these days it is very uncommon to see a man attired in this way. "Telefomin trousers" was the name given among MAF pilots of the day for men's traditional attire in that area. A hollowed-out gourd was used to cover that which makes a man, a man. The gourd would be worn with very little else. More disturbing was that the gourd doubled as a pocket or a wallet! Receiving cash payment in those days was not for the faint of heart. Even today, if one knows where to look and whom to ask, it is possible to find those of the older generation who have experience as head hunters: cannibals.

In the April River area, Immanuel Jude's home, houses were constructed up in the trees; this was purely for safety. The village was comprised of just three tree houses; a couple of identical villages nearby described as "spear friends." Perhaps you have figured this out: head hunters prowling in the dark seeking retribution for some previous wrong, a tiny village in need of an alliance to swell the ranks in the event of such vengeance: "spear friends." The unfortunate would find themselves at the wrong end of a four-foot bamboo arrow tipped with bone or hardwood barbs. At that time, Papua New Guinea was under Australian administration; dead bodies floating down the river were considered worthy of further investigation. Following the trail, the government patrol travelled up the Sepik River, then the April River; and so at the age of seven, Immanuel met his first "wait man" (white man). This must have been thoroughly terrifying for these isolated people. Their tiny world consisted of just a handful of people; unknowns were always to be feared, treated as "kill or be killed." But these with a different skin colour were undoubtedly viewed as something even more terrifying: unwelcome visitors from the spirit world.

Many miles away in the Goroka valley of the Eastern Highlands live the Asaro people known as the "mud men." Folklore suggests that in the distant past, there was war between the Asaro tribe and those farther down the valley. Hopelessly outnumbered, the Asaro covered their entire bodies in white mud to achieve an advantage over their enemies. As the Asaro approached in the dark of night, moonlight reflecting off the white mud produced an ethereal vision of creatures not of this world. Interpreted as spirit warriors, the enemies of the Asaro would have fled in fear. Almost certainly this was the reaction of Immanuel's family on encountering the Australian army patrol.

Twenty years later, Immanuel Jude brought me his VCR to see if I could fix it. Just twenty years from the Stone Age to the computer age. For those of European descent, this journey encompassed thousands of years, a slow progression of advancement: Bronze Age to Iron Age, the Middle Ages transitioning to the Industrial Revolution. For the people of developing nations, most of these intermediate progressions were leapfrogged, jumping from tree houses direct to electronics. Changes in culture occur alongside transitions in machines, so the bypassing of technological steps results in the exclusion of stages in cultural growth. The harsh terrain and impenetrable jungle means that, for years, the tribes of PNG have existed in isolation. Family was everything. All types of support and security were found in the extended family. The "wan tok" system developed around this. For an individual, prime responsibility was to those who spoke the same language: "wan toks" (one language). The challenge in PNG is that there are in excess of eight hundred languages. The result is eight hundred special-interest groups. While the technology leap has been huge, the far greater test is handling the cultural jump.

In purest, original form, the won tok system is good. In many ways, it is ideal socialism in action: from each according to his ability to each according to his need. The old and the weak will be looked after. New houses are built by a team. Children are raised by the village. However, as paying jobs have become more prevalent, the divide between "haves" and "have-nots" has appeared. Those with higher personal motivation see their personal wealth increase. Those with less motivation take advantage of the won tok system to demand a share for which they have no need and have made no contribution. If society had the opportunity to develop slowly, the transition out of the negative aspects of "wan tok" would have been spread over multiple generations. This has ramifications for government, which further stunts growth of the people as a unified country. With less than 120 seats in parliament and 800 special-interest groups, elections inevitably involve significant strife. We need to understand that the "wan tok" system means that I must vote for my relative; and if elected, my relation must prioritize the needs of his family. It is impossible for an MP to truly represent the majority of his constituents when his priority is for a minority.

And so from the outside, we look into these countries and wonder why there are law and order issues, why education is poor, why health care is substandard, why corruption is rife. It is simply this: the pace of change outstrips the ability of people to cope. Maintenance of airstrips is a large issue for the operations of Mission Aviation Fellowship. Cutting the grass runway is an arduous back-breaking chore that, when done by hand (bush knife ) takes hours. In general, the more remote and isolated a community, the more likely they are to maintain their runway. Locations with a government station or larger school tend to have a better notion of how government works in the wider world. At one village where we were having a struggle getting cooperation in having the grass cut, one man told me "we aren't savages, this is the government's job." As a small business owner. I wanted to ask him how much tax he paid. And yet the longer we were in PNG and the more I learned about the people and culture, the more convinced I became that people are just people.

A friend of ours, another pilot, often drove his motorbike to the airport. Cresting a hill, he came upon a van stopped on the side of the road. These fifteen-passenger vehicles are the PNG equivalent of a privately run bus service. An individual can purchase a vehicle and a "bus" license and begin carrying passengers for hire. A lady just off the bus darted across the road in front of the bike without looking. There seems to be zero traffic awareness among pedestrians, and the incredible optimism of life leads people to believe that they couldn't possibly get hit by a vehicle. Our friend swerved to avoid the lady and came off his bike. In PNG, fault for an accident is rarely laid with the one who caused it. The driver of a pickup that hits someone racing across the road can be beaten to death on the spot.

If the driver is a foreigner, they will often be blamed regardless of circumstance. In Canada, leaving the scene of an accident is a crime; in PNG, remaining at the scene is dangerous beyond words. For our friend, his backpack was stolen even as he lay in pain on the road. In Papua New Guinea, they call it compensation; in Canada, we call it a lawsuit. People are people.

One night, I was driving back from the school with our son Nate. It was dark and rainy, very difficult to see. A dog darted out. I tried to miss it, but the back end of the MAF vehicle started to go around. Unfortunately, the dog didn't make it. A couple days later, I received a call from our office. Apparently, the owners of the dog had arrived looking for compensation for the loss of their "best hunting dog." "Excellent," I told our office manager. "Tell them I want to see them too. I want compensation for the terror they inflicted on my son." The claimants disappeared in a hurry. Sometimes you just have to play the game!

For Papua New Guinea, a land whose people I have grown to love, the growing pains continue. The pace of change is staggering and will persist. When faced with the controversial, incomprehensible, and of course, unexpected, I remember my friend Immanuel Jude. I recall his story and pray a little harder for the land of the unexpected.

# JULIET

## -Joining Hands-

A LIFETIME AGO, yet just yesterday, our young family arrived in Papua New Guinea to a plethora of foreign sights, sounds, and smells. Those physical assaults on our senses were, however, cast into the dark shadows in comparison to the alien customs we encountered. To us, these traditions ranged from funny to bizarre, outlandish to perplexing. Some were just plain uncomfortable.

We had landed our aircraft in Green River: just another forgettable landing, a nondescript day in the life of MAF. But in true PNG fashion, that was about to change. A man approached us, clearly agitated over something of which we were about to be made aware. As he entered my space bubble, it became obvious that his disquiet was stimulated by a not insignificant amount of alcohol. It seems to us outsiders that the PNG way is approach any dilemma, any query, with offensive. There seems to be a feeling among some that belligerence, passion, and vigor are the answers to all of life's problems, as if bullying will result in acceptable resolution. So one of the challenges for an MAF missionary is reading the situation and determining how to meet this display of aggression: the strong demonstration of power or the consoling display of assistance.

At times, it is fitting to stand up to the posturing ritual, to call it out for what it is, a simple exhibition of male plumage like a bird of paradise strutting his stuff to overcome a rival for a female's affection. This rarely works with a drunk. It is far better to enter that part of

108

culture that makes us uneasy: the holding of hands. To be clear, we are not talking about a prolonged handshake. We are describing the holding of hands as I do with my dear wife when out for a romantic stroll: left hand to right hand. So I stretched forth the olive branch. My right hand clasped his left and led him away from the gathering crowd, away from the inspiration of the audience, just a couple of guys having a conversation. It never ceases to amaze me how this simple act diffuses a potential powder keg of emotion.

With its Melanesian ways, Papua New Guinea functions on the power of relationships, bonds that are manifested not simply in words or expressions but in physical contact. And while this touch can quiet a stormy sea, it can also be banked, used to build a relationship. Some memories fade with time, but my first real encounter with this tradition is burned into my mind. Our PNG coworkers love to be part of our education, helping us to become fluent in Tok Pisin and in our understanding of who they are. Within our first few weeks, Francis took me by the hand, literally by the hand, to increase my knowledge of and love for his homeland. Many others followed suit, and it was out of these impromptu times that my relationships with our PNG coworkers matured. I wish I could share all of them with you, the names that meant so much to us, friends that cared for us beyond reasoning. Here I choose but a handful, faces that reflect the spirit of those that labour alongside as we seek to bring transformation to the isolated.

*JB.* To me, John Bekopwai is the epitome of the power of PNG relationships. The longer we called PNG home, the more I came to realize that people the world over are Melanesians in disguise. We all work better for those we trust and who trust us, those for whom there is reciprocated respect. I worked with JB during our Vanimo years. That period was one of intense business. We flew our Twin Otter relentlessly, cramming seemingly impossible numbers of flying hours and landings into each day. I was, I suppose, still full of fire and young energy, ignorant of long-term fatigue and the need to really pace myself. On reflection, perhaps my buddy JB was the wiser: a steady worker but sometimes too slow for me. I learned that allowing JB his pace was essential. It was critical not just for my health but also to our relationship. I gradually came to understand that if I let JB work at his tempo, then when necessity demanded we ramp up the pace JB would respond. If I had failed to invest in the relationship, resorting to being a slave driver, then the harvest would simply have been one of frustration, for JB would have clung to his default tempo, regardless of circumstances.

One of MAF's ministries is supporting schools through the delivery of supplies, including food. In its wholesale size, rice comes in twenty- kilogram bales. A Twin Otter can easily carry in excess of 1,500 kilograms: 30 bales of rice. Even Papua New Guineans, who are on average shorter than Westerners, cannot stand erect inside a Twin Otter, which makes it a challenge to lift with one's legs as is safest for one's back. I suppose it is possible to crouch down, straighten the back, lift with the legs, and do a sort of duck waddle towards the cargo door of the aircraft. The rice bales at the front sit a good four meters from the exit, so the duck waddle is as uncomfortable as other means of unloading the cargo. The simpler method is to hurl the rice bags from the front, using the twenty-kilo momentum to sail it towards the back door. This method has the advantage of potentially being able to empty the aircraft incredibly fast. JB and I did this on many occasions. We would leave the right engine running with the other pilot in his cockpit seat monitoring the gauges while JB and I ejected thirty bags of rice. Time on the ground? Eight minutes from touchdown to takeoff. Only relationships have that kind of power.

I am glad that I was not born sooner, for in the old days, the MAF pilot did everything for himself. By the time we arrived in PNG, many tasks were being capably performed by PNG coworkers. A key task in the efficient functioning of MAF is programming. Flight programming is a bit like attempting to complete an organic jigsaw puzzle, one that seems to shift shape, with the picture changing even as the puzzle is being put together. And each day there is a new puzzle. It is the process of aligning requests for service with resources available in the most efficient manner. An aircraft rarely goes in and out from its home base; it will regularly have intermediate stops en route. There will be passengers and cargo from the main base to several remote locations, with pickups of people and their goods at a number of communities and also one's travelling between those remote communities. With a base serving fifty or more airstrips, the potential combinations are infinite. A good programmer will be able to visualize in his head options and possibilities not just for the next day but stretching out to the next month.

*Albert Malken*, leader of the team at Vanimo, was the best I ever saw. As the land of the unexpected, Papua New Guinea infects flight programs with its uncertainty. Yet somehow Albert tamed this wild creature. Pilots would recount tales of their flight programs changing multiple times in one day. This concept was entirely foreign to me as Albert Malken programs always worked. Except for weather and medevacs, in five years, once begun, my program might have changed on two occasions. The downside to Albert's plans was the fearsome demands on his pilots. In a ceaseless quest for efficiency and a desire to serve as many as possible, my friend Albert crammed our days full. Like a slowly rising flood, the number of landings in the program would rise day by day: eight then ten, eleven then twelve. A warning shot to Albert that things were looking busy; might be hard to get it all done. Then it would sneak up to thirteen and fourteen landings. In a race with the sun, we would push through the day, endeavouring to accomplish all that had been set for us. At some point, the race became too much, and a conversation with Albert would ensue. The next day, the program would have been carved back to eight landings, and the tug of war would start again.

*Ludmer Mieko* was possibly the best C/A I ever worked with. In our earlier years with MAF PNG, a Twin Otter crew was comprised of a captain, a first officer, and a cabin attendant. One should not be tempted to picture a major airline flight attendant when I discuss an MAF C/A, for while the C/A was responsible for passenger briefings as on your nation's airlines, there was neither food service nor complementary drinks. Our cabin attendants were more like load masters. One of the challenges in jungle flying is ascertaining weights of passengers and cargo. With limited runway length, there is zero margin when it comes to aircraft weight; the aircraft must not exceed maximum allowable takeoff weight. Our tool for determining weights was a simple bathroom scale. Find a piece of flat ground, stand on the scale to see if it registers your own weight accurately, then start weighing people and their belongings. To weigh bags, we would stand on the scale with the bags then subtract our own body weight from the total.

At many locations, MAF has a representative, an agent that will weigh everything prior to the arrival of the plane. The Twin Otter has front and rear baggage compartments, lockers, that each has its own maximum weights for cargo. To load these properly, a person would really need to know the weight of each bag, but there are no baggage tags recording weights. There is, however, one other technique for determining the weight of freight: the calibrated hand. It is amazing that after handloading an aircraft for a few years, it is possible to be rather accurate in estimating the weight of an object. With his responsibility to load the aircraft, we would wait for Ludmer to report how much cargo he had placed in the front and rear lockers. This is essential information in calculating the balance of the aircraft. If it is too heavy in the front or rear, the plane will simply not fly. Too much cargo in the nose, and the aircraft will not take off; it will stay firmly planted on the ground and go straight off the end of the runway. Too heavy in the back locker, and the nose of the airplane will come off the ground as it is supposed to for takeoff, but it will keep going up till the airplane is vertical, at which point it will return to the ground in a state that will leave it rather unflyable. Most C/As would report weights to me to the nearest ten kilos. Not Ludmer. He would tell me numbers like 122 or 131. I did, of course, wonder about this level of accuracy; so out of curiosity, I decided to check it out. At our destination, I unloaded and weighed the cargo. I did this a number of times because, quite honestly, I could not believe the results of my experiments: Ludmer's approximations were never out by more than a couple kilograms, and that could have been the bathroom scale that was wrong!

I learned lots from our PNG guys about PNG culture. This was not a formal education, but things I discovered as life happened. Ludmer was from a village near Nuku, a community we flew to several times a week. His *wantoks*, relatives, would often send him back to Vanimo with some produce from their gardens. Now in Vanimo,

Ludmer's house was off the road. We would drive him home, as close as we could get; but with the quantity of food he had been given, he needed help to get it home. We would unload the vegetables beside the track that passed for a road, and Ludmer would disappear into the bush to get his kids to come help carry the load. I never waited as Ludmer assured me no one would steal his things. Knowing PNG and just human nature, I was rather surprised at his confidence. I noted that Ludmer would always place a stick or a banana leaf on top of his cargo before he left it beside the road. Further enquiry yielded the explanation that a marker of some sort sent the message that these vegetables, bags, or boxes belonged to someone, and no one would touch them!

Papua New Guinea can be a difficult place to fathom: a people that can be a real enigma to those from Western countries. Where Ludmer could, with assurance, leave his boxes beside the road and walk away, certain they would remain till his return, I could not leave items outside my house. Even within a fenced and secure compound, toys and tools would grow legs. This is a conundrum for many missionaries, for the thieves could only be those we trust: those that we employ to work in our houses or the security guards that watch over us at night. And yet it makes perfect sense when seen through different eyes. If I leave things lying around, then I am sending the message that they are not important to me. And if they are not important to me, then I won't mind if they are taken. And if I don't mind if they are taken, then someone who would like those things might as well have them instead of me. Of course, if I had simply left a banana leaf…but this struggle with honesty is a very real issue for missionaries. We have our idea of what truthfulness looks like, yet perhaps it is not as simple as we first think.

Traditionally, Papua New Guinea families hold wealth in community. There are the richer and the poorer, but those with more are expected to help out those with less. If I have a need, then my family has an obligation to help me out. In the minds of some of our workers, this extends to their workplace, their other family. Further complicating the situation, those with jobs are closer to the "have" side of the equation than the "have-not," so if relatives are in need, the ones with jobs are approached for assistance. In PNG culture, you really can't say no to a family member, so if you can't meet the need, then perhaps an unapproved loan from the other family, the employer, will resolve the issue. It takes a real strong person to stand up to the levels of pressure brought to bear, but *Matilda* was strong as Samson in that regard.

As the main guardian of the purse in Vanimo, and later with us in Goroka, I never worried about her dipping into the pot for personal gain. You might have formed a picture of Matilda as rather a formidable physical presence, but nothing could be further from the truth. Matilda was born lame. With an emaciated and ineffective leg, Matilda navigated life with a crutch. With no car and no taxis, transportation limited to minibuses of questionable road worthiness and drivers of even more questionable skill, just getting around was a challenge for Matilda. Yet I never heard a complaint, never saw anger at her condition. I would see her around town with moisture glistening on her brow, yet she would throw me a smile and keep on going. I have been on crutches three times in my life, and not once did I act with the level of grace my friend Matilda projected every day.

We had already been in PNG for nearly seven years when we moved to Goroka. It was only when we moved there from Vanimo that I met *John Ipi*. In the MAF PNG world, Goroka is at the far east edge; and in our seven years, I really had not had need to visit there, and the few times I had were before John began to work for MAF. There is a song performed by the group Point of Grace that talks about "being Jesus to those He came to save." That would be my friend John. The more I worked alongside John, the more I came to realize that this man had truly been transformed. I often reflect on the "fruit of the Spirit" written about by Paul in the book of Galatians. I think most of us would struggle to say that we reflect those qualities that Paul lists, yet in the life of John, I see evidence of all of those traits. When events would frustrate me, when people would anger me, I would look to John and wonder who the real missionary was.

They say that missionaries remember events based on places rather than time. Similarly, when I reflect on the myriad of things I have carried, loaded, into an MAF Twin Otter, I can't help but recall the people that I worked with in man-handling those items onto the aircraft, for everything that goes in and comes off does so through simple manual strength. We were asked to help out with the transport of supplies for a hydroelectric project in Marawaka, a community that sits at the extreme top end of the Marawaka valley. The vast majority of what we were to deliver was plastic water pipe. Now, over the years, MAF has flown many thousands of meters of water pipe all around the country, but none like this pipe. If you are picturing the pipes in your house that bring water to your sink, then you need to multiply that in size seven or eight times. If you link your hands together and place them in front of you to make a circle, then you will get a concept of the girth of these pipes that we were to make fly. Being made of plastic, you may think they would be light, but extending to five meters in length, each tube tipped the scales in excess of one hundred kilograms.

In order to maximize the load, we of course wanted to be at maximum allowable weight, but these pipes were extremely bulky and inflexible. To fill the space and weight made this the mother of all puzzles. Each unit was slid in through the side cargo hatch at an angle, like threading a needle. The first few were straightforward, but as the stack grew and as space inside the aircraft diminished, each unit was harder than the next. I suspect without *Heron*, it would have been an impossible task. When I first met Heron, I thought his name was Aaron; just with the PNG accent, it sounded different. Later on, I discovered that his given name is actually Heron. In checking out what this name means, I was surprised, first of all, to even find it listed, more so when I read the detail. You see, *Heron* means "hero" or "stone," possibly derived from *Haran*, which would be "mountain." If ever a name reflected its owner, Heron would be it. I am not overly tall, barely average these days, yet still I am taller than Heron. However, Heron is a genuine tower of strength. Besides his work with MAF, Heron plays semipro rugby, and I would not want to meet him on the field of play. Loading those pieces of polypipe, Heron sat on the floor of the Otter, in the doorframe; and as the tubes slid in, pushed by three or four men, Heron would support the end and lift it backwards over his head to those waiting inside the plane!

I met *Doris* within a couple months of arrival in PNG. She worked in the MAF office at our pilot base in the north coast town of Wewak. It perhaps fitting that Doris's name means "gift of the ocean." Wewak was our first PNG home and the place I became a real MAF pilot. Our family had spent our first four months in Mount Hagen undergoing language learning and cultural orientation, as well as my initial pilot training. We only spent one year in Wewak, but for that year, I was the only MAF pilot that lived and operated from there. Being a real babe in the woods, I relied heavily on my PNG coworkers to guide me through cultural minefields and also the maze that describes MAF procedures. We moved on from Wewak after just twelve months, transitioning to Vanimo, which would be our home and a defining period for our family. Our flights from Vanimo sent us to Wewak two or three times a week, so I still interacted with Doris regularly. Like Matilda, Doris was one of those people that I trusted in all things. As is the case in MAF, an acronym alternatively expanded to "move again, friend," after five great years in Vanimo, we were on the move again to Goroka, from where I rarely ended up in Wewak. I guess Doris left MAF somewhere in there, but when I became chief pilot for MAF PNG and was in need of a new administrative assistant, Doris appeared for an interview, and I knew right away this was the lady I needed as my right hand. As she was in Wewak, so again in the chief pilot's office in Mount Hagen, I am not sure what I would have done without Doris.

During our time with MAF PNG, many families came and went: nearly one hundred pilot families alone, not to mention engineers and managers. We were also privileged to work alongside many Papua New Guinean folk, as you have just read. But no chapter on this would be complete without mentioning *Joy*: John Yark. John was with MAF when we arrived, and still there when we left PNG. Alongside a couple others, John has ministered with MAF PNG longer than anyone, including missionaries. John hails from Enga

province, an area known as perhaps second only to the Southern
Highlands for the volatility of its people. Yet I know John as nothing
but a quiet, gracious, unassuming man. It is for this that we took our
young children from our home to the other side of the world: to be
part of the transformation that God makes in the lives of people that
come to Him.

I could tell more tales of my friends in PNG. There is Richard,
running a close second to Albert as the best programmer I worked
with; Suzie in HR, who was always so kind with my late requests for
help with airline flights; Sarah in accounts; Wesley, our jack-of-all-
trades fix-it man in Goroka; Agatno, our haus-meri; Pastors Japalis
and Michael and Gabriel and Peter at our church. But there really
is only one way to end this chapter. I have written, shared about my
experiences, what these folks mean to me. When our kids graduated
high school, they were able to invite some friends to attend, and it
was these ones they chose to invite. "The base guys," as they called
them, and the pastors from our church, our haus-meri Agatno—
these were the ones our children chose to share in their celebration.
What greater privilege than to have had these brothers and sisters
impact my children in such a meaningful way.

# KILO

WE ROLLED ONTO final approach at Kanabea, and it was like we had jumped onto one of those rodeo bulls: up and down, rolling left and right, edging towards the worst turbulence I had experienced in my time in PNG to that point. Prior to that day, Tifalmin was the record holder.

Several years earlier, we had conducted a flight from Tabubil to Tifalmin. Tifalmin sits in an offshoot of the Telefomin valley. As airstrips in Papua New Guinea go, it is fairly benign. Relatively long and comparatively flat with reasonable separation from the surrounding mountains, it really has just one problem: when the wind blows, the ride gets emotional for passengers and is a practical assessment for pilots, where pass is the only option. Except for a handful of airstrips, wind is not normally a huge thing for pilots in PNG. There is a select group of locations where later in the day, wind is known to be a factor. Tifalmin is not among those. It is on the rare occasions when there is a low-level jet stream wind that the breeze at Tifalmin creates difficulty.

Jet streams are winds in the higher levels of the atmosphere inhabited by airliners and are invariably extremely strong. In the midlatitudes of the Western world, it is also common to be subject to winds of reasonable strength all the way to the ground. In equatorial regions, winds at the surface tend to be robust only where the terrain causes localized increase in wind speeds. But when the jet stream descends out of the higher altitudes, interesting things occur. Over PNG, the jet stream will run west to east, straight along the central ranges that form the spine of the island of New Guinea. The Tifalmin valley and its runway are oriented west to east. Unfortunately, the dead end of the valley is to the west and is terminated by mountains rising to well over ten thousand feet: more than five thousand feet above the valley floor. The low-level jet stream roars across the Indonesia-PNG border, flies over Busilmin, then finds the open space of the Tifalmin valley, down into which the airflow explodes. This of itself would not necessarily be massive concern, except that shortly before touchdown, there is a small gulley. As the high wind hits this, it creates a very substantial downdraft that catches the aircraft and threatens to trigger a premature landing: crash.

The flight to Tifalmin was entirely uneventful, and even as we oriented ourselves for landing, the turbulence could only be described as light chop: unsettling for passengers, ho-hum for pilots. On final approach, the ride became more interesting, and late final, we needed to increase power substantially to combat the downdraft and maintain our distance from the ground. Wisdom being the better part of valour, we elected, in pilot jargon, to "give it away" and return to Tabubil: mission incomplete, but everyone still alive and no extra paperwork, as would be required if we bent the plane. Naively perhaps, we thought the worst was behind us. Then we went back over the wall. The ride went from swimming-pool smooth to class 4 rapids in less than a heartbeat. They say that planes don't fall out of the sky, but I tell you on that occasion, the bottom certainly fell out. Despite my secure four-point-harness seat belt, my head hit the ceiling, alarms and warning lights flashed in the cockpit, and those passengers that could find voice involuntarily screamed. As fast as it happened, it was over, and the rest of the flight was completely unremarkable.

As bad as Tifalmin was, it paled in comparison to Kanabea. The runway at Kanabea sits parallel to and hard up against a ridge to the south, backstopped by another one to the west that makes the runway one way in and one way out. There is a lower ridge perpendicular to the runway that the plane must blast over halfway on final approach. I say *blast over* because if the whites of the eyes of birds roosting in the trees are not clearly visible, then the plane is too high to make it to the runway. Unfortunately, this reduces the margin for error, and margin is required when the wind is howling at Kanabea. As at Tifalmin, the wind interacts with that final ridge in an unhelpful manner. Crossing that ridge on that unforgettable day, the aircraft descended at a rate that was unacceptable. In the space between two heartbeats, thoughts raced through my mind. More power. More power! Maximum power! Power levers forward as you would put your foot right to the floor. The slight hesitation as the engine accelerated before roaring to beyond maximum power, combined with a very hard right bank away from the airstrip and towards the providentially deepening valley as the aircraft continued to descend in the grip of the downdraft. The engines caught up and won the battle, and then we were through it. Clearly, the reward was not worth the risk that day, so we bade a less-than-fond farewell to the community and returned from whence we had come: older, wiser, and thankful once again to the folks that built and designed the Twin Otter and to those that pray for our safety each day. However, as far as Kanabea adventures are concerned, that memory falls behind two other occasions when the surface of the strip conspired to ruin our day.

The MAF PNG Route and Aerodrome Guide does advise pilots of runways that are slippery when wet. When wet, all grass runways are more greasy than when dry. That is perhaps obvious. But the ones with the "slippery when wet" warning applied become like skating rinks after a good dose of rain. Kanabea is one of those. The difficulty is that the only predictable part of slippery is that it is unpredictable. So pilots are expected to execute their very best judgment in evaluating the wisdom of attempting a landing on any given day. One such day, we arrived overhead Kanabea after a night of rain had left the runway very clearly wet. Having landed successfully and, more importantly perhaps, uneventfully in similar conditions on previous outings, it seemed reasonable to assume that with an appropriate level of caution, the outcome would be the same. They say that a good approach is the precursor to a good landing. Additionally, pilots are cautioned that the landing is not complete until the aircraft is slowed to a walking pace. In any landing, the objective is to have the descent rate decline to zero feet per minute at the point the wheels touch the ground. If you have flown on any commercial airliner you will recognize that this is actually more difficult than it sounds. When faced with the conditions found at Kanabea that day, the importance of putting the wheels on straight and smooth reached the imperative. The approach was textbook stable, actually quite good, even if I do say so myself. There is a time in every landing when a pilot can feel if it will end well; unfortunately, this doesn't happen till after touchdown. The wheels caressed the ground with a feather touch that may place it in my top one hundred landings: all to no avail.

The tires slipped onto the grass, rolled a short distance, then slipped on the grass. But this is PNG, so of course the unexpected followed: the aircraft started to skid sideways. At some airstrips, this would be merely an inconvenience; Kanabea does not fall into that category. To the right-hand side, a mere handful of feet from the runway edge, the mountainside drops away at an alarming rate. To the left-hand side, it is the opposite: there is a vertical escarpment. Between a very literal rock and a slippery slope, even if we had full control of the aircraft, the choice was really no choice at all. So it became a game of reactions: could I match my reactions to the aircraft's gyrations? A swing to the left counteracted with right rudder and a slight increase in right engine reverse thrust. Then quickly retracting those inputs in anticipation of the aircraft veering back to the right. Followed by left rudder and left reverse thrust. A contest where intuition supersedes conscious thought. Control recovered, landing complete.

During landing, the aircraft is slowing; so even if it all does, as the New Zealanders say, "turn to custard," the impact at the end will be low in energy and most probably survivable. When taking off, the converse is true in all respects. Should directional control become problematic on takeoff, the question of safe abort arises. On many of Papua New Guinea's remote airstrips, an aborted takeoff will have the same result as loss of control on landing. However, on many highlands airstrips, like Kanabea, an aborted takeoff will be catastrophic. A directional control problem on takeoff results in another set of rapidly evolving options: poor options. My most memorable experience at Kanabea, trumping both the turbulence and the landing, involved this very scenario.

I increased engine power, and as I sensed that the brakes could no longer hold the aircraft stationary on the slippery surface, I released the brakes and carefully but assertively increased power to that required for takeoff. Working the rudder pedals like a tap dance with no music, I kept the aircraft straight. I also employed judicious adjustments of asymmetric left and right engine power to contribute to the rapidly increasing complexity of the directional control conundrum. The time-space equation altered as a sizeable tree in line with the trajectory of the left wing entered the picture. Judicious power adjustments transitioned into energetic as the gap closed. As we reached liftoff speed, I pulled the aircraft into the air and dropped the right wing as much as I dared to increase our separation from the looming tree. It was over as quick as it had happened, just another memory of the unexpected that is a fundamental aspect of flying in Papua New Guinea.

And yet there are other memories, people really, that render Kanabea a special place to me. Vanimo had been our home for five years when we departed there for furlough in Canada. When we returned to Papua New Guinea five months later, it was to the town of Goroka, which, as it turned out, was our home for the next ten years. The flying in Goroka was the same, only different from Vanimo. During the first few years in Goroka, we also served the people in the communities around the coastal city of Lae. Lae is the second largest metropolis in PNG, and although it is coastal, all the airstrips around it are hidden in the mountains. The old airport in the middle of Lae City closed several years ago, replaced by a new facility built outside of town on the site of a World War II airstrip at Nadzab. To the north, the spectacular Finnestere Mountains rise rapidly from the floor of the Markham Valley. The strips of the Mongi Valley are to the east, with many others to be reached only after negotiating the Saidor Gap to the northwest. But it is thirty minutes' flight time to the southwest, in one of a series of tight, deep parallel valleys that Kanabea is to be found.

Matt and Becky had arrived in PNG a short while before our move to Goroka. Particularly in their early years, we were privileged to support the ministry that God had led them to in the village of Kotidonga. In my mind, Kanabea is Kotidonga, but that is just bad geography. In fact, the airstrip of Kanabea is just the closest runway to their little village. A "road" winds its way up from Kanabea, up and over a ridge then back down the other side. As aircraft fly down final approach, they follow this track, covering in seconds what takes hours on the ground by foot. Over the years, we flew all sorts of things into Kanabea for the family and the ministry. I don't actually remember when I first met Matt, but I do remember when I met his parents. John and Selina came to PNG to visit Matt and Becky and their young children one Christmas. But the most amazing thing was when John and Selina heard God's call to join Matt and Becky in the ministry in PNG. They went back home, left their jobs, and prepared to move to Kotidonga to become partners in the "That They May Know" mission. From Matt and Becky's early days, the ministry has grown to include church planting, a Bible school, and a medical clinic that cares for some eight hundred patients a month.

When we moved to Papua New Guinea, we packed our belongings into seven drums and one wooden crate. We had no need for furniture as the house provided by Mission Aviation Fellowship included furniture. Not so for John and Selina. They had to pack not just personal belongings but furniture as well. As a nurse, Selina was going to expand the ministry to improve health care for the entire valley, so there were plenty of medical supplies to go too. Additionally, there are no stores in the back of beyond where Kotidonga is located, so there also that pesky little matter of needing food, groceries, for a couple months. Fortunately, that is the kind of job at which the Twin Otter excels.

Lae is a major seaport, the gateway to the highlands. There is a road from Lae through to Goroka and on to Mount Hagen, a link not available from the capital city of Port Moresby. John and Selina's belongings had arrived by ship into Lae, so we flew the Otter to Nadzab to provide our assistance. Airplanes are limited not just by space but also by weight, so we worked on the ramp selecting items that would maximize our load within both those constraints. As I recall, it actually took a couple of flights to complete the job. That was not the last time we were able to partner with these families. There were groups of work teams and also the time we carried a bucket, scraper blade, and hydraulic controls for a Bobcat that had previously been slung in under a chopper. In addition, somehow, a couple of small off-road vehicles had made it into Kanabea, reducing the ground time from Kotidonga to forty minutes each way. Even with this, it still took several trips to move an Otter load of cargo from Kanabea to Kotidonga. Because of the time spent—wasted— in transporting to and from Kanabea, it seemed to the Kotidonga missionaries that perhaps for the long-term efficiency of the mission, it might be wise to invest in the building of a runway at Kotidonga. This was the reason for the Bobcat.

Perhaps the most interesting visit, however, was the day I actually had the chance to go to Kotidonga and see the runway under construction. Three years before my visit, the site of the new strip was still hidden by jungle. Construction began with the clearing of the trees and proceeded at the pace of hand tools. Two years later, we flew in the equipment for the Bobcat. In balance with all the demands of ministry and aided by the arrival of John and Selina, the pace of construction increased to the point where it seemed prudent to get a little input from the folks who would be asked to land there. I had recently assumed the responsibility of chief pilot for MAF PNG operations when Matt and John requested MAF to come have a look at their runway in progress. So early one Friday morning, I boarded one of our Cessna 206 aircraft with another Richard, also a pilot from MAF Canada, and departed Goroka for the fifty-minute flight to Kanabea. We were praying for the impossible: good weather all day. Kanabea is usually a morning strip, especially for the lower-performance single-engine Cessna, in that by lunchtime, the runway and valley are often obscured by cloud. We were going to need about five hours on the ground to complete the transit from Kanabea to Kotidonga, then trek to the runway site, have a look, and then complete the journey in reverse order.

Richard and I were very glad for the buggy ride from Kanabea as it sure beat walking up one side of the mountain then back down the other. Having said that, it was not the most comfortable of journeys with the road being little more than a rock-strewn path. It was, however, a poignant reminder of why Mission Aviation Fellowship exists. The airstrip site is located above the village and required a short walk. It commenced immediately with the crossing of a "raging river." The photos exhibit more of a quiet little creek five or six meters in width and approaching waist deep, but the concealed current threatened to knock us off our feet and send us on a merry and very cold ride downstream. Across the river, we climbed up a muddy track to the ridge that was being transformed into a runway. The effort required to carve a runway out of the jungle is unimaginable for most. Phenomenal amounts of labour had been completed to clear the trees away and then slice the crest off the ridge. But there was at least as much again to be completed. The strip needed to be longer, and a double-dog leg straightened to make is useable for an aircraft. I estimated that to take out only the double-dog leg would require shifting at least five hundred cubic meters of dirt. In perspective, that is the top ten centimeters of earth from an entire football field: line to line, side to side, American, Canadian, or English football. To relocate that much dirt takes something like 1,800 trips with a wheelbarrow.

After dispensing what we hoped were words of both wisdom and encouragement, translated by John to the many community members that were with us, we once more braved the river. It reminded me very much why I fly. Prayers for good weather were answered, so we were confident in accepting a gracious invitation to have lunch in Matt and Becky's home. As I recall, it was an unexpected feast to enjoy so far from civilization.

These are the kinds of people that are my missionary heroes: the types of people that leave everything to go to the uttermost, unreachable parts of the earth to share the love of God with those who are isolated spiritually by physical barriers. And I had the privilege to partner with these dedicated folk in overcoming at least some of the physical barriers.

Me with Richard Jano, my friend and flight programmer
at Goroka, Eastern Highlands province.

A sinsging at Nagri airstrip, Eastern Sepik province.

Nate at his high school graduation with friends
from his church volleyball team.

My fond farewell from Lumi, Sandaun province.

# LIMA

## -A Lumi *Education*-

I LEARNED A lot in Lumi. About flying. About people. About miracles of God's timing. I got to know Lumi during my first year in Papua New Guinea. It is at the far west edge of what was my check-in area, the places to which I was permitted to fly. Lumi is found on the backside, the southern side, of the Torricelli Mountains. It is cradled in a corner where the Torricellis end and the Bewanis begin. The map would lead you to believe that the divide between these two ranges is obvious: large. In reality, it presents as one continuous range, with a slight bend punctuated by a low point. As PNG villages go, Lumi is one of the larger; and as PNG airstrips go, Lumi is one of the simpler. Atypically, with a slope of just 1.3 percent, Lumi is a two-way strip, meaning aircraft can take off and land in either direction. The runway is eight hundred meters in length, more than double some of the very short ones.

Once we moved to Vanimo and I was flying the Twin Otter, Lumi became very familiar. It was the first stop on our RPT flight that went Vanimo-Lumi-Aitape-Anguganak-Nuku-Wewak and return three times a week. We kept the name RPT long after the reason for the name passed into history. Years ago, MAF held a license to run a regular public transport flight along the route described. The law changed over time, erasing the need for the license, but the name stuck long after. The RPT was a well-organized and fast-paced affair. We had MAF agents, with radio contact at each location, so it was easy to plan in advance. Even as the day progressed, we could advise the folks on the ground how many seats we had available for their passenger bookings. It was very common that we only shut down the left engine, that being the side for passenger access, to expedite our time on the ground. We would regularly spend less than fifteen minutes from wheels on to wheels off. In that time, we would do the shutdown checks, unload what we were bringing into the community, complete the paperwork and load what we were taking out, restart the left engine, complete all our checks, and be gone. While very busy, it was great fun being part of a team that was functioning well—seeing if we could go fast enough, making up sufficient time to be able to slide in an extra flight to help out more passengers or carry food in for one of the little "trade stores." This would have been impossible without our agents.

On the ground at Aitape, we had Jacob and Luke. Linus was at Nuku; Isaac was our man on the ground at Lumi. Although it has been many years, when I close my eyes, I can still see Isaac walking towards the aircraft from perch in the captain's seat of the Otter. He always had a bilum (woven or knitted bag) slung across his right shoulder to underneath his left arm, carrying the passenger manifest on a clipboard in his left hand with a pen held in his right, still working away to finish up the manifest. He had a very sort of upright posture with a short-stepped gait. Isaac wasn't actually from Lumi but around the corner, so to speak, from Yebil. Isaac was a wontok of Matilda, who worked in the MAF office in Vanimo. As the bird flies, it is ten kilometers, but Isaac would regularly make the walk back home. In contrast to Lumi, Yebil is one of the hardest strips in PNG. It is in a very confined space, and the runway has two steps—slope transitions—in its very short 402-meter length. The slope overall is 5.5 percent, but it starts flatter then gets steeper, then flattens out, then gets steeper again before flattening out one last time at the very top.

All aircraft—regardless of size, power, or purpose—must be operated within their design limits. Those design limits may vary, but each aircraft has a maximum allowable takeoff weight and a maximum allowable landing weight. The maximums may be trimmed on a given day due to weather conditions. Air temperature affects the load that an aircraft can carry: the hotter the temperature, the longer runway an aircraft will need to take off. If runway length is a problem, then the aircraft must carry less weight. The same is true for wind, when it is blowing behind the aircraft. Planes get airborne when there is sufficient air flowing over the wing. When taking off into the wind an aircraft gets off the ground much sooner. I have seen small aircraft, pointing into a strong wind takeoff from almost a standstill. Operating with a tailwind is the opposite. A wind from behind the aircraft will cause it to gobble up the runway when taking off or landing. Pilots prefer to take off and land with a headwind, but in PNG, this is often not possible because the runways are located on the sides of mountains. Aircraft also must usually land on flat runway, or alternatively land going uphill and take off going downhill. It is possible to land downhill when the slope is minimal, like at Lumi; but this is not easy, quickly leading to problems if the pilot makes a mistake, as I found out on one occasion at Lumi. Fortunately, the only thing hurt was my pride. For a landing downhill, the runway just seems to keep falling away from you, refusing to meet the wheels of the aircraft.

Our standard arrival from Vanimo into Lumi, and indeed often the way we got there from Aitape, was by way of the Sissano gap. Inbound from Vanimo, we would carve a track that was slightly north of the direct route, descending along the mountainside towards the flat bowl area that separated the Bewanis from the Torricellis. When the weather was poor, this was the only way to get from the north through to the south side of the mountain ranges. When the clouds sat on top of the ridges, we would slide underneath in the space between the cloud base and the ground, passing through the Sissano gap. To do this safely, a pilot really needs to have done it several times in good weather. It sounds like an exaggeration to say that the pilot needs to know every tree and every little stream, yet when the weather is uncooperative, it is imperative that you can recognize exactly where you are. Breaking out of the Sissano gap, we would execute a right-hand turn to place the aircraft immediately in the landing pattern. The day of the mudslide, it was very confusing. Fortunately, the skies were reasonably clear, for overnight the landscape had shifted—literally, it had moved. After a series of rains, the storm of the night before had been too much for entire hillside. An area the size of two football fields had simply slid down into the tiny lake that rested at its base. The lake was now a river. It was very perplexing, for at first we could not tell what had changed; we just knew something was not right. The grass was all intact; even the trees stood upright. The whole hillside had just crept down into the lake.

The north coast of PNG in particular was heavily Catholic during the years we spent there. Without the Catholic mission, life would have been very different—worse—for many of the people living in the remote villages of Sandaun and East Sepik Provinces. The Catholics provided huge amounts of health and education in needy areas. They were also a source of some interesting experiences for mission aviators. It started in my Cessna 206 days when flying out of Wewak. MAF does not carry alcohol on any of its flights. Alcohol and developing countries just do not match. Drinking ends in rape and murder, as a rule rather than as an exception. So when Father Austin arrived to check in with a few bottles of sacramental wine, I was a bit stumped. Father Austin, later Bishop Austin, was at the start of a trip to visit a number of villages, where he would celebrate communion. A quick check with my boss, the chief pilot, clarified that sacramental wine was acceptable, so into the pod went a few bottles, along with Father Austin's nine iron. Apparently, the good father liked to have something to do while out bush, and runways made good fairways to practice his swing. Also out of Wewak was the time we loaded a three-foot-high Madonna into the cargo pod. Once upon a long time ago, the Catholic diocese operated their own aircraft. Their aircraft registration letters reflected the diocese, so Diocese of Vanimo was DOV, Wewak was DOW, Aitape was DOA! Perhaps not the best thing to paint all over an aircraft.

Eight kilometers north of Lumi, halfway up the side of Mount Sulen, lies the little village of Fatima. My map shows an airstrip at Fatima, but there was never any evidence of one in my flying time; must have been back when DOA was flying around. While there may not have been an airstrip at Fatima, there was a school operated by the Catholic mission. Over the preceding months, we had flown some building materials into Lumi, to be carried to Fatima, for the construction of a new classroom. Such accomplishments are celebrated in New Guinea, so a big sing-sing was planned to mark the opening. Such an event could not happen without a "mumu," which would need to feed a lot of people. We were requested to fly two cow carcasses from Aitape to Lumi for the event. That was the only time I ever had a whole cow in the plane, and I was glad they were already dead. I was equally pleased that I did not need to be part of the team that carried the meat those eight kilometers up the mountain.

The Catholic missionary I got to know best was Brother Leo. If memory serves, Leo was a Franciscan monk. We usually saw Brother Leo when we landed at Lumi. He would stop by for chat, exchange his incoming mail for his outgoing letters, or maybe collect some spare parts for something he was fixing. Despite living a solo existence as the only missionary of any stripe for miles around, he was always cheerful. On occasion, Leo would need to go down to Aitape, perhaps for supplies, perhaps to meet with his leadership. All I know is the he could not wait to get back to Lumi. Brother Leo had no time for the big city; population of Aitape might top out at two thousand, if you include the stray dogs. I never did figure exactly out what Brother Leo's role was, but he invariably showed up to greet us, looking like he had recently jumped out of a bath of oil and dirt. It was therefore a huge surprise the day Brother Leo met us in the parking bay wearing his "official" monk garb: coarse brown robe with rope belt. Leo had been in Lumi for years. He must have been seventy if he was a day when I first met him. With all the escapades and anecdotes accumulated over the years of mission flying in PNG, one thing that I have learned is that in many cases, it is the people that make the place. Brother Leo was one of those people. Just quietly getting on with God had called him to do.

As with many of the 303 airstrips I have been to in PNG, there is one event, one memory, one experience, that stands out from all the others. And often that thing has very little to do with the airplane. So it is with Lumi. Many of my tales start out with "it was day much like any other." That is, of course, because that is how they start. As a pilot, I am sure I looked at the plan the night before. As it was going to be an RPT day, it was expected to be fairly straightforward. We started the day with a check of the plane, making sure all the bits were still attached in the right places, that the tires were inflated, that there was oil in the engines and fuel in the tanks. We filed a flight plan and loaded the cargo. At eight-thirty or so, with the passengers on board and the CA delivering his passenger briefing, I called for the PRESTART checklist. As it was the first flight of the day, we completed the extra once-a-day checks prior to takeoff: autofeather, beta backup, and overspeed governor systems. We lined up runway 12 and rolled down the paved runway, lifting into the clear morning sky. With the deep-blue of the Pacific to our left and the lush green of the Oenake Range to our right, we climbed to six thousand feet, leveled out, and set cruise power. After five minutes, we completed the engine trend monitoring check; then as turbine engines are more efficient at altitude, we slipped on up to nine thousand feet for what remained of the twenty-seven-minute flight to Lumi. We didn't linger long at nine thousand feet, for soon it was time begin our descent into Lumi via the Sissano gap.

With the engines shut down in the Lumi parking bay, the unexpected emerged in the form of a conflicted mother, distraught and relieved in equal measure. I never knew her name—oh, I suppose I did from the manifest perhaps, but not in a way that I can recall now many years later. But I didn't need to know her name, for her it was enough to know that I was "pailot bilong MAF." She wasn't from Lumi but from a village without an airstrip some kilometers away. She had very little money, but she had travelled with hope. Cooking in the jungle is done over an open fire, a fact that is familiar to children right from birth. But the night previous, her young son had fallen into the cooking fire and suffered rather severe burns.

The nearest hospital was Aitape, only fifteen minutes by air; but for this poor lady, it might as well have been the moon, for her son would have been dead before she topped the first mountain peak separating Lumi from the coast. There had been no radio call to us of a medevac. There had been no information from the agent. The lady had just arrived at the strip. When I enquired about why she had come to Lumi, she replied that she knew the airplane would come that morning because that is what it always did. A half hour later, the little child, wrapped in his bandages, was in Aitape and headed to the Catholic mission hospital.

Between Wewak and Vanimo, we spent over six years serving the people in the isolated communities of the Sepik. I got to know some of the people by name, but thousands knew me. When the time came for us to move on to Goroka, many of those people we had ministered to shared a word of thanks as I flew my last days in the area. One of my most cherished pictures from my Sepik days was a spontaneous snapshot taken by the pilot I was flying with for my last landing at Lumi. It is of a "Sepik-mama" giving me a huge bear hug. Sepik ladies can be "solid," so it was a substantial clinch. While PNG folk can be emotionally demonstrative, contact between men and women would normally at most be a side-on embrace. For this lady, whom I had known for years, that would not suffice to express her appreciation. It was far from what I imagined when she approached me beside the Otter, but then this is the land of the unexpected.

# MIKE

THERE I WAS, buried in the depths of a conundrum, solidly jammed between the proverbial rock and a hard place. Airborne in my little Cessna 206, I was attempting to navigate a path along the Jimi Valley in search of the Yuat Gap: the gateway to freedom from the mountains of the Western Highlands to the relative safety of the broad expanse of the Sepik plain. Clouds hung stubbornly to the mountains that guarded either side of the valley through which the Jimi River snakes its trail. The gray-white screens seemed to barricade the route at every twists and turn of the gorge. There was no chance of ridge hopping, of cutting corners. Today it was follow the valley. In these conditions, the wary pilot will keep a constant eye on the "back door," being certain that retreat remains a viable alternative to progress. Advancement being the objective, however, I took careful stock of the options. Often climbing a little more would be helpful, although these clouds seemed to challenge that option, demanding a rather considerable altitude to gain a clear course above the cumulus. Descending to seek a path below appeared less than inviting as the clouds were pushing off the slopes, further constricting the already narrow valley.

Scaling the cloud wall looked like the best selection from my menu of options except for one factor: the reason for the flight. I had been given the responsibility of flying a mother, father, and newborn baby back to their home in Wewak on the north coast. The infant was suffering from some illness that inhibited its ability to breathe properly. At higher altitudes, the air is thinner; there is less oxygen, which would not be helpful for a young one already experiencing breathing issues. Large aircraft overcome this problem of oxygen deprivation at altitude through a system of pressurization: the air inside the plane is at a higher pressure than that outside, which enables passengers to breathe as if they were much lower than the aircraft. For this to work, the aircraft structure must be very strong, sealed completely leak-free, and of course, some sort of pump to pressurize the interior. None of this is financially viable for small aircraft that spend much of their lives in the zone where breathing is unaffected. So there I was in my unpressurized single-engine aircraft, barred from descent because of the clouds, unable to climb because of the condition of my tiny passenger, and denied my current road due to the swirling mist that filled my windshield. It was either turn around or find a hole in the veil ahead.

Medevacs come in all shapes and sizes but basically fall into one of three categories: expected, unexpected, and preemptive. Mission Aviation Fellowship regularly receives requests to fly to a village to pick up the sick or injured for transport to hospital. When these flights are not extremely time-sensitive, they are often woven into the flying program for the day as a matter of efficiency. On occasion, time is of the essence, so we launch a special dedicated flight. Sometimes we land at an airstrip for one purpose, only to discover a person in need of medical attention waiting in anticipation of the aircraft arriving. There are also flights that aren't really medevacs per se; they are flights carrying medical staff to conduct clinics and medical operations. In some African countries, these are regular events referred to as "safaris." The pilot joins with a medical team and flies to several communities over a period of days, camping out away from main base.

One of my early medevacs on the Twin Otter was at Buluwo. Although 95 percent of destinations in PNG would be classified as isolated; some are more remote than others. Buluwo would certainly fall into the category of extraordinarily secluded. It hangs on the edge of the north coast ranges, maintaining a toehold on the Sepik plain. The runway is unremarkable in every respect. As a lowlands strip, the runway is basically flat; and measuring 790 meters from end to end, MAF pilots consider it more than adequately long. Uncommonly for PNG, Buluwo runway is unobstructed on both approaches, permitting aircraft to land in either direction. The small group of houses that constitute Buluwo village sits in the near distance down a narrow path carved through the kunai grass. People rarely congregate at the airstrip. Planes are few and far between at Buluwo, so when the plane circles overhead, the young come running, the older at a pace more commensurate with their age, certain that having taken the trouble to find Buluwo, the pilots will wait.

That day, we knew the purpose of our visit: a pregnant mother in difficulty. Perhaps the majority of medevacs in Papua New Guinea are birth related: still births, retained placentas. Arrivals at bush communities do not exactly follow a schedule, so the patient remained in the village till the aircraft was on the ground. The lady was transported in some style, a stretcher fashioned from branches and other bush materials. Even by PNG standards, this stretcher was unique. It was created more like a tent: two long poles forming either side of the base and extending out as handles. There was a farther pole at the pinnacle tied to the base poles with shorter sticks. As a whole, it was almost cage like, perhaps intended to be sure the lady could not fall out during the walk over the rough path. This presented a problem for us: there was no way the entire contraption was going to make passage through the aircraft doors. Explaining this to the men, and before we could hardly draw breath, a man raised his ubiquitous bush knife and began the process of removing the canopy. A level of mild panic gripped me as I imagined a slip that would compound our patient's trials. As if the birthing turmoil was not enough, a wicked bush-knife cut would make things much worse. I should have known better than to be afraid, however. The man's aim was true, honed by years of practice. He cut the stretcher down to more acceptable dimensions.

The machete carried by practically all Papua New Guineans from a tender age through to the grave is not always used for good.

In a society ruled by family loyalties and not far removed from Stone Age civilization, the presence of a weapon readily to hand is a temptation that is too great for some. Karimui is a government station in Chimbu Province, but that doesn't mean it is free from trouble. Still only accessible by air, as a center, we visit Karimui more often than other communities. On arrival at Karimui, we are accustomed to being met by a substantial crowd. This day was no different in that regard, but what happened next was unquestionably a problem. As the passengers deplaned and we unloaded the cargo, three men separated themselves from the crowd and proceeded to express their displeasure over something that was completely lost on me, but apparently we were not the object of their wrath. The personal baggage of our passengers was the immediate target of their swinging bush knives. A response from the owners was no surprise, and what had been a normal, peaceful day erupted in total mayhem. Teams were rapidly drawn, although to be honest, my feeling was that those on the side of the instigators were doing their best to bring resolution rather than escalation.

As the minibattle flowed away from the airstrip, we decided that departure was the best course of action. With everyone drawn to the community drama, preparation for departure was simple; but just as we closed the doors, someone came running up, breathlessly announcing that we needed to delay our takeoff because of a medevac (why was I not surprised?). A man was helped to the aircraft parking bay with blood streaming down his head from a very serious scalp wound. Probably lucky to be alive. It was obvious that medical attention was necessary before we went anywhere. The local health workers were conspicuous by their absence, so any first aid was going to be pilot administered. My medical training is limited to a Saint John Ambulance First Aid course when I was in Scouts, renewed two or three times during my pilot career. We broke open the first aid kit and did our best to stem the flow of blood. Head wounds are notorious bleeders, and strapping a bandage to a head is like attempting to tie a scarf on a balloon. Sharing the story with a paramedic some years later, he suggested that a trauma bandage jammed under a ball cap would have worked the best. Being ignorant of this trick at the time, we did manage to stem the flow, guided the patient onto the aircraft, and departed for Goroka. Somehow the story made the papers, complete with a cartoon depicting the angels of MAF.

My medical skills are representative of most MAF pilots, but there was one who flew with us for a few years that was a trained, licensed doctor. My first meeting with Hui was a great surprise: as a Singaporean, I was stunned when he opened his mouth to hear a Glaswegian accent. Dr. Hui had studied medicine at the University of Glasgow and had been infected by the strong accent prevalent in this Scottish city. We were crewing together on the Twin Otter on a flight that passed through the Southern Highlands community of Kelebo. In all of PNG, the Southern Highlands is the most volatile. On landing, we encountered one of those unexpected medevacs. Short story, two brothers had come to blows over a pig. Seems that the pig belonging to brother 1 had ravaged the garden of brother 2, including breaking through a fence. Brother 2 had lost patience with the pig's repeated destruction of the vegetable garden and administered discipline to the pig. Brother 1 took offense, and brother 2 ended up with a cut on the back of his right hand, a slice that severed tendons to his middle and ring fingers. Fortunately, our next stop was Telefomin with its small hospital.

There is a joke about a pilot that unfortunately had an engine failure. Fortunately, he had a parachute. Unfortunately, it failed to open. Fortunately, the man was heading for a haystack. Unfortunately, there was a pitchfork in the haystack. Fortunately, he missed the pitchfork. Unfortunately, he missed the haystack too. Well, for our medevac patient, fortunately, we were headed to a hospital. On arrival, unfortunately, we discovered the doctor was just leaving. Fortunately, my copilot was a doctor. Unfortunately, he had never done surgery. Fortunately, he was willing to give it a go. Unfortunately, he had to learn how to reattach tendons from a textbook. Fortunately, the surgery was a success. Sort of. You see, tendons are elastic, sproingy. When cut, they have a nasty habit of disappearing back from whence they came. So while it is possible to grab the tendon and stretch it back to reconnect, they aren't marked; so when there are two, it is a guess as to which tendon belongs to which finger.

We landed at Telefomin, and Hui disappeared into the office to conference with the departing mission doctor about the process for reconnecting tendons. Now, this may seem strange, even perhaps irresponsible; but in the land of the unexpected, the choice is often between the less than ideal and nothing at all. In this case, the option for brother 2 was take his chances with Hui or go through life short of two functional fingers. The story goes that on completion of the operation, with anaesthetic worn off, it was time to check the results. The doctor pointed to brother 2's ring finger, who proceeded to wiggle the middle finger. Switching to the middle finger, the patient waggled his ring finger. They say that misaligned tendons are not the end of the world; that, given time, the brain figures it all out.

Fortunately, some surgical procedures are planned a little better; some are planned far in advance. Hauna is a tiny community buried in the middle of the Sepik Plain. Actually on the Sepik River, the village is established on a couple of small islands and either shore of a tributary, the "subdivisions" united by rope bridges. Single-lady missionaries had been serving in Hauna for many years before I made my first landing on the island that held nothing but the airstrip. It was my first year in PNG, and I was flying a Cessna 206 based in Wewak on the north coast. I had flown the fifty minutes to Hauna several times loaded with cargo that seemed out of place in the tropical jungle: cement, wire, conduit, and even floor tiles. Turns out we were building an operating theater in preparation for a medical mission that I would have the privilege to support for more than a decade.

The annual mission team comprised of eight or so professionals: a mix of doctors and nurses headed by a skilled plastic surgeon. It may be that a plastic surgeon seems out of place in country with larger medical concerns, but in a society reliant on subsistence farming, two functioning hands are rather critical. I saw a man with two thumbs on one hand granted the gift of normal functionality due to the skill of my doctor friend. Thousands of people would travel by canoe, up to one hundred kilometers along the crocodile-infested river to receive the services of GPs, OB-GYNs, ophthalmic surgeons, general surgeons, nurses, and an anesthetists. The people of Hauna graciously hosted the many visitors over the week the team was "in town," providing food and shelter to complete strangers.

One year, 1,164 patients went on the record over the seven days of the mission. Hysterectomies, hernias, thumbs, and—I kid you not—knotted intestines, all fixed in 115 operations in a fully stocked operating room in the middle of the equatorial rainforest. Everything needed for all the ops was brought in on two Twin Otter trips and one GA8 Airvan. Supplies included ninety kilograms of highly specialized ophthalmology equipment that was used to return sight to sixty-four blind people. Imagine: once I was blind, but now, *now*, I see. How cool it was to be a part of that.

Sometimes a medevac is very different. We don't normally fly on Sundays. The chief pilot can't approve it. Only the general manager can okay Sunday flights. Saturday night, I received a phone call from Leah, one of the missionaries we support. I had flown Leah and husband, Doug, to Wewak from their home in Ambunti a few days previously. While here, Doug started having problems with a rapid heartbeat. The doctors said that he needed to go to Australia for specialist help as Doug's heart had failed to respond to the drugs they had tried. The problem was that passports etc. were still in Ambunti, thirty-five minutes' flight away. Sunday dawned with clear blue sky, so at eight o'clock, we were on our way. The bad news was that on the other side of the Torricelli Mountains, the morning fog had thickened up since our weather report. In fact, there were no breaks at all the whole way out. We were doing some serious praying—with eyes open, of course! Miraculously, a hole appeared with three miles to go, and the mission was a success. With proper documentation in hand, Doug and Leah were able to get to Australia and see the specialist. A little over a week later, I returned the couple to Ambunti in perfect health.

My favourite though, the best, was being able to do something totally outrageous. In the land of the unexpected, one never can be sure what the new day will bring. There were about four Saturdays in a row when there were requests for medevacs that we had to coordinate. The last of those was particularly challenging. I received a phone call from Christian Radio Missionary Fellowship (CRMF) to say that a health worker from Mount Aue was requesting a medevac. CRMF monitors their high-frequency radio network every day of the week, 365 days a year, from sunup to sundown for such eventualities. As is often the case, a lady was suffering birthing complications.

Aue is little airstrip about eight kilometers (twenty minutes' flight time) from Goroka. It has a deserved reputation as a strip requiring even more respect than most. The runway can be quite soft and unpredictable. Several years ago, one of our 206s hit a soft spot on takeoff, resulting in a prop strike: the hole was so deep that the normal clearance between the spinning propeller and the ground was reduced to less than zero. The community is located in a mountain bowl that looks a little like a frying pan, where the handle is the opening into the bowl. Cloud usually clings to the mountaintops such that entry to the strip is only by way of the handle. Further, the straight line track from our home base of Goroka does not line up with the handle, so flights between the two require a circuitous route, a more expensive route. For dedicated medevac flights like this, we prefer to launch a small plane as the patients rarely have sufficient funds to cover the cost of the flight. Unfortunately, on this particular day, for a variety of reasons, none of our single-engine airplane pilots were available. We tried contacting some other missions with aircraft, but none of them were available either.

We were now impaled on the horns of a dilemma. The patient and guardian (travelling companion required for admission to most hospitals in PNG) had two hundred kina ($70) between them to pay for the flight. In the single-engine planes, this would be less than a third of the total cost, but really not a big loss to send the plane out. On this day, the only plane on hand was the Twin Otter. The money that the people had was barely enough to turn the engines. But this is Mission Aviation Fellowship, so we launched the big bird. A quick right turn after takeoff saw us heading for the Watabung gap and beyond that the western edge of the Mount Elimbari escarpment. We didn't really expect to have a clear run into Mount Aue, yet as we

142

cleared Elimbari, we could see all the way through to the Mount Aue basin—an unheard-of direct flight.

We had been in Aue late the previous afternoon and so were mildly confused as to why the patient had not travelled with us at that point. The lady was not a member of the little Aue community but had arrived as it got dark late on Friday afternoon, travelling from her village to Aue as the nearest medical aid post and airstrip. It turns out the lady had gone into labour four days previously. Twenty-four hours later and still in labour, five men began to carry the lady to Aue. After three days of walking, they arrived in Mount Aue. These heroes carried the patient on a bush stretcher for three whole days. The next time I was in the area, I looked around from the lofty perch of my office in the sky and tried to picture from where these folks might have come. All I could see was jungle and mountains in every direction. It was great to be able to be a part of this outrageous thing: flying an airplane to save a life of someone who trusted that Mission Aviation Fellowship would be there for her.

This is the great challenge that is faced almost daily by mission pilots: to go nor not to go. We are required to assess the risk of every flight, not just medevacs, to decide if the risk is too great for the purpose of the trip. Most times, it is quite a simple decision, but the medevacs are hard on the heart. That is why MAF has some limits on pilot authority, why sometimes special permission is required. A late-in-the-day call for a medevac flight in poor weather that will push the concrete boundary of available daylight is a decision best left to someone removed from the emotion of the pleading voice on the radio. Mission pilots are, by definition, mission focused. We left home and family to bring support, aid, and comfort, but a dead pilot is no use to anyone. As chief pilot for a period of time, it was part of my job description to make those judgments. I clearly remember one such request. I evaluated the circumstances, the situation, and declined permission for the flight to proceed. I heard the voice on the phone tell me, "If we don't go now, you know the patient will be dead by morning." Yes. I was fully aware of the consequences of my decision. I was also fully aware that the chances of the pilot dying were equally high, and with him would go the lives of all the people he would save into the future. They say that the mantle of leadership is heavy, and indeed it is; but in PNG, we can expect nothing less.

This story would not be complete without recounting the funniest medevac I was part of. *Funny* and *medevac* should perhaps not be used in the same sentence, and yet in this case there is no choice for me. We were on our way from Vanimo to Telefomin with a flight plan that called for everything to run smoothly. In the land of the unexpected, anticipating a trouble-free day is a touch naive. Of course, halfway to Telefomin, we got one of those radio calls: "Medevac at Miyanmin, can you drop in on your way for a quick pickup?" In reply, we requested further details. Expecting a pregnant mother, instead we were told, "Arrow in the eye, but not from tribal fighting." We swallowed hard, looked at what we could cut from our day if time ran short, and diverted to Miyanmin. On landing, we shut down just the left engine and ejected our cabin attendant JB to find the patient and guardian. In truth, I was afraid our patient was going to present with three or four feet of bamboo projecting from the center of his head. As the couple approached the aircraft, I was thrilled at the absence of lumber in the man's eye, a simple bandage covering the wound. I was in a bit of hurry, motivated to be on our way by the pressure of time, yet JB was moving rather slowly in boarding our new passengers, paralyzed by intermittent fits of laughter.

Doors closed, I called for a status update, but JB was unable to communicate coherently due to his high level of amusement. Persuaded that the passengers were at least secure, I restarted the left engine, ran through our checklists, and departed for Telefomin. Established on our way JB was now recovered enough to share the root of his laughter. In our short time on the ground at Miyanmin, JB had gleaned the key details of the story: how a man manages to stop an arrow with his eye when there is no tribal fight. It seems that the patient and his best friend had sourced some home brew and were having a good time. They observed some rats moving around in their little hut and decided that bow and arrow was the best resolution to this minor infestation. They say don't drive while impaired, but an addendum to that sage advice would also be not to hunt rats while impaired. The level of intoxication must have been substantial as one man apparently took his friend to be the mother of all rats and loosed a bamboo arrow in his direction. Our patient was fortunate to have kept his life and vision in both eyes.

Returning to the swirling mist filling my windshield en route to Wewak, prior to my departure from Hagen with the baby, I had checked the weather as much as is possible in PNG and drawn the conclusion that this flight was going to be less than straightforward. Our ministry with MAF being for us a family venture, I had called home to ask Jennifer and the kids to pray for the flight. It wasn't till much later that I understood what had transpired. Around our dinner table, I told the story to Jennifer and our three young children. Samantha was barely five at the time but perhaps still best placed to grasp the need of her dad, so she had prayed what to her was the obvious cry: "God, please make holes in the clouds." So as I wrestled with my options and prepared to retreat, a hole appeared in the clouds. Not one of those "sucker holes" that lure a pilot into a pit, an honest-to-goodness clear hole through which I could clearly see to the next bend in the river with plenty of room to turn back around. Popping through the gap, I was able to continue for a few more miles until the next curve, where once again I was faced with the conundrum: down, no good; up, not an option; straight ahead, barred. But again, as I prepared to withdraw, a beautiful tear appeared in the clouds, promising space to safely fly on the opposite side. As before, I assessed the opening and, confident as before, proceeded through.

This is going to sound like one of those bad never-ending jokes with which I tormented my children, but for a third time, the clouds closed around, suggesting that a return to my start point was in order. But for a third time, the finger of God reached down from heaven and split the veil for my tiny plane to burst through, this occasion clear through the Yuat Gap into the Sepik Plain with visibility stretching to the coast some 140 kilometers to the north. Ah yes, expect the unexpected.

# NOVEMBER

## -*Meningitis Miracle at* Nuku-

I ALWAYS THOUGHT it would be a great name for a daughter. For a little girl, it would be cute, perhaps with a slight ring of whimsy. For a teen in that transition from child to woman, it would set her apart, hopefully in a good way. Possibly grant a sense of unique identity and confidence that might help her avoid some alternative damaging methods of standing out in a crowd. And for a young lady seeking to make her way in the world, the name could conceivably grant an air of sophistication and grace. Yet for a woman who has successfully navigated the developmental years, the name would remain remarkable. A name unable to be sullied through short forms, nickname, or strange associations. Yes, I always believed that *Nuku* would be a timeless, visionary, exceptional name for a daughter. Of course, I never asked my daughter if she wanted to change her name. Besides it being messy legally, it would have been very confusing to all those relatives. Although, we did know a family where everyone referred to the youngest daughter by one of her given names while the dad called his daughter by her other name. So I could feasibly have just called my daughter *Nuku* anyway. But Samantha was already five years old by the time I was introduced to the community of Nuku, and I had long since coined my special diminutive for her. We used to play peak-a-boo, as parents do with their toddlers, and even though our lovely daughter commenced talking intelligibly at ten months, peak-a-boo was launched when all she could do was gurgle.

Sam's first forays into the aural side of this time-tested ritual was "pa-boooo." Perhaps, therefore, somewhat expectedly, she became, and remains, my boo.

*Nuku* is the name of an airstrip in the East Sepik Province of Papua New Guinea. Well, actually, it is the name of a community; but as an MAF pilot, communities are airstrips to me. In truth, as with all PNG runways, Nuku actually serves several surrounding related villages. It is generally believed, even by some pilots, that the lowlands airstrips are less challenging than the highlands airstrips. I think the theory is that mountains equal hard and flat equals easy. The truth is quite far removed from this assumption. The shortest and steepest runway in Papua New Guinea is found in the Eastern Highlands Province; however, the next three on the list of most demanding by length and slope are all found in the Sepik Provinces that delineate the northern lowlands. In addition, many lowlands strips are plagued by high water tables that can generate soft and slippery conditions.

Nuku is not really any of these. It is actually considered to be quite benign in PNG terms. Oriented northwest to southeast and composed of reasonable quality grass, Nuku measures 709 meters in length and 40 meters wide. At just 6 percent slope, it is quite straightforward. Picturing this may need some help. Forty meters is about the same width as ten lanes of road side by side. Six percent slope means that when an aircraft touches down, it then climbs forty meters to the other end of the runway. This gradient is about the most you will encounter when driving a major divided highway. Seven hundred nine meters is equivalent to the length of seven football fields, eleven ice hockey rinks, or nine wide-body airliners. This may seem to be plenty of stopping distance; however, for those more accustomed to flying on major airlines, passenger jets require level runways over three thousand meters in length. In light of that, Nuku may still seem a bit on the extreme side.

In reality, any experienced MAF pilot would consider operations at Nuku to be pretty average in terms of difficulty. It is when poor weather conspires with the terrain that a pilot will sit up a little straighter for landing at Nuku. At such times, the pilot will need to do a little more of that "piloty" stuff, combining a slightly better-than-average decision-making process with a reasonable level of what is aptly termed "manual aircraft control." Nuku is closely surrounded on three sides by terrain that rises a few hundred feet above the runway. Final approach, those last few seconds of flight where the aircraft is lined up with the runway, is flown through a saddle in the hills. Picture a horse saddle, and you have the picture: the aircraft flying across the horse through the lowest point of the equestrian's seat.

As the aircraft crosses the saddle, little children on the hilltops laugh and dance as they look *down* on the plane; people on the walking track invariably dive for cover. On those days when the clouds are low, hugging the ridge lines and obstructing the saddle, it might be possible for the pilot to catch a glimpse of the runway from the northeastern side. An experienced captain, one very familiar with Nuku's personality, may perhaps consider a ridge approach. This involves flying tight inside the saddle ridge with the left wing tip seemingly brushing the tree canopy. With a tight right turn to align with the runway just prior to touchdown, the landing is complete. Takeoff again in these conditions is not advised so the extra effort for a nonstandard approach may be futile.

Amid hundreds of flights into Nuku, there is one that stands out not for the challenge or heart-pumping adrenaline hit but for the shear unexpected quality. Whereas some experiences generate feelings of apprehension, relief, or excitement, this episode simply made me giggle. The sky was that pristine blue: deeper than sky, more brilliant than lapis, perhaps a shimmering cobalt. Departing from Wewak 130 kilometers to the east, we rounded the southern slope of Mount Turu and established the Twin Otter on a westerly heading level at 6,000 feet above sea level. Visibility was well beyond the horizon some 175 kilometers distant. What we saw, while not completely uncommon, was nevertheless noteworthy. A plume of smoke rose in the middle distance. Seemingly random bush fires are a familiar sight in PNG, especially in dry season. When I have attempted to count those types of fires, I run out of motivation approaching one hundred. The solitary nature of this fire was what made this situation unique. From horizon to horizon, the gray pillar was an orphan. As the kilometers to destination clicked down at the rate of 4.9 per minute, I began to wonder if the fire was burning at Nuku. It could mean anything from the simple clearing of a garden plot to a full-on tribal war accompanied by the burning of houses. In truth, the visual presented did not match up with either of those scenarios. My concern mounted that it could be something far more problematic.

MAF generally operates in developing countries where most of the airstrips from which they operate would be optimistically termed "unprepared." This is not entirely true or entirely fair. I am sure that the people who cut trees, pulled stumps, and flattened ground over periods extending many years would suggest that a lot of preparation had been undertaken. Regardless, the airplane operates from grass, which grows and must be cut and cleared. Back then, lawn mowers were scarce as hen's teeth, and the cutting of the runway was accomplished by back-breaking labour with a bush knife. Sometimes then, the final clearing is assisted by incineration. Wildfires just don't happen in New Guinea. Perhaps there is just too much moisture, but whatever the reason, fire as a tool in PNG is generally not reckless.

Indeed suspicions became reality: the runway was on fire. I suppose that perhaps I should have been surprised, but if memory serves, the emotion was somewhere between annoyance and humour, but probably weighted towards annoyance with a pinch of disbelief. The arrival of the aircraft was far from unexpected. We had left Nuku scarcely two hours previously to fly to Wewak with a return straight back to Nuku. What were they thinking? Although it was clear from some distance that the fire would inhibit the landing, we continued on. There is no telling from afar exactly where a fire is nor how long the conflagration will continue. Accompanying the faint odour of smoke, there was a touch of fancy in the cockpit, that perhaps the fire would die prior to our arrival, or that possibly it would be so close to the threshold that we could fly over it and still land with plenty of runway. Arriving overhead Nuku, all optimistic illusions were washed away. Although the majority of the airstrip remained bathed in sunshine, it was clear that the smoke would create an impenetrable wall to our approach and would remain that way for some time.

Options. When faced with such conundrums, a pilot's thoughts immediately shift to options. There are usually three alternatives: wait, go back from whence we came, select an alternate destination. The decision process considers fuel, which is equivalent to time and distance, weather, and what we actually have on board the aircraft in terms of passengers and cargo. An assessment of our situation rapidly revealed that waiting was not a viable option. While it was quite safe to conduct lazy doughnuts overhead the field, the fire would likely continue to hinder arrival for quite a period, causing us to burn through all our contingency fuel. In the land of the unexpected, pilots get to be old by always maintaining their fuel margins. There are plenty of alternate landing sites much closer to Nuku than our departure point of Wewak. The obvious choice was to head to Aitape. Just fourteen minutes away, and with refueling available, it made perfect sense.

The addendum to this tale is that we had on board with us as a passenger an MAF middle manager who is a Papua New Guinean from Nuku. I couldn't help but catch his eye as we passed over his home village and deliver a knowing smile. In typical PNG fashion, I received in return a shrug, a grin, and an expression that clearly communicated, "Hey, you're in the land of the unexpected."

The experience with the fire was a rather random event, certainly not the norm. It remains clear in my mind, but not for any significant difficulty it posed. Conversely, the weather encountered flying over the jungles and mountains of PNG supplies a considerable daily challenge. In Canada, we are accustomed to predictable weather patterns. We watch the news, the weather channel, and check the weather app on our phone. We hear words like *low pressure* and *cold front*. We can receive an hourly forecast that will predict with reasonable certainty the arrival of a rainstorm, including items of specific value to pilots such as cloud heights aboveground and visibility distance.

Papua New Guinea lies between two and eleven degrees south of the equator. As such, it does not experience weather and climate as we know it in Canada. Countries that lie close to the equatorial belt are subject to tropical weather patterns. Seasons are split into wet and dry rather than the traditional spring, summer, fall, and winter. The combination of what is known as air-mass weather with the precipitous terrain results in unpredictable patterns. One mountain valley can be clear sailing. Turning a corner, a pilot can be faced with a gray rainy wall. Pilots are trained to check weather reports and forecasts prior to launching on a flight. In countries like PNG, this practice assumes a different face. While aviation forecasts are available, it is just not possible to predict weather when there are so many localized geographical features that interact with the atmosphere to generate local weather patterns. Pilots in PNG seek to gather reports from many little villages to construct a mental picture of current weather. They then overlay this on their previous experience to assemble a likely weather picture. Wise pilots will then compare this with the mental images built by other pilots. Still, there are times when we get it all wrong.

In contrast with the highlands, the lowlands regions of PNG might more frequently be subject to widespread poor weather consisting of low cloud and rain showers, hindering visibility. On the north coast, the scenario is complicated by the presence of the coastal mountains that stretch 380 kilometers from the border with Indonesia on the west to beyond Wewak on the east. This particular stretch is technically a combination of three ranges—Bewani, Torricelli, and Prince Alexander—but the geography belies the name change, the three sections combining to form a single feature as far as the meteorology is concerned. North side versus south side will often present contrasting weather conditions. However, this is Papua New Guinea; pilots must always be primed for the unexpected.

Preparation for a day of flying is a variable recipe of checking the program, verifying aircraft airworthiness, preparing the load, and of course assessing the weather. It was one of those days where weather reports from around were all less than ideal. Mediocre weather on both sides of the mountains did not bode well. However, there were indications, hints, that improvement might be forthcoming. So once all was ready, we launched from our home base of Vanimo just thirty-three kilometers from the Indonesian border for a direct flight to Sibilanga. Forty-five minutes later, the cloud and rain were not conducive to a landing. Consequently, we were back once again to options. The conditions were clearly identical over an extensive area. Returning home was not an awesome alternative due in part to our intentions for the day but also because of deteriorating weather at Vanimo.

The Sepik Provinces were in fine form that day. Our usual alternate of Aitape fourteen minutes away, while acceptable, from a weather standpoint, had become a lake. Flooded for most of its 844-meter length, we would have needed floats on the plane to pull off a successful landing. Nuku lies a short 20 kilometers from Sibilanga, but at 1,400 feet lower elevation and slightly farther south of the coastal range, it looked like the best option. The landing at Nuku was accomplished with little fanfare and only slightly elevated adrenaline levels.

Safely on the ground, the challenges did not evaporate. Fuel was now the question. With Aitape out of the equation, options to get more fuel were limited to Wewak twenty-nine minutes east or Vanimo thirty-seven minutes west. Both were probably oaky, but in the land of the unexpected, *probably* is insufficient. Viable alternates for Vanimo or Wewal require at least twenty minutes fuel even in under clear skies, and that extra fuel was absent from the tanks due to our issues at the start of the day. We were going to need guaranteed weather conditions to consider a takeoff from Nuku. The wait for better weather extended past midday and well into the afternoon before we received a good report from our staff on the ground at Vanimo. So the day went into the logbook as Vanimo to Nuku and back to Vanimo, and into the financial accounts as MAFWX: "weather turn back." They say it is better to be on the ground wishing you were flying than to be flying wishing you were on the ground. Similarly, it is better make a loss safely than to make a profit dangerously.

Amidst all these memories, however, the one that stands out has little to do with flying the aircraft. In my mind, it is filed as the *meningitis miracle*. From the chapter L ("Lima"), you may recall that

Nuku was a regular stop in both directions on the Vanimo-Wewak RPT. The flight would depart Vanimo about eight forty-five in the morning, with stops at Lumi, Aitape, and Anguganak prior to the first landing at Nuku. I cannot begin to count how many times I flew that route, but I would estimate well in excess of five hundred times. Probably 499 instances, we followed the regular route. Except for one day. One day in the middle of five years of flying the RPT. One day, we flew a different order. One day, when all the myriad puzzle pieces aligned in the mind of our flight programmer to suggest that it would be more efficient to fly a different order. One day when our customers would be better served if instead of Lumi as our first landing, we went direct to Nuku. One day when Nuku went from number four to number one.

It was my privilege to work with many Papua New Guineans during our time with MAF PNG. In general, I had very little to do with the details of the flight program for the day. I would plan our altitudes, directions, and leg times for our flights. I would decide how much fuel was required and how much payload we could manage. But the order of stops was decided by our Papua New Guinean programmers. Some of those men and women were extraordinary in terms of their abilities to assess often conflicting service requests and create a plan to assist isolated communities in a very efficient way. Matilda, Richard, and Famiri were all very, very good; but if I were forced to pick the best, I think it would have to be Albert. So if Albert said we should go skirt Lumi, bypass Aitape, and overfly Anguganak for direct Nuku, then while I might have asked why, it would be for information, not for argument.

After Nuku, the plan was to proceed to Aitape. As part of the RPT, the Nuku to Aitape leg routinely happened on the return flight. Passengers travelling from Nuku to Aitape could expect to arrive in Aitape at about two in the afternoon. Aitape is located on the north coast, right on the Pacific Ocean. It is the closest town to Lumi, Anguganak, and Nuku, all of which lie on the south side of the Torricelli Mountains. Goods arrive in Aitape via ship from Wewak and Madang, so people travel there for food, medicine, educational supplies, and pretty anything else that doesn't grow on tree or in the ground. Of key importance, however, is the Catholic-run hospital found in Aitape. The next closest health facilities of note would be the main hospital for the East Sepik Province in Wewak and Vanimo General Hospital, the only significant hospital in all of Sandaun (West Speik) Province.

Unbeknownst to us, a young man in a village in the catchment area of Nuku airstrip had become gravely ill overnight. Early symptoms of fever and severe headache accompanied by significant stiffness in the neck had matured to include nausea, vomiting, and seizures. Clearly, the man needed help, so his relatives loaded him in a stretcher fashioned from tree limbs for the trek to Nuku. With no hospital or means of contacting a doctor, this was their single option.

In developed countries, people experiencing symptoms in line with severe flu will almost certainly visit their family doctor long before it progresses to seizures. This involves picking up the phone and making an appointment, then crossing town to arrive at the scheduled time. Should the patient have waited overly long to make the call, and should the receptionist understand the severity of the situation, they may well tell you to call an ambulance for a quick trip to the hospital. A second phone call and a few moments' wait will see the patient in the hands of trained medical professionals. In developing countries, especially ones with significant transportation challenges, the transition from feeling bad to seeing a doctor usually takes much longer.

In Papua New Guinea, by the time a person understands that they are seriously ill, the chances for recovery may be quite slim due to the efforts required to reach proper medical care. And so it was for this man. The RPT route and times were well known to the people of the Torricelli Mountains, so the best that friends and family could do for the patient was to carry him to Nuku and hopefully get a spot on the MAF plane for a ride to Aitape.

What no one could know was that the man had contracted meningitis. This is a condition characterized by the infection of the membrane that enfolds the brain and spinal cord. While there are a number of reasons for the infection, and thus different varieties of meningitis, if left untreated, meningitis will lead to death. And therein lies the rub. The time line from infection to demise for this man meant that an arrival at Aitape hospital at 2:00 p.m. would be too late. However, getting to treatment six hours earlier could almost certainly be the difference between life and death.

It is not in my recollection that there was really anything special, good or bad, about the weather on the day. It may be that the events that would unfold simply pushed those details to the irrelevant section of my memories. It was not until we had successfully completed our landing at Nuku, shut down the engines, and opened the passenger door that we became aware of the battle for survival that was taking place. The pace of preparation for departure increased dramatically as our clarity of understanding of the situation grew. Following a time on the ground that would have qualified us as a Formula 1 pit crew, we were on our way. Clear skies, calm winds, and a dry runway encouraged us on our way. A short climb to five thousand feet and a straightforward negotiation of the Tadji gap saw us safely on the ground at Aitape.

Forewarned by MAF ground staff, the Catholic mission was on hand with their ambulance for the short—not smooth but short—trip to the hospital. When I say "ambulance," you will need to wipe that mental image of a cube van-like vehicle with Day-Glo yellow or red and topped with a veritable galaxy of lights, and replace it with an illustration more akin to a large SUV topped with a 1960s cherry light. Of course, it was not until much later that we heard a confirmed diagnosis and how close our passenger had been to the end of his appointed days on earth.

On reflection, what is very clear is that without a change in the flight plan for our aircraft on that day, that man would certainly have succumbed to his infections. How thankful we are that the Lord foresaw the need and used MAF as his instrument that day to bring life out of what I am convinced would otherwise have been death. One of my favourite Bible verses is found Exodus chapter 5. Verse 1 very simply states, "Afterward Moses and Aaron went to Pharaoh and said…" I always find that so incredibly amazing.

Imagine, if you will, what it would take to get an audience with the queen, a president, or the prime minister. I think there is a huge probability that should I send a message to the prime minister, that I want to chat with him about a change that would likely ruin the economy of the country, my appeal would be refused. I doubt it would even make it past the mailroom. And yet in the case of Pharaoh, God prepared the way such that Moses and Aaron could apparently just walk right in. As I compare this story to others in the Bible and how little detail there is, the conclusion I reach is that getting into the palace was not a drama. God is able to know and arrange far in advance of what we can imagine. On that day, in a tiny unheard-of community in a small, little known country, God miraculously redirected the path of a small plane to save the life of a nameless man.

Unexpected change of plans. Unexpected miracle.

# OSCAR

Control Locks ...................... Removed
Parking Brake........................Set
Avionics .............................. Off
Power Levers ........................ Idle
Propeller Levers .....................Feathered
Fuel Levers .......................... Off
Beacon ................................ On
Master Switch ...................... On
Battery Switch...................... On
Hydraulic Pressures .............. Above 1,200 psi
Fuel Selector........................ Normal
Fuel Quantity....................... Sufficient
Boost Pumps ........................On, Lights Out
Doors and Tail Strut............. Secure

AND SO THE patter goes: a routine and rhythm repeated four, eight, twelve, fourteen times a day—one pilot challenging, the other checking and responding. A breath, a pause, as I prepare for the sweetest sound in aviation: the *whoosh* as a Pratt & Whitney Canada PT6, a turbo prop engine, lights up.

Reaching above the windscreen, I grip the start switch; and with a slight tug to unstow it, I am able to move it to the right. I am rewarded with the pleasing high-pitched whine of the engine compressor turbine

157

turning, sucking in great mouthfuls of air, and the rhythmic *click*, *click*, *click* of the ignition. The free-turbine three-blade prop begins to spin lazily through its seven-and-a-half-meter rotation. A quick check of the engine gauges reveals sufficient engine speed and battery power to expect a successful start, so I reach up to the ceiling between the pilot seats and move the fuel lever forward to the "on" position. I count the seconds, and before I reach "five Mississippi," I hear it: that pleasing *whoosh* as the aircraft wakes, the fuel and compressed air mixture catching fire inside the combustion chamber. I turn a keen eye to the T5 temperature gauge to watch that the engine doesn't get too hot: if it goes past 1,090°C for more than two seconds, we have just turned nearly a million dollars into recyclable scrap.

Small by airline standards, the Twin Otter is the largest plane that Mission Aviation Fellowship anywhere in the world. I would admit to a certain bias, except that everyone agrees; at least all Twin Otter pilots concur. There really are only two kinds of pilots: those that have flown a Twin Otter for its intended purpose and those that wish they could! Developed from its predecessor, the single-engine Otter, the de Havilland Canada Twin Otter is the ultimate STOL (short take off landing) bush plane. It is a nineteen-passenger utility aircraft capable of operating from the worst airstrips Papua New Guinea has to offer. A true go-anywhere, do-anything aircraft, it can take off and land in little more than three hundred meters. Give it some upslope for landing and a little downslope for takeoff, and it will do both in much, much less than three hundred meters. And the "TwOtter" will do it with whatever you can imagine being carried inside. There used to be a television commercial in PNG for the Toyota Hilux pickup truck that asked the question, "Need to move (fill in the blank)?" and provided the answer, "No problem, I've got a Toyota Hilux." Well, for the missionaries, church workers, and remote communities of Papua New Guinea, the answer is, "No problem, MAF has a Twin Otter."

We have told stories of medical-evacuation patients on stretchers and, unfortunately, coffins; related tales of a Noah's Ark menagerie of animals and birds and reptiles. X-ray machines and five-meter-long rigid pipes for a hydro project have also flown to new homes. Fridges and generators, quad bikes and tractors, school materials and medical supplies, even suspension bridges and houses. No typographical errors: *tractors, suspension bridges,* and *houses.* MAF partners with thousands of churches, missions, and nongovernment organizations around the world, and so it is toward the fulfillment of their objectives that we squeeze these unthinkable cargos through the restrictive doors of the plane. MAF pilots become rather adept at maximizing space when packing, but in fact, my first attempt at packing too much into too small a space was just after Jennifer and I were married.

Returning from our honeymoon on Prince Edward Island, we knuckled down to the task of packing our meager collection of earthly belongings into our Plymouth Reliant, which we named *Betsy,* for the journey from the Atlantic to the Pacific coast. We had our wedding gifts, bedding, clothes, pots and pans—all to squeeze into that poor car. Everything that could travel out of a box was removed from packaging, boxes with air space were filled: a practice that later became routine suitcase-packing custom during our various transits to and from PNG. A mouse would have struggled to find space in the car trunk, and the rear-view mirror was useless with the back seat literally packed to the roof. That poor four-cylinder engine dragged the Reliant, all but riding on the bottom of the rear shocks, for six days without falter. Several months later, mind you, the engine blew a connecting rod deep in the mountains of British Columbia, its life no doubt cut short by the westward trek that forced it beyond its design limits.

What we didn't have to do was cram an ATV into Betsy, along with everything short of the kitchen sink. ATVs, quads, four-wheelers—they come in multiple shapes and sizes. Some fit into an Otter with little fuss; others are more tedious. The maximum width of the floor inside a Twin Otter is just over 1.3 meters. A big four-wheeler is just under 1.3 meters wide. The weight of a full-size quad is heading towards two hundred kilograms, so simply lifting it up to the floor of the Otter, which sits at 1.3 meters above the ground, is out of the question—so ramps. Pushing the vehicle up the ramps is not too hard, given enough strong backs; but once at the top of the ramps, the Otter isn't wide enough to swallow the bike straight ahead: the rear wheels hang out the door. So while some people hold up the back end, another team inside has to jimmy the front around to get the right rear wheel inside. With three wheels safely in the aircraft, the loading team can take a breather in preparation for the next stage. Phase two is not pretty: tremendous quantities of pushing, pulling, grunting, bouncing sees the four-wheeler safely inside. We did this in several occasions, but in the one that I am picturing, we jockeyed not one but two nearly identical machines into the aircraft for a group of missionaries in Simbai. Getting them into the plane is one thing; crawling all around in very limited space to secure the bikes to tie-down rings is another. Straps must be carefully placed and tightened since ATVs rolling back and forth in a plane is a scary proposition. Usually, the process of loading consumes far more time than unloading, but large ATVs would be the exception.

Much less complicated in terms of packing and unpacking are mosquito nets. In our family, four out of five of us have felt it and suffered as a result: the chills, the fevers, the aches and pains. She is no respecter of persons. Age means nothing to her; social status is irrelevant. Except for a brief kiss, she is long gone before you will feel the effects of her little gift. She is the female anopheles mosquito, and she leaves the unprotected with a dose of malaria. Properly treated, malaria is no longer a killer; but when you are far from the nearest drugstore, it is life threatening. There are several prophylactic drugs and many herbal remedies that seek to defend against this disease. However, the reality is that the only sure way to not get malaria is to not get bitten! Being outdoors at dusk in humid climates is a certain way to contract malaria. For people living in the tropical rainforest of the lowland areas of Papua New Guinea, in houses with no windows and no window screens, there is very little that can be done to combat the female anopheles mosquito.

One way is to be sure the whole family sleeps under a treated mosquito net. Rotarians Against Malaria have entered this conflict. By supplying mosquito nets to these remote communities, it is now possible for these people to "not get bitten." MAF regularly partners with Rotary Australia in flying these nets out into the jungle villages. The nets are packaged in bales weighing forty-seven kilos each. We would often dedicate an entire day delivering nets to multiple airstrips, with each airstrip serving multiple villages. On one flight to one airstrip, we carried thirty-seven bales.

Simpler yet are schoolbooks and boxes of medical supplies: cartons of twelve to twenty-three kilograms throw in and stack like Lego. Many smaller communities have their own primary school and medical aid post that need to receive regular infusions of supplies. Aid posts are supplied with prepacked boxes that comprise a standard kit of provisions from Band-Aids and pain relievers to saline and bandages. Schoolbooks are sent out in a similar manner. While the actual handling of the materials is simple and the aircraft is often underweight since we run out of space and therefore less demanding on short airstrips, the administration can be time-consuming. Since logistics companies are contracted to ensure delivery, everything must be signed for by the health worker or school headmaster as applicable to meet the terms of the contract. A representative of the company flies along with us to take care of the paperwork, which usually also includes a photo and recording of the GPS coordinates of the school or aid post as proof of delivery.

The medical supplies are, however, just so much useless junk without people trained to use them. Community health workers (CHWs) are the mainstay of village health programs. These folks are mostly volunteers that are trained in assessing illnesses. Their assessments help others in the health network determine appropriate treatment and if there is a need for a medevac. They are also trained as midwives, birthing difficulties making up the vast portion of MAF's medevac calls.

On one occasion, eighteen ladies on a CHW course were flown into Goroka from the Simogu District, about twenty minutes' flying time. The alternative transport method was about two days' walking through jungle, up and down mountains, and across rivers to get to the start of the "road," then a day on that road packed into a "PMV" (public motor vehicle [fifteen-passenger van]). The course was presented with a biblical foundation by Christian instructors. While most of the ladies had previously been exposed to the Gospel—and a number were definitely Christian—the fact that the course was taught from a Christian perspective will bear additional fruit. The ladies were presented with new shoes and clothes and a CHW "tool kit" to enable them in their work. On completion of the course ten days later, we flew the ladies back to the Simogu area.

While boxes are easy to load and passengers self-load, the ability to picture a load fitting into a defined space came to the fore when CARE approached MAF about the possibility of transporting the materials for building suspension bridges into some very isolated communities. CARE is a worldwide humanitarian organization "dedicated to saving lives and ending poverty" (CARE vision and mission). In Papua New Guinea, MAF works with CARE on transport for various projects including health-care worker training, drinking water supply, and building of suspension bridges.

Whether flying in the Finnestere Mountains or in the Bismarck Range, I loved the good-weather days. It wasn't just that the flying was easier; it was that I had time to sightsee: time to look out the window to enjoy what I may never have seen before. Steady at cruise altitude, I could afford to partition my concentration, permitting a little bit of attention to be diverted to enjoying the amazing scenery. Where the mountains are so rugged, vertical in places, one can be fairly certain that no one has ever been there, that the experience has been limited to those who have been airborne spectators. It was the waterfalls that really captured my imagination. There are streams which plummet two, maybe three, hundred feet in a narrow band. The thing is, the density of the jungle canopy conceals the river that births the cascade; it is as if the waterfall appears out of nowhere. There are places where the rivers flow underground and only pop into view as they pour off a cliff. At the terminal end, the water splashes into a small pool and once again vanishes from sight. But there are other spots where the trail of water is obvious: turbulent, furious, and perilous. For some communities, these rivers are mean serial killers, snatching lives of unwary children, of adults forced to hazard a crossing to reach a vegetable garden. The villagers build bridges, but due to limited choice of materials, these crossing points afford only a slim increase in safety. One of CARE's projects in their partner communities has been to provide materials and construction expertise for permanent safe links to span these brutal torrents. Simbari was one of the locations that received a bridge.

Simbari is located partway along a small valley to the east of Goroka. The strip is somewhat unique in PNG in that it lies across the valley. By contrast, the runway is similar to many in that the approach requires driving the aircraft in extreme close proximity to the jungle mountain slopes. The runway is not the best, but not the worst. It has a clay base, so when very wet, it does become an adventure to keep the aircraft on the runway. The valley sides are crenellated with minor spur ravines through which the lethal little brooks wind their course. If you know where to look, the bridge is visible from the air, tucked away in one of those inconsequential gullies. Yet if you were to attempt it on foot, neither the canyon nor the river would be trivial.

It takes a number of trips even in the Twin Otter to transfer all the necessary bits for a complete bridge. The stacks of components are only mistakable as a bridge if you are familiar with the process: twenty kilogram bags of cement, rolls of braided wire cable, steel grate plates about two-by-four meters, steel rod, a welding machine, and bags of tools. Dropped at the runway, everything is then carried by hand over jungle trails to the river's edge.

If that sounds challenging, it is nothing compared to moving an entire house, from one isolated village to another remote village. Missionaries of New Tribes Mission have been in Sendeni for years, but as the ministry became established, fewer missionaries were needed. At the same time, a new ministry was being established in Menyamya "just over the ridge." Sendeni is located in the Marawaka Valley about twenty-five minutes' flying time east of Goroka in the Eastern Highlands Province. This is the airstrip where an MAF aircraft suffered a hard landing due to some nasty and unpredictable winds. Menyamya is located in another valley system little more than forty kilometers to the east of Sendeni. Awkwardly, those few kilometers are bisected by a range of mountains whose twelve-thousand-feet stretch is invariably cloud covered.

Talk about the unexpected. I was surprised on my first visit to Sendeni to see an old Land Rover rusting away off to the side of the runway. Investigation on later visits revealed that "back in the day," there was a road from the coastal city of Lae all the way to the Marawaka Valley. The road tracked across the flat Markham

Valley, then rumour suggested past Tsile Tsile and snaked through the valley systems to Menyamya, from which it began an exhausting ascent towards the Umba Gap. Cresting the breach in the mountain defenses, Sendeni would have looked enticingly, agonizingly close, yet not so. The route descended from the Umba Gap, weaved towards the top end of the Marawaka Valley, crossing to the opposite side. Then paralleling the track but in the reverse direction, the track climbed to the midpoint of the mountainside, zigging towards and through Usarumpia with a zag and a curl to Sendeni, which would have been in view probably for nearly an hour. But by the time of the house move, the road option was a distant memory. While still navigable on foot, the demise of the road for vehicle traffic would no doubt have fallen into the expected, being little more than a dirt path.

The idea was to deconstruct rather than destruct the house, the difference of course being the intention to reconstruct. Should the road have been passable for a flatbed truck, then the house could have been taken apart in module fashion to simplify the rebuild. But of course that option being unavailable, the house had to be cut to fit through the aircraft door: an opening 1.25 meters by 1.4 meters. By the time the house was ready for transport, its resemblance to a building was passing at best, it having been reduced to a pile of plywood and a collection of lumber.

It might seem to some that this exercise was not merely labour-intensive but also appreciably more costly. Regardless of source, supplies into Menyamya needed to travel by air. The recycling of a house, long since paid for, is evidently better stewardship than leaving it to rot while purchasing new materials for a new house. New plywood, lumber, roofing iron, and all the myriad of items required for a house were available for purchase in Goroka or Lae, but flight time from Sendeni to Menyamya is a third of that from either town. Having concluded that reuse was best from the materials standpoint and flying less-expensive over the shorter distance, the decision fell to the viability of flying the house from Sendeni to Menyamya.

While the personality of Sendeni encourages pilots to approach with caution, on paper, Menyamya is straightforward; but this is PNG, so therefore there is the element of unexpected. The runway of

Menyamya is very long and nominally quite flat, except that it rolls and corkscrews like a rowing boat on the high seas. Furthermore, the last minutes of the approach entail flying close to the terrain in the midst of a natural venturi. The valley bowl in which the runway rests is at the terminal end of a long valley that narrows just before the bowl. Wind racing up the valley towards Menyamya picks up speed as it passes through the narrowing valley: the venturi effect. As the pilot manoeuvres the aircraft to align with the runway, the wind gives it a kick in the tail then causes the plane to drift. It turns side on to the wind to line up for landing. The pilot must then assertively continue the descent across the last ridge, battling the wind to plant the plane on the first third of the runway: the flattest, most level third. However, neither Sendeni nor Menyamya airstrip presented an abnormal challenge to the Twin Otter, so giving wings to the house became the next challenge for MAF PNG.

Throughout these adventures, this great airplane has never let me down and has saved me more than once. Way back in my early hours as an Otter captain, we were attempting an arrival at Lumi in Sandaun Province. The weather was fine, except for fog veiling the runway. Fog is an insidious blanket. Looking down from above, it can be thin, translucent, giving hints that to penetrate its cloak will be harmless. Yet down lower, looking straight into the fog, the illusion of visibility is dispelled as the world disappears in a swirling gray mantle. With that in mind, we were in no great hurry to descend into the mist. Morning fog in the low-lying areas typically dissipates as the sun climbs in the sky, and so we circled around and around overhead the runway, expecting that patience would yield clear air.

We kept catching glimpses of the field, the parking bay, and the waiting crowd. In time, a large hole appeared and lingered, enticing me to attempt a landing. I learned a serious lesson that day about temptation, for as we approached for landing, the picture faded a little, but I felt we were still in good shape. It wasn't until the aircraft settled into the hole and the wheels were caressing the grass that I reached the startling conclusion that the break in the fog was much farther down the runway than I had estimated. Too late to do anything else, I planted the wheels on the ground, prayed to God, and trusted in the aircraft designers at de Havilland. We gobbled up the remaining runway at an impressive pace. I stood on the brakes as hard as I dared and applied a sizeable measure of reverse thrust. We did stop in time, but I had never really seen that end of the grass runway before, and thankfully never again since. At least one passenger was aware how near we had come to ruin and expressed to me his judgment of my decision-making skills. Many years on, I still carry those words and the feeling embedded in them on every flight I make. And when faced with similar decisions, the words ring in my ears, bolstering my determination to make the hard choices: the safe choices.

And so with engines running and pre-takeoff checklists in progress, it is time for another highly critical aspect of our preparations: the takeoff briefing.

This will be an MPS power 50 takeoff with speeds of 70 and 80 from runway 34.

We are at maximum gross weight with wind below maximum allowable for takeoff.

We can safely abort prior to the school buildings on the left-hand side.

Any problem prior to that point or a power loss below $V_1$ of 70 knots, we will abort the takeoff.

I will bring power levers to idle and apply maximum braking, initially stopping straight ahead.

If we are going to run off the end of the runway, we will head to the left to avoid the houses and select fuel levers off, FESOVs off, DC master, and battery switches off. We will then evacuate as necessary, remembering that the medevac patient will need extra assistance.

For a power loss after $V_1$, we will reduce power as required to control yaw.

Through VMC will then go max power to the first red line, flap 10, speed V2, and check for auto-feather.

If auto-feather has not occurred, then we will confirm the failed engine and feather the propeller manually.

There will be no further action till we are through 400 feet; then we will conduct the ENGINE POWER LOSS AFTER TAKEOFF checklist or other checklist as applicable.

In the event of a fire, we will be returning back here for landing. Otherwise, evaluate our options for single-engine flight back to base.

For normal operations, we will climb in the valley till we are clear of the ridges then set course at 10,000 feet.

Standard calls will be auto-feather armed, power set, $V_1$, and 400 feet. Pilot monitoring is to observe caution and advisory lights and call out any abnormalities of malfunctions.

Any questions?

Unless you are a pilot, you probably have heaps of questions; but for MAF PNG operations, that is just the first crew briefing of what would probably be repeated four, eight, twelve, fourteen times a day, always preparing, expecting the unexpected.

A medevac patient from Andakombe airstrip in the Eastern Highlands.

landing the Otter at Lengbati Morobe province
(Brent Dodd, used with permission)

As seen from the air, Hauna village, Eastern Sepik province.

Our daughter Sam, with Kodiak, our Doberman-Rottweiler.

# PAPA

## -Pets *Are Family Too-*

WE NEVER REALLY had pets as a child. Jennifer always had a cat, but my childhood home was devoid of animal entertainment. As the youngest, I am not entirely sure of the reasoning; the precedent was well established by the time I was in any position to express desires about the relative value of a pet. I am not quite sure what would have happened should I have returned home from the country fair with my prize from the coconut shy: a water-filled plastic bag containing "Sir Glub-Glub." The lack of pets in my young life may be, of course, that, as a family, we were just incapable of delivering reasonable care to something with fur and four legs, or even as untaxing as a free goldfish. A reasonable person would suggest that the evidence does bear this out.

In their infallible wisdom, Berkswell Church of England School had decided that education would be enhanced by the presence of incarcerated rodents in the classrooms of the youngest grades. No doubt we learned something of value by having a gerbil learning the times tables alongside us. Perhaps for our family, what we learned is that, as mum and dad had decided, we were not, in fact, animal people. You see, those adorable little desert rats needed a home during the school holidays. The gerbil may have actually been a hamster for all I know, but somehow, whether it was the furry friend from my sister's class two years ahead of me or from my class, we managed to receive the honour of rodent-sitting for one of those glorious school-free vacations.

As animals go, gerbils are relatively low on the maintenance side: a bit of food in the morning, a refill of the water bottle, and off we go for a day of running loose in the neighbourhood. Except for the weekly chore of cleaning the cage: this involved the removal of said creature from his home for the replacement of the litter. If you have ever attempted to hold on to a gerbil or hamster, you are probably smiling already. The pesky creatures are ridiculously wiggly, and being so small, they are not equipped with handles for restraint. Family folklore suggests that on cage-cleaning day, the rambunctious fellow, loathe to be held, fashioned an escape. The hunt was on. Perhaps they are slightly more intelligent than they appear, for the tiny beast made tracks for the smallest and nearest bolt hole. In this case, the toaster! Fortunately for us, unfortunately for him, the toaster, while wide enough for his head, did not permit passage of his body. So there he was, head down, tail up, neither in nor out. I was just a young lad, so I have zero recollection of how we extricated the oversized mouse. He was, however, returned to class at the start of the new school term in the same physical, if not emotional, shape as we had received him.

I suspect that normal people learn from their experiences; it would seem that our family needed a second opportunity. In all fairness, it was probably the incessant pestering of young Richard that instigated a do-over. So once again, we were granted the opportunity to care for the class darling. This story is very much a déjà vu as we once again arrived at cage-cleaning day. In a repeat performance, the cunning fiend made his getaway. Whether this was the same gerbil or not, I have no idea, but this one headed not for the toaster but off the kitchen table around the corner towards the back door where lurked the washing machine. Darkness beckoned to our little friend, and he made straight for the darkest spot of all: the drainage hose. Failed in his appreciation of space versus body mass, once again we were faced with stuck head and madly pedaling rear legs. I imagine that school term began with the class pet in his proper place, but those are the only two occasions I remember pet-sitting. I don't know if it was my parents or the school that put an end to us looking after the creatures.

By contrast and by all accounts, Jennifer's family always had a cat. "Mittens," "Snoopy," and all the others belonged to siblings; but at age eight, Jennifer became the proud parent of "Phantom." To render his full appellation, *Phantom Dusty Conway Kitty*. I feel like the entire clan had a hand in that name. Phantom was a Christmas present. Jennifer is the youngest of five, twelve years separating her from the eldest, and seven from sibling number four, so what happened next was probably understandable, possibly inevitable. As the family sat around Christmas Eve, someone asked, out loud, about kitty litter. Eight-year-olds don't pick up on all the clues, but they can certainly smell a cat. And they can be devious, underhanded, and manipulative. In an Oscar-worthy performance, young Jennifer feigned sadness and sorrow to the point that Phantom was delivered on the eve of Christmas.

Phantom was certainly at the bigger end of the gene pool. A large cat, he was also blessed with significant longevity, surviving right through till just before we were married—which is where the intersection of lifestyles occurs. Every newly-wed couple has adjustments to make as they blend two sets of heritage. Money, food, church, holiday are potential conflict points; add to that pets. Jennifer wanted a cat to fill the void left by the passing of Phantom; me, not so much.

A couple years into our married life, I was persuaded that we should adopt two cats that would otherwise be headed for the pound. The original deal was that we would select one of the pair. The loser, however, looked so forlorn that Jennifer just couldn't, which meant, by default, that neither could I. So we now had two felines in our lives. "Spitfire" was my cat. She was a Siamese cross, full of attitude, and the epitome of the cat stereotype where dogs have owners and cats have servants. Slightly cross-eyed, Spitfire could jump supremely high and was totally fearless when it came to heights. "Mugsy" was the other extreme: a simple, domestic shorthair; in dog language, a mutt. She was fat, to the extent that, without fail, people meeting her for the first time would enquire as to her due date. Despite differing in most ways, the two were like inseparable twins.

On their first road trip we had, the friends separated in two different car carriers. One was a commercial venture, the other a homemade effort. Mugsy, in the homespun transporter, was not at ease and, like the gerbil from years before, facilitated a jailbreak. We had no choice but to bunk pair in one box, which is how they travelled from that point on for the next several years, even when Spitfire got road sick over Mugsy's head. When our family moved to Papua New Guinea, I thought perhaps it was my turn: time for a dog. I always wanted a dog, a real dog, something big and proper. So we became the proud owners of "Nugget." Somewhere buried in her heritage, there might have been New Guinea singing dog. Certainly not a purebred, she carried all the markers of the type that bear resemblance to the Australian dingo.

Nugget came to us as a puppy from Telefomin. As she grew, we discovered that she wasn't exactly normal. Much later, we heard that even as a newborn, she was "different." Would have been nice to know that earlier. Nugget was one of those dogs to whom strangers should not turn their back, especially when we were around. She was severely overprotective, and I loved her as my first dog. I could do anything with her and to her with impunity. If I put my hand in her mouth, she wouldn't even close her mouth, but that was for me. Due to where we lived, Nugget had to be on a wire run so she couldn't get away. The son of the man that looked after our gardens thought that teasing Nugget was great sport. He could harass from close up knowing that Nugget couldn't get him. That was until the chain came loose one day. Without a bark or any other sound, in a move that would make a ninja proud, Nugget exacted her revenge. The cost to us was a pair of boy's shorts and a bit of antiseptic. The profit to Nugget was freedom from torment.

When we moved the 275 kilometers west along the north coast to Vanimo, Nugget came with us. Life there for her was much better as our house was contained in its own fenced-in yard, so she was free to run without restraint. Unfortunately for all of us, Nugget's character of distrust was now fully embedded to the extent that anyone not a member of the family must be the enemy. When I would go and come from work, the kids were responsible to man the gates for the van to get in and out. The gates were large and heavy, iron frame with iron wood pickets. The children were small and light. On occasion, the gates got away from them, giving Nugget a chance to make a break if something interesting caught her interest.

One day, a young man was walking down the road, minding his own business, when the gates opened. Nugget was gone in an instant. On the opposite side of the coral-gravel road was a tree. Really more of a sapling with a trunk no thicker than your arm. The innocent young man took to his heals with Nugget in hot pursuit. Nugget's speed matched her craziness, so the obvious solution for escape for the lad was around the tree. Round and round the sapling, the dog chased the teen. Noting the narrowing gap, the hapless youth elected to go vertical, leaping up the tree. Barely able to support his weight, the tree bent, leaving him clinging for dear life, suspended above the grass with Nugget waiting for the inevitable collapse. As a cartoon, it would have been hilarious. Inappropriately, that is how I was seeing the events, so doubled over in laughter I couldn't call the dog off despite Jennifer's clear and impassioned directions for me to do so. I collected myself with sufficient time margin to save Nugget's target from physical injury and to rescue us from a potentially nasty compensation negotiation.

While we limited our selection of companions to the classic dog-and-cat scenario, others were far more adventurous. In a nation like Papua New Guinea, the controls on pets are far less restrictive. In theory, there are rules against farm animals in the backyard in towns, but that doesn't seem to stop people from keeping chickens and pigs. MAF families have been known to keep chickens and guinea pigs, but one family took full and complete advantage of the opportunity to have their own miniature aviary and zoo. A hornbill and a variety of snakes formed the bulk of the collection, but pride of place surely had to go to the crocodile. It may be just urban myth, but they say that crocodiles will only grow to the size permitted by their environment, so there really was little chance of waking one morning to find the reptile bursting out of his enclosure. At little more than thirty centimeters from snout to tip of the tail, he didn't seem all that intimidating, except for the teeth. Crocodiles spend a significant amount of time immobile, tempting one to slide a finger through the wire mesh to see how that scaly armour feels. Best to be alert, however, as the tranquility is deceptive—crocodiles able to transition from apparent comatosis to violent action in a split second.

Our housing compound was watched over by guards during the night. They arrived at 6:00 p.m. for a twelve-hour shift. The work period began with the sentries patrolling the perimeter to check for breaches and a stop by the crocodile cage to verify the presence of the prehistoric predator. This process was repeated several times through the course of the dark night. It seems that highlands men are not thrilled with the potential of a crocodile, no matter how small, stalking them in the dark. Another friend of ours, imbued with a streak of mischief, was very tempted to remove the crocodile after the setting of the sun, then watch for a reaction when the guards noted the disappearance of the crocodile. Perhaps his conscience got the better of him, for the plan was never enacted.

Mount Hagen hosts the headquarters for MAF in PNG. It is the center for administration, training, and aircraft maintenance, so pilots often pass through, spending the night. A well-oiled system of hospitality for visiting people provides a bed and meals as required. One night, returning from dinner to my assigned house, I was met by two glowing points of light barring my path. That part of that compound is poorly lit, so I was traversing the ground by memory and feel, so it was rather startling to note two tiny pricks of light apparently floating in the inky black. Caution seemed the best course of action, but without flashlight, there was little to do but proceed at snail's pace.

As the distance narrowed a shadow grew around the beams forming the outline of a tree kangaroo. I stared at him; he stared back. I edged forward; he stared back. Suddenly the impasse dissolved as the creature gave way and disappeared into the dark of night. During our early years in Papua New Guinea, someone in Mount Hagen had this tree kangaroo as a pet, and he had liberated himself for a taste of freedom. Measuring at most two-thirds of a meter from head to root of the tail, with the tail adding the same. Again, the tenkile is not the largest of animals and does, in fact, look docile and friendly.

Fortunately for me, that evening, as a prey animal, the tree kangaroo is actually quite timid.

Prior to our first furlough in Canada, Nugget passed from our lives, so on our return to PNG, we began to look for another pet, perhaps one with a little more accommodating personality. About that time, a couple that was "going finish" (leaving PNG permanently) was searching for a new family for their dog, Bear. This is one of those problems integral to owning a pet as a missionary: sometimes the animal's lifespan exceeds the time of the missionaries on the field. As dogs go, she was fairly no-descript. Border-collie size, she was light brown and very fluffy. As the dog of a couple with no children, she had been rather spoiled; and as an eight-year-old when she came to us, Bear was rather set in her ways. However, Bear seemed to adjust to the different lifestyle associated with living with young children. But then came our quandary.

Shortly after our first arrival in PNG, we met Lady, a beautiful, mild-tempered Doberman-Rottweiler cross. We decided on the spot that if she ever had puppies, we were in. Fast-forward a few years, and our opportunity arrived. Bear was now more than ten years old, which for a bigger dog is old age. While we wanted one dog, two was more than we had planned. This was perhaps our sole chance to get the puppy we wanted, so anticipating that Bear may soon leave us anyway, we took the plunge and brought "Kodiak" into our home. She arrived as a puppy, all feet and tongue, so tiny that she couldn't even climb the stairs to our second-storey home. For the first weeks, Jennifer tucked Kodiak under her arm as she went up and down the stairs. Being so small, Kodiak believed she was a lapdog, which became a rather large problem as she herself became, well, large. What to name this puppy was the source of a serious family meeting. The three kids were old enough to have a say. My vote for "de Havilland" was soundly defeated, but with us already having Bear, Kodiak seemed to be a reasonable tag: cool-sounding and appropriately strong for what would become a rather sizeable pet.

Bear struggled in those early days. Kodiak just wanted to play, and Bear just wanted to chill. Fortunately, our kids were young at that time and always ready to run around outside in the equatorial sunshine. Kodiak developed a habit that she maintained right to the end. She would lie inside on the cool hardwood floor, giving the air of being soundly asleep, but any sound of children playing brought her head up and slightly cocked to one side as she evaluated the noise. Having determined it was children playing, she would rise to her feet in a mad spaghetti of legs and tail, fly to the window to double-check, then blast out the door and fly down the stairs, it being a wonder that she never ended up on her nose as she cascaded all those appendages down the steps. Since she liked nothing better than to be in the midst of playtime, it was best to dive out of her path once she got moving as her size, energy, and low center of gravity would bowl over any obstacle between her and fun.

Her energy was, in fact, insatiable. Neighbourhood dogs would appear on the back side of the fence, and Kodiak would race at full speed up and down that fence line time after time after time. The years we spent on the north coast in the little town of Vanimo are full of great memories. On a weekend, we would drive out the coast road towards the border to a little beach we called Sandfly. Kodiak loved those afternoons. The beach was actually a sandbar between the surging ocean and a cool mountain stream. Kodiak would tear around the beach, in and out of the lagoon, nonstop, not wanting to waste a single moment. Back at the house, she would just collapse, utterly wasted yet completely content.

We did our best to train young Kodiak, and for a family with little to no idea what we were doing, we were actually reasonably successful. We started with training her to wait for our command at feeding time. We would prepare her food, tell her to sit, put down the bowl, and then have her wait for the command prior to eating. I say "eating," but it was far more akin to inhaling or vacuuming. But it was Kodiak's anticipation that actually made this entertaining. Her teeth would chatter while she waited, and great tears of gelatinous drool would escape her voluminous jowls as she begged permission to satisfy her hunger. We usually fed Kodiak outside and just before family dinnertime. Having consumed her vittles during our meal, which she would find refuge under the table, hoping for any morsels that might fall, which, when the kids were younger, was more than a possibility. She would eat practically anything that came within sight or smell, with the exception of pineapple skin. Kodiak wouldn't eat banana skins either, but she loved bananas, teaching herself how to peel any that fell from a ripening rope to gain access to the sweet, soft flesh hidden inside.

As if two dogs were not enough, we fell prey to the most beseeching set of eyes you have encountered. When I say we fell victim to, I do, in fact, mean Jennifer. Another family had accepted the role of slave to a cat. When they left PNG, the cat "Zachy" moved to the airport in Mount Hagen as the MAF hangar cat. Zachy was not satisfied with this arrangement and contrived to return to his childhood home at the MAF housing compound just down the road. I am sure he believed that there had been a dreadful error, so Zachy went back to his house. The new residents of the house, while sympathetic to his plight, were rather allergic to cat hair. Feeding of Zachy just encouraged his repatriation, but keeping him outside was a constant battle.

Enter Jennifer fresh from an encounter with the animated movie *Shrek 2* starring the character Puss in Boots. With younger children, this was our level of family entertainment at the time, but the scene where Puss looks deep into the camera with titanic, radiant, beseeching eyes was too much for Jennifer. The reignited desire to once again have a cat may well have died with the children's attention span drawn to another movie, except that we were off to Mount Hagen for annual staff conference—and an unintended encounter with Zachy. We stayed with our friends in Zachy's house and were entertained with his sad story. Jennifer met Zachy. Zachy looked deep into Jennifer's eyes with a look reminiscent of Puss in Boots, and just like that, we had another cat: pet number three.

Returning to Vanimo, Jennifer thought it wise to introduce Zachy to Bear and Kodiak. Bear really couldn't have cared, but Kodiak, while full grown in size, was still far from mature in personality. I left the house to go flying for the day when Jennifer carried Zachy out onto our back deck for a meet-and-greet with Kodiak. You may remember that our house's main living area was on the second floor, as was the deck. Kodiak just had too much energy for Zachy, who got barely a whiff of the Doberman-Rottweiler before making his escape from what I can only assume he perceived as certain death. Leaping from Jennifer's arms, he launched himself straight off the deck into space. Surprised he may have been to not find solid ground for the next four meters, but Zachy was not deterred. Touching the ground but twice as he covered the eight meters to the back fence, the cat was up and over the fence and gone from sight before Jennifer could draw breath. Besides the height of the deck, what Zachy had failed to appreciate before he embarked on his getaway was that behind the fence, the ground dropped away to a gully at an alarming rate. Having survived the first vault into thin air, catapulting himself off the back fence propelled the poor cat into nothingness for the second time in as many seconds.

I returned home later that afternoon to a rather depressed household. Zachy had failed to make an appearance after his rather energetic departure. I was dispatched into the tangle of trees and weeds behind the house in a futile search for the cat. It was dark when the family gathered at our table for family dinner. A more subdued bunch, I don't believe I have ever met. As we sat there, some of us more forlorn than others, the squeak of a meow was heard at the front door. Under cover of darkness, Zachy had made a stealthy return. And so began a routine that lasted almost till the end: Zachy would stay inside during daylight, disappearing outside when it was dark, and he held the advantage over the dogs. During the day, he remained safely ensconced indoors, where all animals knew that the eating of the cat was forbidden. Zachy stayed with us right to the very end of our PNG experience, reaching a ripe old age before heading to his final resting place in the garden just outside the back door.

Kodiak too was with us right to the end, but it was a very close call during her tenth year. Kodiak had long since outlived all her siblings when she fell ill with something that was beyond our diagnosis. Vets are not common in PNG, but fortunately, there was an MAF pilot who had been a vet in his former life. It was a Friday morning just before Christmas when Kodiak's lethargy turned into a nasty-coloured discharge from her tail end. I phoned our friend, the former vet. My layman's presentation of the facts was sufficient to render a diagnosis that required an immediate hysterectomy. Things being what they were, the best we could do was hope that poor Kodiak would survive the day till our friend could arrive to attempt the surgery. The outlook was not good at all, considering the circumstances and Kodiak's age. The dog clung to life till the late afternoon when the pilot-vet arrived. Even then, chances of success were not high.

With Kodiak sedated, we hoisted the heavy body onto the dining-room table, that being the only possibility for the operation. I got far more education and up-close understanding of dog's anatomy that day than I had wished for. The offending part would normally be the size of your thumb. The inflamed and heavily infected organ had swollen to over two meters in length, the size of a loaf of bread in girth and several kilograms in weight. The operation complete, all we could do was wait and see. Still sedated, we barricaded Kodiak in our kitchen and went to bed. In the darkness of the early morning, we were awakened with a slow rhythmic thump emanating from the kitchen. It was poor Kodiak, on her feet yet very disoriented. She had walked into the corner of the kitchen and bumped into the cupboards. She backed up and tried again. And again. And again. Come sunrise, she was still somewhat dopey and clearly not out of the woods. But the recuperative powers God has bestowed on animals are a miracle. Sunday afternoon, Kodiak was out running with the kids. She probably overdid that day because she did relapse a little, but by the end of the week, she was completely back to her full and unstoppable self. In due time, Sam and I removed her stitches; and before too long, the scar had disappeared as well.

The year of the surgery was Sam's grade twelve year, and Kodiak continued on to see both Matt's and Nate's high school graduations. But that was all she had in her, so when we left Papua New Guinea, she too found her final resting place in the garden just outside the back door. In a twist of irony, we buried Kodiak and Zachy together, cuddled up in a way that was only possible in death. There are many strands that made our time in PNG so very special, but for me, I think it would be another unexpected that our four little fur balls are such a part of our family folklore.

# QUEBEC

Do you have any of those "I remember where I was when" memories? It was grade nine. I was walking home from high school, nearly two miles, but that is another story. I was almost home, at the last set of lights. Because of the junior high school and elementary schools close by, this intersection was monitored by a crossing guard. It was the same lady that had been doing the job since we moved to Trenton in grade seven. She said to me, "Did you hear?" Often these recollections we have are of unhappy events. It's like those people that were around in the '60s might remember where they were when JFK was shot. Or for others where they were and what they were doing in August of '97 when they heard about the death of the Princess of Wales. We do remember good events too. I have absolute crystal-clear recall about when I asked Jennifer to marry me. I can picture in my mind the births of our three children. Funnily enough, I don't really remember my first flight at the start of my pilot training. It does seem, however, that more often than not, our "remember where" memories are of distressing or sorrowful events.

On 17 January 1991, Jennifer and I were having dinner at the Canoe Club in downtown Kingston. As the saying goes, we were poor as church mice. I had finished flight training May the previous year, then worked for a hot-air balloon company for a few months until we moved to Kingston for me to take further training to become a flight instructor. That was finished, and I was looking for a job. Our income was limited to what Jennifer made working for a bank, and we had big debt from my flight training. There was zero room in the budget for restaurants. But the local TV station ran a daily contest with the evening news' "Question of the Day." We became avid news watchers in the hope of winning a free dinner out. So we ended up at the Canoe Club, having dinner courtesy of the evening news. As we sat there, the wall TV switched to one of those "Breaking News" graphics. "Operation Desert Shield" had become "Operation Desert Storm": the invasion of Iraq. That memory, however, is vague and hazy in comparison to what I remember of where I was and what I was doing in the afternoon of 22 February 2005.

We were coming up on the sixth anniversary of our arrival in Papua New Guinea. I started the day in Vanimo on the north coast where our family had been happily living for four and a half years. My routine was well established; I had flown all the routes many times, some hundreds of times. The airstrips were all familiar, and the program for the day held no suggestion of real surprises, except of course the normal expectation of the unexpected. I remember nothing from the first half of the day, the information being gleaned from the pages of my pilot logbook. With my Korean first officer, we flew our Twin Otter to Ok Isai, then Telefomin, Tabubil, Ok Isai, and back to Vanimo. I do know that the weather was super easy. Ok Isai lies in the same little valley system as Blackwara, a very simple fifty-minute flight southeast of Vanimo. In PNG terms, that is a long run, double the average sector flight time, in fact.

In good weather, the flights between Ok Isai, Telefomin, and Tabubil are very enjoyable. In the sunshine, the view of the mountains and rivers is exceptional. We made great time in the clear skies and were back in Vanimo around one o'clock. The Vanimo program was very demanding at that time with requests for flights far outstripping our capacity. So an early afternoon landing was far from day's end. The team at Vanimo loaded the aircraft for flight to Green River and back. The only real thing of note in Green River is the high school. Like most high schools, it is a boarding school and in need of regular supply flights for food for the students. I really don't know if that was the purpose of the flight that day, but I do know that we only picked up a couple people with very little baggage for the return to Vanimo.

There is a repetitive routine and flow of items that the crew must complete as they prepare to transition the plane from sleeping tin can to miracle of flight. Cargo is loaded, passengers are boarded and briefed, doors are secured. The captain calls for the prestart checklist, then goes through the familiar process of bringing the Pratt & Whitney Canada PT6a turbo prop engines to life. After start checklist follows, and the aircraft is ready to move under its own power. Somewhere in the process, the first officer will make some calls on the radio. There is a transmission on the VHF frequency advising other aircraft in the area of our intentions. Far too small for a control tower, most PNG runways are uncontrolled; pilots are required by law to broadcast their intentions to avoid conflicts. Very high-frequency radio waves only travel in light of sight so have limited range.

In PNG, to communicate with the flight service station, pilots must use their HF radio. High-frequency waves are able to bend and reflect, making long-distance conversations possible. On rare occasions, I have heard radio calls from San Francisco while flying in PNG. Papua New Guinea regulations require us to advise the government employees at the flight service station of our intentions and also the number of people on board. This is normally acknowledged in a routine fashion. However, on 22 February 2005, the response to our call was nonstandard: "Contact company Mount Hagen before departure." Of itself, this too was not something to raise alarm bells. Curiosity, yes; apprehension, no. Staff on the ground sometimes phone flight service with a request for us to call them when there is some change to our route or expected passenger load, perhaps when a medevac request has been received. In those cases, flight service usually waits till after takeoff to pass on the message, so this was a little different, but still not significant. Flight service asking us to call our Vanimo office, or even Telefomin or Tabubil office, would have been quite unremarkable. "Call company Mount Hagen before departure" was, however, out of the ordinary. So we put our preparations on hold and made the call. That was when the things got interesting, and not in a good way.

When the radio is answered by the chief pilot, it is not often good. There is a person whose job it is to monitor our MAF company HF radio frequency, and that person is not the boss. The chief pilot at that time was a Canadian, but there was no stereotypical exchange of pleasantries. What the boss had to say was short, sweet, and to the point: "Dump your load and go direct Telefomin. We have an aircraft missing." A command that strikes fear into the heart, words I had hoped to never hear—an order that suffers no questions, an instruction that calls for action. For me, it was relatively simple to slip into my shell of detachment and focus on the job, but it was much more of a challenge for my inexperienced copilot.

Green River sits equidistant from Vanimo and Telefomin, so fuel was no issue, the amount required to head for Telefomin the same as that to head home. With limited explanation but much haste, we unceremoniously ejected our passengers. Wheels up in record time, we turned south, climbing around ten thousand feet to clear the series of ridges separating the Sepik plane from its headwaters in the Telefomin Valley. As the wheels kissed the gravel and grass runway at Telefomin, it was clear that not all was well. The usual welcoming committee was swollen beyond all measure, with clear signs of distress: it seemed that the jungle telegraph was reporting bad news. Twin Otter "Mike Foxtrot Quebec" was overdue for its landing at Wobagen, and the agent there was transmitting accounts via HF radio of the aircraft crashing into the trees on the steep slope that bordered the southern edge of the valley.

To the north, the main river is the Sepik; to the south, it is the Fly River with its large tributary, the Strickland, that are the key features. In the midst of the central range, the Strickland, named after Edward Strickland, a onetime vice president of the Geographical Society of Australasia in the 1800s, flows roughly southwest. Like a backwards *F*, two valleys branch to the northwest, the northern one hiding the community and airstrip of Bak, the southern arm holding Bimin and Wobagen. Although the valley is narrow, it is further subdivided at its end by a short spur descending from Mount Kweirok. The original airstrip was located at Bimin, tight against the northern slope of this minor spur.

Several years earlier, under the force of heavy rain, part of the slope had given way, effectively bending the runway in the middle and making it unusable. Undeterred, the community worked to create a new runway on the opposite side of the spur. On completion, it was named Wobagen. It was to this airstrip that pilots Chris and Richard, together with their cabin attendant Stanley, had been heading with their load of cargo and a handful of passengers. At 579 meters in length and just 6.6 percent slope, Wobagen would not be all that challenging in the PNG context, except that it can be slippery. More importantly, its surrounding geography makes it a magnet for morning fog and afternoon rains.

Despite the overall pristine weather conditions, fog at Wobagen persisted until well after the arrival of "Quebec." It remains unclear exactly what happened, but in manoeuvering to land in the cramped and fog shrouded hills, the aircraft collided with tree-studded mountainside to make its final landing. The pilots gave their lives, but miraculously everyone else walked away. But when we landed at Telefomin, we knew none of this. As the leadership of MAF struggled to manage the immediate effects of this tragedy, my copilot and I were dispatched towards the area of the accident. A helicopter from the nearby Ok Tedi gold mine was also en route, so instead of landing at Wobagen amid some security concerns, we were instructed to proceed a few miles farther on and land across the Strickland River at Agali. It was there that we were met by the chopper carrying the bodies of our friends. The community at Wobagen had made haste over the ridge and across the river, a not inconsiderable feat considering the terrain, and recovered the bodies back to the airstrip. The Bell 412 had picked them up at Wobagen and transported them to us at Agali.

As the chopper touched down, we were surprised to see the cabin attendant climb out, obviously in a complete state of shock. The bodies were transferred to our Twin Otter, and with the day moving towards its close, we lifted off and turned the aircraft west towards Tabubil. Telefomin is a remote community with no facilities for handling bodies, so it was to Tabubil, home of the Ok Tedi mine, that we flew. News travels fast even in PNG, so our arrival in Tabubil was no surprise. Most of the flying in the Telefomin area actually takes place out of Tabubil, so the two pilots were well known too and loved by many. Met by a large crowd of folks now distraught by the passing of "their" pilots, we handed our friends over to representatives from the local hospital to care for the bodies.

Last light now imminent, we made haste to depart for the short twelve-minute flight up and over the wall to Telefomin. As we rose into the sky, crossed the Ok Manga ridge into the chute, and made tracks to curl around Bolongong for the low point, we found our little plane surrounded by a rainbow. We normally experience rainbows as arcs, but this was a perfect circle that stayed with us as we flew. But that is not accurate, for there were two perfect rainbows that marked our path. It would be uncommon to see a complete rainbow halo like this, extremely rare for it to be so crystal clear in its colours and bordering on impossible to see two, one inside the other.

As if that were not enough, even as we changed directions, the rainbows remained with us. But yet there is more. Rainbows, placed in the sky by God as His promise to never again destroy the earth by flood, are visible as the sunlight passes through rain that diffuses the light into its seven-component colours. But that evening, as the sun retreated into the western horizon, there was neither rain nor cloud. The formation of a single rainbow would defy the laws of physics, yet there we were, flying in the midst of the two of the rarest of rainbows, a certain indicator that even in this, God was present.

The following days were spent in activity rather forgotten. First thing the next morning, again in clear weather, we flew back to Vanimo. Our other pilot family based in Vanimo was good friends of the family of one of the pilots who had died, so we brought them to Telefomin to support and uphold in this time of terrible grief. Then we were again from Telefomin to Tabubil. The purpose of this visit was very somber: the bodies needed to go to Telefomin for the community haus-cri. There was a huge outpouring of grief and support, and it was a cultural necessity to bring the bodies. By the end of the day, needing to return the bodies to the morgue in

Tabubil, my young copilot was overcome. Fortunately, another pilot was by now on hand to fly with me as we made yet another sad trip over the wall down to Tabubil. The day was well spent, so we stayed the night with friends of MAF in Tabubil.

The next morning, threading their way through an honour guard formed by coworkers and friends, the coffins were placed on the aircraft of the regional airline to make their journey to our headquarters town of Mount Hagen. We followed on, travelling via Telefomin to pick up the families. Again under clear skies, we flew the hour to Mount Hagen, where, on bringing the aircraft to a stop in front of our maintenance hangar, I was finally able to pause and let my own sorrow find its vent. I completed the checklists as required for aircraft shutdown, installed the control locks, stepped from the aircraft, and slid around the backside. I was met by a friend, who asked me, "Have you cried yet?" I collapsed in tears, finally free of my duty and the need to be a stoic professional.

At that time, there was a commercial on EM TV, the Papua New Guinea television station that talked about mud: "To some people, mud is mud…to others, it's what you do with it." A couple weeks after the accident, we landed at a tiny community called Yebil. We were greeted by several ladies, their faces covered in light-brown mud. The instant the engines stopped turning, the sound of loud, mournful wailing reached my ears. I was unable to leave my seat as the ladies were at my door; my legs soon covered with mud transferred from their faces and arms. The mud on the face is a sign of mourning and respect for someone who has passed away. It was a difficult time for us, but in the days and weeks following the accident, we experienced an incredible outpouring of support from the people we serve.

The scene from Yebil had been repeated many times in the days after February 22. The Min group of tribes in the Telefomin area were extremely generous in their gifts to the families of the two pilots. It was their pilots who had died. Theirs was recognition of the sacrifice made by these men and their families to serve the people of the Min area. What made Yebil different was that these people didn't know the two pilots that died. Yet they were grieved on our behalf. They understood how we felt. At Aitape, I was given a big hug by another lady, someone who flies with us regularly. She was moved to tears by our loss. These are the faces that you serve through us. You may never see them. They will likely never meet you. But the service of MAF is so vital to them that when we cry, they cry with us because we are a part of them.

I had known that this type of tragedy was a possibility. Ten years earlier, four prior to our arrival in PNG, MAF had suffered an even worse accident. Yet we always believe it won't happen—not us, not to those we know. And yet I should have known better, for even while working as a pilot in Canada, pilot friends had passed away in aircraft accidents. Still, the possibility seemed remote at best. Perhaps then you can gauge my horror and shock when, on 23 March 2006, one year, one month, one day after Wobagen, there was another call. Another accident. Another death.

These are the stories that are hardest to recount. These are the experiences that sear our souls. There is a book I like: *The Robe*. It is a fictional account of the Roman soldier that commanded Jesus's crucifixion squad. In the story, he is the man that won Jesus' robe, the robe for which the soldiers drew lots. The character is emotionally scarred as he recognizes what he has done in killing an innocent man and becomes unglued, randomly interjecting in conversation the question, "Were you there?" For those of us that were with MAF PNG in 2005 and 2006, it is very much like that; for if you weren't here, you can't understand how it affected us, how it continues to influence the way we fly. Those of us that lived through those dark days are more cautious, more risk-averse, more certain to have firm options before penetrating into murky weather. We try to explain their mortality to the younger pilots. We do our best to persuade them that there is no heroism in pushing too hard, no valour in completing what should not even be attempted. Papua New Guinea remains the land of the unexpected. It is, in part, as a result of the sacrifice of my friends that, to the end of my aviation career, I will fly expecting the unexpected.

# ROMEO

## ~Relationships: *The Melanesian Way~*

I AM THE youngest, the youngest of four siblings. I have two sisters and one brother. I am the youngest, the youngest of nine cousins. I have two cousins on my father's side and three on my mother's. My children have eight cousins on each side of the family: thirteen aunts and uncles in all. That is by my count. By their reckoning, Sam, Matt, and Nate would contest that their aunts and uncles number possibly in the hundreds. This is the dilemma: what do you call adult friends of your parents that you live beside, work with, and go to church with? Families with whom you share Friday-night rituals and beach trips. Families whose children are your playmates, and in him whom you find best friends. *Mr.* and *Mrs.* seems way to formal, yet first names are disrespectful. So they become *aunt* and *uncle*. And what of the lady who helps in the house, who has done as long as you can remember? What should your kids call her? In Papua New Guinea, the answer to that is *auntie*: Auntie Agatno.

For some, having someone help around the house seems wrong for a missionary, yet the truth is that in PNG, it is almost wrong not to have one. Agatno was our "haus meri" for the ten years we lived in Goroka. She graciously helped with laundry, washed our floors, and cleaned our bathroom. It is quite hard to explain the difference she made in our lives. In a country where food is often made from scratch, feeding the family is itself a time-consuming task in excess of what it would be in Canada. Bagels, buns, muffins, tortillas, cookies, yoghurt—all made from scratch. While Agatno kept our house clean, I cannot begin to describe the blessing she was to our family.

Our experiences with haus meris in Vanimo had been less than successful. We had one that never seemed to figure out that Nate was "Nate"; she always called him "baby Nick." Another that we tried to train stole, among other things, Jennifer's engagement ring. I went to her house and found the ring on her finger. She never understood why we didn't want her working for us anymore. But Agatno was a gem, a ready source of education on PNG culture. And our kids loved her. She was with us as our children travelled from elementary through high school graduation, and each one of them wanted Auntie Agatno at their graduation.

They say that people often mark memories by time. You have probably said it yourself: "Remember when I was fifteen?" Or maybe something like, "Back in '97…" MKs, and even their parents, think, reminisce, catalogue our memories kinda differently. For us, it is more likely to be, "Remember when we were in Paris and Mom couldn't find Notre Dame?" Or, "I bought my first camera at Sim Lim Tower in Singapore." Or, "That was funny when the cow chased Matt, and he levitated over the electric fence." We also mark the passage of time by those we knew, those who are part of our family narrative, who contributed to the tales we tell.

During our PNG years, we lived, worked, and played with ninety-five pilot families. But in addition to pilots, there were multiple others: aircraft engineers, administrators, managers. They came from a wide variety of countries, cultures, and backgrounds: Canada, US, UK, Germany, Netherlands, New Zealand, Australia, Sweden, Finland, Switzerland, Singapore, and even Korea. Among these folks, hiding in the crowd, are our role models, our heroes. For each one, I have stories.

On reflection, I am compelled to start with Patrick and Alison. Having said so, I will begin with them, though I find myself at a loss to know what to say. Patrick was born into the tail end of the "troubles" in Northern Ireland, a Protestant with a Catholic name. Alison is Australian. How they met is a mystery. Patrick came to Mission Aviation Fellowship as a finance manager. If it were sports, then MAF clearly won the trade as Patrick is quite brilliant. He had been working London's financial district, and as the story goes, his expense account was worth more than his MAF salary. After they left MAF, they took up residence in Cairns, and it was to them I placed my call for help when I ruptured my second Achilles tendon.

It is generally advisable for missionaries to go outside PNG for major operations, and so to Cairns I went for a week to get my piece of "elastic" reattached. When I was chief pilot, Patrick was my boss, quite possibly the best boss I have ever had. He somehow figured out how to get the best from me and keep my worst in check. In the words of Canadian fictional icon Anne of Green Gables, I think Patrick was my kindred spirit. I loved working with him, seeing what we could accomplish to make MAF better at our ministry of reaching isolated peoples. On many of my frequent visits to our headquarters in Mount Hagen, I would end up at Patrick and Alison's place, which I found as a place of refuge from the craziness that identified my office days in Hagen.

Colin and Rosemary were in PNG long before we ever thought of going there. Their family was similar in makeup to ours yet a few years ahead of us. It is hard to say why I remember them with affection. Perhaps it is the many times I shared a meal in their home when away from my own. Possibly it is simply that as we watched them, we learned how to make Papua New Guinea home, a place beloved by our children; how to survive the ups and downs, negotiate the troubled waters, and celebrate the good times. For me, Colin was one of those guys that just helped. As an engineer, he had a grasp on the emotional side of making an aircraft fly. Unbelievers think planes are just objects, but in the hands of an artist, an aeroplane sings. When broken, it sometimes takes the hands of an artist to feel what is making the bird sick. It takes more than a book to fix a plane, and when mine wasn't behaving, sometimes it needed a coffee, a chat with Colin, who knew what to ask to figure out the mystery illness—an engineer who didn't need to check the book to know how to set up a gizmo. It was like he could feel when it was right.

When I was chief pilot, Colin was the maintenance controller, sort of the interface—interpreter, if you will between pilot and engineer. It must be understood that pilots and aircraft engineers are natural enemies. The pilots break the planes, and the engineers fix them. The pilot whines that "it doesn't feel right" while the engineer opines that he can find nothing wrong with the plane. Colin seemed to have the gift of bilingualism, speaking both pilot and engineer. Colin was more than that though. I think he understood my passion for doing the right thing, for serving, for finding a solution to the problem at hand.

Larry and Ruth were our host family when we arrived that first time into Mount Hagen. The assault on the senses and emotions for a young family taking up residence in a developing country is beyond imagination for most. The simple volume of things to learn is astronomical. Language is the easy part. What to eat and where to buy it—have you ever cooked on a gas stove? Awarding recipes at sea level are flops at five thousand feet. Driver's license. Banking. Security. Housing. Water. Electricity. All these and more need to be learned, need to be taught. And Ruth was our teacher. She had conducted new family orientation a million times, yet she answered our questions and belayed our concerns as if they were all fresh and new, never before heard.

Like Colin, Larry was a plane whisperer. I am convinced that the "rigging" of a Twin Otter is a black art. To get the power lever working with the fuel control unit and the propeller lever operating with the governors and the blade angles set just so require a multitude of minor adjustments. Each sixteenth of a turn of tiny set screw has knock-on effects to several other tiny screws. Adjusting one means adjusting three others. "The book" says what to do, but occasionally it takes the touch of a master craftsman, the special sense gained through years of experience, to know exactly what to tweak to make it all come together in sweet harmony.

Greg was my coworker, buddy, jokester supreme, and all-around nice guy. I really don't know when we first met Greg and Jacqui and their two kids. I keenly remember being with Greg at Agali airstrip as we waited for the chopper to bring the bodies of our friends following the accident at Wobogon. Their son Louis was like an older brother to our three when we all lived in Goroka. If I needed to tell Greg something, I could never be gone five minutes. Jacqui would offer a coffee; and half hour later, I would return home, and Jennifer would give me that look, the one that says, *I knew it would be more than five minutes*. Although Greg and I shared many flying adventures as crew on the Twin Otter, there is one that needs telling.

We landed our aircraft at Maimafu. That of itself is a major feat. Lying in the shadow of Crater Mountain, Maimafu airstrip is 460 meters of nastiness. The runway is steep; the surface can be soft or rough or both. The wind can whistle around the craggy terrain to create a schizophrenic lake of air that seeks to bend the aircraft to its will. But on this day, none of that is recorded in my memory banks. What I do know is that on that day, we ran into a little snag. We were scheduled to pick up something in the order of thirty-two bags of coffee, each containing fifty-five kilograms' worth of the finest Arabica coffee beans. Normally, the coffee is stored in a shed in the parking bay, near the top of the runway. Unfortunately, coffee had yet to make the trip to the parking bay. It was still in a shed at the runway landing threshold. With its 11 percent slope even, walking up and down is a week's worth of gym exercise. To carry a fifty-five-kilogram bag up the equivalent of seventeen-odd stories is not for the faint of heart or weak of back!

The people of Maimafu were encouraging us to taxi the plane down the strip to the coffee house. However, taxiing an aircraft down an 11 percent grade on a grass and dirt surface is neither easy nor very brilliant. You see, at the bottom, when we ask it to stop, the plane has a tendency to keep going! In an amazing display of servant leadership, Greg headed down the hill with some of the guys to get the coffee. At this time, my ankle was still not 100 percent recovered from my first Achilles tendon rupture, so I was certain my doctor would have recommended against this kind of exertion. Grateful as I was for the excuse, as I waited patiently by the plane and watched the coffee bags march up the hill, I was struck by a thought: if Jesus had come to earth as an MAF pilot, I believe he would have been there carrying one of those heavy bags, just like Greg. Ministering as a pilot with MAF in PNG doesn't afford many opportunities for preaching, but physical demonstrations of the love of Jesus are our stock and trade.

Tim and Carol were our neighbours in Goroka for several years. In fact, ourselves, Greg and Jacqui, and Tim and Carol overlapped for a while. In many ways, those years were Jennifer's favourite in terms of community. Her best friend, Carmela, was with us in that period too. When Jennifer's dad passed away, those three ladies were the ones that came to our house, brought chocolate, and cried with her. Carol is one of those people that sincerely lives in an attitude of prayer, speaking to God in all things as if He were physically present.

I remember training with Tim when we first moved to Goroka. He introduced me to all the strips in Goroka and Lae areas. I think we did fifty new places in two weeks. Tim was raised in PNG as an MK and had many great insights into PNG culture and how to live there as a missionary. We shared our frustrations and fixed our cars together. Sometimes those were the same things. The most memorable event with Tim and Carol must certainly have been the tree-scepade.

The Goroka housing compound had started life as the home of LutherAir, the mission aviation arm of the Evangelical Lutheran Church. In times past, possibly even before I was born, although I don't really know, LutherAir's operations were assumed by MAF. The compound became the home for MAF Goroka families. Growing outside the compound fence were three trees that were doubtless as old as the houses. They were tall and straight, yet apparently at least one of them held a dark secret, a weakness. One Saturday, in the midst of a wet-season afternoon downpour, the weight of the mighty tree became too much for its roots struggling to keep purchase in the sodden ground. Without warning, the tree tipped, ripped itself right out of the ground, and toppled, crushing the security fence and coming to rest on the roof of Tim and Carol's kitchen. The kids were playing in the house down the hall. Should the tree have uprooted an hour or two later, Carol may well have been standing there, at the kitchen sink, as the silky oak plummeted toward her. It may be that the steel fence saved the house, for although it stove in the roof, inside the only visible evidence was a dislodged ceiling. As I looked at the damage, I was amazed first that this had happened, but second that it had not been worse. I think Tim and Carol immediately saw the hand of God at work, arresting the descent of that tree and setting limits to the destruction.

It is in times of crisis that we see what we are made of; in struggles that the strengths of the team prevail or the fragility of the group is revealed. I study the photos that we took over the next couple days of cleanup, and nowhere do I see aggravation or dissension. I see men striving literally shoulder to shoulder—MAF missionaries, Papua New Guinean friends, coworkers from other missionaries, all pulling together to remove that oak. I see ladies standing together, smiling, joking. I see our kids sitting on a truck watching it all happen, not inside playing video games or watching TV, but outside with the family, presiding over the refreshments set out. I see people using gifts and talents of which I knew not. I learned that day all the things that others could do that had remained hidden until the need arose.

Michael and Nicki were in PNG when we arrived, and along with Brandon, I believe they were the only MAF missionaries still there when we left. Initially, it was an unexpected discovery for me that all mission pilots were not born to it like I was; perhaps as many as half were second-career people. And Michael was one of those. Formerly a vet in England, Michael had turned his back on a career with the Ministry of Agriculture, travelling to the States with his young family to learn to fly in pursuit of a ministry in missions. It is to Michael that we owe a debt for saving our baby Kodiak with the operation on our dining-room table. They were well established in PNG prior to our arrival on the scene; at that time, Michael was holding the position of operations manager. It was Nicki that we knew first, however, for she was our Tok Pisin teacher. It was from her that we learned the language and so much of our initial understanding of the culture of Papua New Guinea. Jennifer and I would meet with Nicki in the mornings for our language study, pausing for morning tea with her haus meri to practice our few faltering phrases and learn a little more about what makes this country tick. We experienced our first mumu with Nicki, although a "giaman" (counterfeit) one as it was cooked in the oven. After our move to Goroka, Michael and

I spent many of those years working together: me as chief pilot and Michael as manager of crew training, then Michael as chief pilot and me as manager of crew training. The hours we spent wrestling with operational problems and training plans are too innumerable. I guess their impact and meaning in our lives is best gauged by Matt using one of his limited allotment of invitations in asking Michael and Nicki to be his guests at his high school graduation.

No narrative on our PNG relationships would be complete without Lowell and Gail. Also members of MAF Canada, we met Lowell and Gail for the first time within days of our arrival in Mount Hagen. Once we left Mount Hagen for Wewak, we saw little of them. I crossed paths with Lowell at annual pilots meetings and with the family at staff conference. But once assigned to the Twin Otter, our encounters became more frequent as Lowell was a senior training captain on that aircraft. Within a couple years, Lowell became my boss as he assumed the role of chief pilot. Over the years, I learned much from him about flying the Otter, about understanding what makes it tick, so I can feel when it isn't happy. From him, I also absorbed the knowledge of, and dare I say love for, the rules and procedures that kept me safe all my years over the jungles of PNG. From Lowell, I learned to understand and apply not solely the letter but the spirit of the principles that guide mission aviation. We travelled through the Mike Foxtrot Quebec accident together.

Our families connected on a personal level too. It was by adopting Zachy the cat that we saved Gail from her feline allergy. Their family left PNG halfway through our time there, relocating to Australia to work in the MAF regional operations administration office. We passed through Cairns numerous times either on holiday or just transiting through on our way to or from Canada, and it was always a joy to spend a few hours with. They introduced us to the game Killer Bunnies, which found its place in our Sunday-evening family games nights. It was to Lowell and Gail that I placed my call for help when I ruptured my first Achilles tendon. Later on, they returned to PNG for a couple years with their younger son Tobin. Matt and Tobin had been friends in passing over the years as our families had connected, but in their junior and senior years of high school, they became closer friends, sharing in those escapades up track and to Kea Falls. They joined up again after graduation, ending up in flight school together.

I hesitate to place labels for fear of offending, but I think it is only fair and proper to say that our best friends in PNG were Holger and Carmela. Holger and Carmela had met in the Philippines, Carmela's home, when Holger was there as a missionary from Germany, before MAF. Their son, Josh, became Nate's best friend, so close that Carmela joked they only had one brain between them, sharing it as the need arose. I don't believe I can explain the relationship between Jennifer and Carmela. Perhaps following the example of our sons, they too shared a brain. On the occasions when Holger and I were away from home, flying elsewhere in PNG, I rarely found Jennifer and Nate at home; they were most often at Carmela's. There is video record of the two of them together, acting crazy, silly as only can be done in the company of a kindred spirit.

By contrast to his spirited wife, my friend Holger is a quiet man. But one of those people you have to watch, for they are mischievous, coming out with a zinger when you don't see it coming. You have to look to see if you heard right, but the glint in the eye is the giveaway. Holger was one of those special people that I had but to ask; for whatever I needed, he was there. There was never a question in my mind that he would refuse; if I needed him, he was there.

One of the things about living on the other side of the world is that you have to travel halfway round the globe coming and going; and if you plan the route carefully, you can see something new every time. That is how we ended up in France and Singapore and how we were able to visit our friends at their home in Germany. Holger and Carmela were such gracious hosts. We visited the Mercedes factory and the site of Auschwitz concentration camp. We ate German sausage and bread. We went to Munich and Stuttgart. They even arranged for our two families to cross into Switzerland and spend the night in a cow herder's cottage in the Alps. All I can say is, "What happens in the Alps stays in the Alps!"

If space permitted, I would tell of Richard and Sue, the couple that first met us in Australia. I would recount tales of their accident-prone son, of how, left in our care, I ended up flying him to visit the dentist as his front teeth were nearly knocked out. There would be the story of moving the rainwater tank in Vanimo with Dirk and Maja, even as it filled up in the pouring rain. I would share tales of flying with Ruben, Thomas, and Yong. Living life alongside Jason and Mel, Brad and Michelle, Mike and Anna, Volkher and Christina—where do I stop? Were you to ask, people that know me would no doubt describe me as "serious," "practical," "driven," most certainly a "type A" personality. All that is true, and perhaps I am not so good at relationships. Yet if I am to be defined by the relationships I treasure, then I guess at heart I am a Melanesian. As Elder Neuwendorf told our PNG church on our last Sunday with them, I may be white on the outside, but I am PNG on the inside.

# SIERRA

## ~ *The* Sibilanga *Pig~*

IT's FUNNY HOW a reputation can be reflective of priorities. Wewak was our first home base in Papua New Guinea. We arrived in Mount Hagen on April 9 for our cultural orientation and initial flight training. By August, our family was on the way to the north coast, to the town of Wewak where we would live for the next year. Due to the unique nature of PNG airstrips, pilots, especially pilots new to PNG, are usually trained for each individual airstrip. Chris, the pilot I was replacing, was not a training captain, and my training captain was normally based elsewhere. Before he and his family departed, he prepared a list for us of the current status of the airstrips served by MAF from its Wewak base. Along with this assessment of current conditions, he provided some personal observations. I can picture to this day the line on the page dealing with Sibilanga: "great bananas, scary when wet." Experience proved Chris correct on both counts.

There have actually been two airstrips at Sibilanga. The original site was down by the river. This meant a hike up a two thousand foothill to where the village actually stands. The "new" strip, the one I utilized, was opened in December 1967—one month after I was born! There is an impression among some pilots that lowlands strips are "easy." The shortest and steepest strip in PNG is Aziana, not far from Goroka in the Eastern Highlands. Back when I was flying the Wewak area program, I regularly landed my Cessna 206 at three locations that held positions two through four in the short and steep directory. In fact, Sibilanga, measuring 433 meters in length, wouldn't even make the top ten, all of those runways coming in under 400 meters.

Sometimes it is not just the length that presents a challenge; it is the ratio of length to slope. The shorter a strip, the steeper the pilot wants it to be, and Sibilanga is only 5 percent slope, which means there is little help from the terrain when it comes to decelerating on landing or accelerating for takeoff. If you can picture a tent, the old-fashioned kind, a triangular tetrahedron, or more commonly Toblerone, then you are on your way to understanding Sibilanga. Flatten the peak of the tent, and that is the airstrip. It is this that makes Sibilanga so interesting for a pilot. Once through the trees that guard the sides of the runway, there is little to stop a wayward aircraft from plummeting a couple thousand feet down the steep inclines to the left and the right. Straight ahead also presents an obstacle or perhaps no obstacle. The end of the runway is marked by a short section fence, vaguely resembling the hitching post to be found outside the saloon in a Western movie. Beyond the bar, a ten-meter vertical to the village plaza below.

My days flying the 206 didn't produce any narratives of serious interest, but the Otter, that was rather a different story. The Twin Otter is two-faced creature: as simple to fly as a basic training aircraft yet doubly complex in systems. On a long paved runway, the Otter lands herself; but on a short grass field, the pilot had best know his craft. I had never heard of an NF cut until I survived one while landing at Sibilanga. I suppose I might have been taught about it, but the transition from a single-engine piston-engined machine to the heavier, larger, more powerful Twin Otter is such a steep learning curve that newbies default to a subconscious prioritization of information retention: simply, the complex system details fall out of the memory bucket. As pilots become more experienced with the airplane, more familiar with its character, more comfortable with its temperament, then they are able to better appreciate its potential for vice.

The day wasn't special in any way. Sibilanga had not been subject to amounts of rain that would dictate increased caution, so the approach and touchdown were conducted with the customary quantity of vigilance. The wheels kissed the surface in the target zone, the nose wheel settled nicely, and I twisted the grips and pulled the power levers to select reverse thrust. Most aircraft in the class of the Otter are equipped with reverse thrust to augment the wheel brakes in the deceleration process. The power levers in the Otter are suspended from an overhead panel. To engage reverse thrust, the pilot twists the hand grips on these levers. This releases a lockout that permits the levers to be pulled towards the back of the aircraft, exchanging forward thrust for reverse. Pulled gently and evenly, the propellers change pitch, and the engines accelerate in an even fashion so the aircraft will track the runway centerline.

Abruptly, with no warning, the aircraft took a vicious swing to the left. I was no longer looking at the hitching post but at the trees bordering the runway. Just as rapidly, things returned to normal, and I was again staring down the hitching post, although more left of runway centerline. Safely parked at the top of the strip, my copilot and I shared some theories, none of which fit the heart-stopping event we had just experienced. A call to the chief pilot on our return to base turned this into an educational experience. It appears that, for a brief instant, the right propeller jumped out of reverse, pulling the right wing forward while the reversing left propeller was pulling the left wing back, providing the wicked swerve. Probably pilot-induced as opposed to a fault with the aircraft, I have since been sure to pass on this possibility and its origin to my captain trainees.

Sibilanga was also the source of a different kind of educational experience: a cultural one. The longer we were in Papua New Guinea and the older I got, the more respectful I became of what I didn't know. I came to expect the unexpected in everything and to ask even when I thought I was in possession of all relevant information. But back then, I wasn't nearly so wise, so when the agent at Aitape informed me that we were transporting a couple policemen to Sibilanga to pick up a suspect, I did a metaphorical yawn and continued adding up all the numbers on the passenger manifest. The flight itself must have been completely run of the mill, for I can recall no details. I would assume we took off from Aitape's bent runway and made a slight left turn to head straight for the Tadji gap. Once through that break in the mountain range, we would have seen Sibilanga perched on the crest of its hill no more than ten kilometers distant.

Everything proceeded as per the script that played out in its various forms multiple times per day, until the twist in the plot that neither pilot saw coming. The two constables disembarked, along with the citizen of Sibilanga who had arranged their visit. The three disappeared over the edge of the runway, and almost immediately a sense of unease and disquiet descended on the gathered community. The tension was quite palpable as the policemen returned empty-handed. The man who had accompanied the police started up the stairs of the aircraft when a man separated himself from the body of spectators and launched himself at the man on the stairs in what to my mind was a cowardly blindside. Whatever control we had been able to exert on the situation evaporated like a water droplet on a hot stove. We went from relative peace to total anarchy in the blink of an eye.

Forty or fifty people engaged in a brawl in the shade of the aircraft wing. Fearful for the safety of the aircraft, we made a vain attempt to reestablish some semblance of jurisdiction over the mob. Strong as my voice is, I might as well have been whispering for all the good my exhortations did. Eventually, the commotion stilled, and we were left all but alone beside the aircraft. Almost alone, but not completely, for there was one lady, back by the tail of the aircraft, just aft of the passenger door, using her skirt to wipe a trail of blood from the skin of the aircraft.

I think it was after we had returned to Aitape, and I made the inquiries that in the future I would make earlier, that I was able to assemble the facts. Aitape would be the nearest metropolitan center to Sibilanga, although with a population of perhaps a couple thousand, it is hardly a major town. It does, however, host a high school, hospital, and a handful of stores. Somewhere along the way, a young man from Sibilanga had allegedly raped a young lady, the daughter of the man that had arranged for the police to travel on our aircraft. Apparently, the plan was for the police to arrest the young man who had fled home to Sibilanga and escort him back to Aitape to face the charges. The accused's most immediate relatives were harboring him in Sibilanga. In this case, sheltering the young man was probably more akin to house arrest, perhaps more probably to save him from the ultimate payback justice: death at the hands of the outraged father.

It transpired that everyone agreed the young man was guilty as charged. From my perspective, the father had shown remarkable restraint in the PNG context, it being unusual to involve the police. The more common practice would have been for the girl's relatives to exact some level of corporal punishment on the offender. In what to a Western mind was a strange twist, an unexpected turn was the root of the angst, the cause of the brawl. Even his closest relatives agreed the young man was guilty and subject to punishment. What divided the village was how this should be undertaken. From their perspective, the offence was within the community and to be resolved within the community. The father's decision to involve outsiders was the source of the conflict. To this day, I shake my head at the logic, the experience, and the lady wiping the blood off the aircraft with the hem of her skirt.

Again, Sibilanga was the setting for an unusual brand of unexpected experience: a miraculous one. To those that are skeptical about the existence of God, this tale will certainly be explained away as coincidence, imagination, possibly even fantasy resulting from overstimulation or fear. Being fairly heavily type A personality, I am not prone to emotional response in the face of adversity; I box up the emotion and dispassionately work the problem. So when the pig came strolling across the runway as the wheels touched down, it was not dread that filled my thoughts but a realization of the inevitability of the outcome.

I was training a new captain for the Twin Otter. Clint was a highly experienced MAF PNG pilot, having been in New Guinea several years longer than myself. He had twin-engine experience and had been flying the Otter as first officer for a period of time as he followed the fast track to the captain's seat. Clint was undergoing his period of line training, flying as pilot-in-command under supervision. I filled the role and duties as first officer while actually in command of the flight. A very capable operator, Clint was a very effortless trainee. He understood how to be captain in a two-crew environment, his many flight hours as an instructor paying dividends in the clear communication skills so necessary to successful two-pilot operations. The speed with which events unfolded left little room for any conversation or direction on my part. Responsibilities in an aircraft with two pilots must be clearly allocated.

For the arrival at Sibilanga, Clint was working as pilot-flying, and I was occupied as pilot-monitoring. Pilot-flying is as the name suggests: the pilot actually controlling the path of the aircraft. As is the case in so many of these anecdotes, the lead-up was unremarkable, the real narrative transpiring in far less time than the telling. It was only after the tires were firmly on the grass that the hog chose to wander across the very piece of turf that we were intent on occupying.

My children tell me that this story is the great original fish legend. According to them, the pig gets ever bigger with each telling. Of course, my position on the matter is somewhat contrary. Regardless, the fact is that the pig was big, very big, the biggest one I have ever seen. In telling the kids about it the day it occurred, I explained to them that she would not have fit under the dining-room table. I believe that my estimation of the pig's bulk is borne out by the attitude of the local people. They told me that in the morning, the pig would leave her pen and wonder across the runway into the jungle. In her own time, the pig would return, back across the runway and home. When I suggested, strongly suggested, that they should not allow this behaviour, the people responded that containing a pig of such dimensions was not really within their power. Lest you be confused, the pig of this tale is not that mimicked in appearance by Miss Piggy of Muppets fame. Nor was it pale pink with the floppy ears, upturned nose, and hunched forehead that gives our stereotypical pig a sort of dopey appearance. It was more like the warthog Pumba from *Lion King*, only not even remotely cute or funny. Just big, menacing, hairy, dark mottled brown, and not endearing or delightful in the least.

So there we were, touchdown complete and rolling out to complete the landing when mama pig entered stage left. Unbidden, my mind reverted to high school physics class and the science of motion, to high school math and the calculations of vectors. The numbers were self-evident: the path of the Otter would intersect the course of the monster pig. In a matter of seconds, the left main wheel of the aircraft would meet the right flank of the pig, an encounter that would certainly cost the pig her life and equally, certainly, savagely amputate the plane's landing gear. As time stood still, I could with clarity see the conclusion: left wheel severed, the aircraft would swerve dramatically left. Option one, the stub of the leg would dig into the soft turf, sending the poor Otter over onto its back, crumpling the left wing like so much tin foil. Option two, the aircraft would spin about, crashing through the thin barricade of trees before plunging backwards over the hill. With no time to give direction and encouragement to Clint, all that was left was to trust in his experience. Not that he was flush with options.

While time gave the appearance of slowing, there is no stopping the march of the clock. Even as I braced for the impending impact, I could sense Clint doing the same. The time my mind had calculated for the encounter of wheel and pig came and went. But for me, time continued to run at a snail's pace. Although I sincerely doubted it, I concluded that my original estimate had been erroneous. Rapidly recalculating, I again prepared myself for impact, the revised resolution to the time-distance equation yielding an impact point between pig and aluminum somewhere just aft of the passenger door. For the second time in as many seconds, the unexpected transpired: the distinct lack of rendering metal and squealing pig. Clint parked us safely at the top of the runway, and I descended the cockpit to express my displeasure. The people were full of apologies, explaining as I have how the size of the beast restricted its controllability. More than that, the onlookers were amazed at the absence of tragedy. Perhaps less schooled than I in the theory of physics, their practical understanding of physical laws had persuaded them also of the certainty of an accident.

The English language is full of descriptive adjectives, superlatives that we employ to explain what we see, hear, and feel. In a society ruled by the sound-bite, many of these terms are overused, reducing their impact and limiting their scope. *Miracle*—a word now abused to record an unlikely event, perhaps a victory in sports or to elevate the outcome of an election. A true miracle is something that defies our understanding of normal physical laws. A genuine miracle indicates the direct intervention of the hand of God. A real miracle confronts our appreciation of what can be explained. Famed author Sir Arthur Conan Doyle spoke these words through his marquis character Detective Sherlock Holmes: "When you have eliminated the impossible, whatever remains, however improbable, must be the truth." From my unhindered view in the right seat of the Twin Otter, I am persuaded that missing the pig that day not just once but twice was not only unlikely but actually impossible. I am convinced that the pig passed under the belly of the plane, behind the nose wheel, and then between the two main wheels. And so like Sir Arthur's famed master of deduction, having eliminated the impossible, all that remains, however improbable it might be to some, is the truth. And the truth is this: God reached out from heaven and gave that massive hog a gentle nudge in order that it could thread the needle between the legs of our fast-moving plane.

Many days, MAF pilots fly into places like Sibilanga then fly out, not knowing if we make a difference. During my first few months as an MAF pilot living and working in the Sepik provinces, I had the privilege of transporting numerous missionaries and national folk to this little village for the fortieth anniversary celebrations of the start of mission work there. As I spoke with one of the first missionaries to Sibilanga, he let me know how important Mission Aviation Fellowship has been to the work and the people. He talked of supplies and travel for the missionaries, of medevacs, and of churches opened up. There are numerous congregations in the vicinity of Sibilanga which have grown out of the mission work started forty years ago. MAF pilots may not often have the chance to be the voice of God, but they are with a doubt the feet of the Gospel to millions around the globe. Without numerous MAF pilots over the years, the people around Sibilanga would not have heard the Gospel. Even today, the only real way to get to Sibilanga is by air. In theory, there is a road, a vehicle track, but it has potholes that can literally swallow cars.

The effect of that day was not lost on my kids. Shortly after the event, one of them wrote about it for a school assignment.

## Why I Am Glad

This story is about God's awesome power and a one-meter-long pig that almost hit an MAF plane.

Once, my dad was flying with a man named Mr. Smith. They were flying to a place called Sibilanga. Everything was going great. They had just touched down when the pig came out on the runway. Dad thought that the pig was going to hit the back wheel. He braced himself for the worst, but nothing happened. By the time he got out of the plane, the pig had disappeared.

Conclusion: he saved the two pilots, all the passengers, and a plane from death. Amazing. If he can do that, he can do anything.

Sibilanga. Scary when wet? Oh yes. Great bananas? Most assuredly. Plan for the unexpected? Always.

My friend Holger and me flying the Twin Otter.

Our farewell PNG mumu.

Flying the approach to Aziana, Eastern highlands.
The shortest and steepest runway in PNG.

Jennifer and me at Sandfly beach near Vanimo, Sandaun province.

# TANGO

## ~Taro *and Other PNG Delicacies~*

"Outwit, Outlast, Outplay"—the motto, the mantra, the aim of the players on *Survivor*, a successful TV series that pits competitors in a thirty-nine-day endurance test in a remote location, not just to survive the elements but also to survive the "vote." Each episode culminates in a vote where one player is eliminated from the game. In addition, each installment of the game pits the contenders against one another in two games: challenges for immunity from the vote and also for a reward. In a game where participants must make their own shelter, start fire, source water and food, the reward challenge is often about food. The winner or winners of the reward challenge are usually ridiculously excited since they anticipate a meal of real food. We never really got addicted to the show, probably because we didn't have TV in PNG for our first few years. We did, however, watch a few episodes of season 9: *Survivor: Vanuatu—Islands of Fire.* We were drawn to this series in particular since as a Melanesian people group, the Vanuatuans have cultural similarities to the people of Papua New Guinea. When a reward challenge of a "traditional feast" was announced, and the competitors were dancing and screaming over the potential for a delectable banquet, we looked at one another across our living room and burst out laughing. A customary spread in that part of the world does not necessarily appeal to the Western palette. The winners were invited to participate in a "mumu." The process of which, the event, is very cool to participate in, but the taste can be disappointing.

In a culture foreign to your own, the simple process of eating can be a challenge. It might be the type of food, the tastes, the availability of ingredients for your own preferences, or even how people eat that causes discomfort. Jennifer's very first Mother's Day was a bit of a disaster. Sam was only a few weeks old and still in the early stages of settling into life. She was not yet sleeping through the night. As first-time parents, we still had a lot to learn. But this was Mother's Day, so we were going to celebrate somehow. We were not exactly flush with cash at that point in our lives, so getting a babysitter was not financially viable, even if our baby girl would have cooperated. Taking her to a restaurant with us did not seem like a great idea either, so we elected to get some Chinese takeout. Great plan, bad execution.

Leaving Jennifer with baby Sam and promises of good aromas on my return, I set out. Unfortunately, the takeout place we had selected had decided to celebrate Mother's Day too—was closing for the day. Pre-cell phone days, I don't entirely recall the sequence of events, but I do know that instead of good Chinese, Jennifer got cold fast-food burgers. I determined to do better for our first Mother's Day in PNG. Now with three children, we were travelling as a herd.

The "Windjammer" was the one and only restaurant in Wewak. My planning skills again falling short, the Windjammer was having a Mother's Day buffet, and the place was filling fast. The five of us were ushered to a delightful table on the patio a stone's throw from the ocean. After a short wait, the waitress invited us to go ahead; this would make us first to the buffet. Feeling that somehow it was not right for us, the foreigners, to take precedence over everyone else, we protested slightly, but the encouragement was strong that we should go ahead. So not wanting to make a scene, we went up and filled our plates. Turns out that when you are an outsider, listening to the advice of locals is usually a good idea. Placed as we were close to the action, Jennifer and I were able to observe how a buffet is handled in PNG. I have never seen so much food piled on one plate. It was like a mountain of rice, vegetables, and chicken on each platter. The dessert was at the end of the table, and either not wanting to return or afraid of being left short, the slabs of chocolate cake went right on top of the main course. As I understand it, traditionally Papua New Guineans eat one meal per day: one large meal.

This theory was borne out every time we had a "base bung." A *bung kai* is, as the English translation explains, a gathering of food: *kai* being "food" and *bung* being "a gathering." This is the rough equivalent of a pot-luck dinner. In PNG, the MAF missionaries live at a number of locations called bases. On special occasions, the team will gather with their families for a bung kai, the team being the missionaries and the PNG staff. These get-togethers are great fun as we mix cultures and share food. In Vanimo, these often took place at our house as the outside space was quite large. The guys would come over early and start a fire for cooking chicken and sausages. After a while, families would drift in with containers of rice and greens and bags of fruit. Everyone was responsible to bring their own cups and plates. Funny, though, at those base bungs, I rarely saw a plate; it was more often bowls that were brought. Not polite little dessert bowls, not even cereal bowls. No, these were more like mixing bowls; one might even call them buckets. I would sit in amazement and watch, no doubt quite rudely, at the quantity of food a small human frame can consume. The chicken roasted over an open fire was great. The cake that Jennifer was also asked to bake was delightful. Yet somehow, neither of those was ever the biggest hit. The winner, the champion of the bung kai, was always the person that showed up with the sak sak.

Jungle game—meat—being a rarity, the dietary staple in Papua New Guinea is one of three things: taro, kau kau, or sak sak. Taro is a root vegetable that I struggle to describe with words. It is larger than a potato yet smaller than squash and of indefinable shape, texture, and taste. Perhaps the size of a bigger turnip and similar in shape but more distorted. Often cooked literally in the fire, the white flesh is drier than a potato. Taro is basically just starch. Kau kau comes in various varieties, the inside colours being different but really rather impossible to differentiate from the outside. It is a bit like a yam in size and shape, perhaps not quite as sweet to the taste. Kau kau is basically just starch.

Sak sak is the process pulp from the inside of the sago palm. The plant looks very much like a coconut palm but without the long trunk: long, classic palm branches sprouting from a central trunk that is hidden from view by the palms. I never did completely grasp the process of transforming the mushy center of a palm frond into something edible. It appeared to me to be very labour-intensive, involving lots of scraping and washing and drying. The final product is a sort of wet powder. Preparation to eat then requires rehydration and cooking to become a sort of gray-coloured sticky jelly. Sak sak is basically just starch. I can eat sak sak, better with a bit of banana mixed in or served with coconut milk, but it is not something I rave over. For PNG lowlanders living in a town, sak sak transitions from a daily staple to rare delicacy, so when it showed up to a base bung, well, it was almost a stampede.

Invariably, it would be Imwe that brought the small green packets: a slab of sak sak the size of your hand wrapped in a banana leaf, almost individual portions. Like a drug dealer on the wrong side of town, Imwe seemed to have a ready source of the gray Jell-O. Imwe was from Green River area, a half-hour flight to the south of Vanimo. With no road access at all and a hike that requires crossing two mountain ranges, I was never certain how he always showed up with those little politely wrapped parcels.

When I was a child, the church where Dad pastored had bats in the belfry. There wasn't actually a bell tower, but there was a sort of steeple that rose above the old furnace room. The bats had claimed this as their home, turning it into their roost. In truth, the little rodents were sort of adorable: tiny, little brown fuzzy creatures with a cute little nose. Most folks considered them other than charming when one found its way into the sanctuary or down into the fellowship hall. Despite the high ceiling of the church, the parishioners found it difficult to concentrate on the sermon when one of God's less-understandable creations was doing low passes over the pews. Worse was when the furnace was turned on for the first time in the fall. During the summer, the flying rats would find their way into the duct work, and when the heating came on, the smell of roast bat was rather unpleasant. Those diminutive creatures are nothing in comparison to a fruit bat.

Alternatively called a *flying fox*, these significantly larger brethren to the bats of my youth occur in vast numbers in some parts of PNG. In Madang town, they are actually a protected species; it's a tourism thing. Throughout the day, the trees around town are festooned with these large "birds," giving the impression of a great harvest. As dusk approaches, they take flight in a great swarm, turning the sky prematurely dark. The fruit bat is found all over the country. We had a regular visitor to our housing compound in Goroka. In the quiet of an evening, the slow *whoosh, whoosh* of its great wings could be heard coming in to land on our guava tree. One of our PNG coworkers once told me they refer to the flying fox as "thief in the night," for they come and steal from the fruit trees. It was that friend, Alex, that gave us our most up close and personal view of one of these bats.

We had seen roast bat for sale in the market in Wewak, but the sheer size of them was lost on us until "that day." We had just returned from our first trip back to Canada and were staying in Mount Hagen while I underwent captaincy training for the Twin Otter. Outside our house, inside our fence, was a large, tall tree. As I sat in the living room, it seemed that a lot of people were walking by—not unusual—but stopping, looking up into the tree, then moving on—very unusual. This continued over a period of hours. Among the crowd, I noticed Alex, not once, not even twice, but several times. I saw him stop and look and move on. A short while later, he returned from the opposite direction and stood for a while longer, obviously pondering. This occurred perhaps a couple more times, till the next time, Alex came with a slingshot in hand.

Well, if I hadn't been curious before, my interest was certainly aroused by that development. I slipped out of the house, over to the fence, and enquired, "Yu lukim wanem?" What are you looking at? This was my introduction to the "thief in the night." Turns out, Alex was hunting a fruit bat that had elected to sleep away the day in the far reaches of our tree. Alex departed without taking a shot. A short while later, he returned, came inside the fence, sized up the target, and let fly with a single stone. He was up the tree in a flash and back down almost before I was aware he had left the ground. On his first attempt, Alex had taken the bat between the eyes. Grasping the tiny hands at the extremity of each wing tip, Alex spread his arms to their full span, demonstrating the dimensions of his prize. "Bai you kai kai em?" I enquired. Will you eat it? "Oh yes," came the immediate and enthusiastic reply. "Better than chicken!"

While we may have been less than enthused with sak sak and roast bat, tropical fruit is truly amazing. On returning to Canada, I would have to restrain my laughter at the "large papaya" on display in the produce section of the grocery stores. What goes for "large" there barely ranks as medium small in a PNG market, and while bananas in Canada make look good, the sweetness of a less-pleasing-looking PNG one is much preferable. We enjoyed fresh strawberries and passion fruit, guavas, juicy pineapples, and sugar fruit—"snot rocks" to our kids. But the best, the very best, had to be mango season. In contrast to practically every other fruit and vegetable that was available, mangoes were the ones that were not available year round. You didn't have to see them; the aroma just walking into the market announced that it was time. For a few short weeks, there was a huge abundance of the sweet, juicy green-skinned delights. As sudden as the arrival, the season was over, and they were gone.

During our season in Vanimo, our family had the pleasure of crossing the border into Indonesia to participate in the MAF Papua staff conference. If you are confused at this stage, you are most certainly forgiven. The island of New Guinea is split down the middle along the 141st line of longitude, deviating only slightly where the Fly River cuts west of the 141st meridian. The western part of the island is the territory of Indonesia, formerly the province of Iran Jaya, now called Papua. Geographically, the southern portion of the island of New Guinea is the region of Papua; hence, why the name can be used by two independent countries and rising to confusion for those not in the know.

For two countries on the same landmass with the same cultural heritage, Papua New Guinea and Papua are very different—and yet similar. There are two almost competing cultures in Papua

(Indonesia). Over the years, there has been a large influx of what I understand are peoples of Javanese descent, giving the province a very Asian flair not found in Papua New Guinea. The population is huge in comparison, with a multitude of motorbikes as standard transportation, something just not common in PNG. Our first night was spent in an MAF housing compound in Sentani. It was the strangest thing because we met some native Papuans, who in facial features and style of dress were exactly what we had left in Vanimo, except we could not communicate, for we spoke Tok Pisin and they spoke Bahasa.

The last day of the conference was set aside for the dedication of a new aircraft hangar and a new Cessna Caravan aircraft. The celebration was set up in traditional Papuan style rather than Asian style. There was roasting of whole pigs, many speeches, and many honoured guests. We were glad not to be considered honoured guests because they were granted what are considered the choicest portions of pork. I am describing massive pieces of pure fat: several inches thick and long enough to be held in both hands.

This was not what the reward challenge winners were given in *Survivor: Vanuatu—Islands of Fire*. They were treated to a "mumu." The variations on this theme are mainly limited to ingredients of the mumu, but all involve the same extensive process. It starts with fire. Well. actually it starts with digging a hole in the ground; then there is fire. The fire is used to heat up rocks, not little gravel but stones the size of a bowling ball. While the stones are cooking, the food is prepared. There are plantains (cooking bananas), kau kau, and taro. Also greens: slightly indefinable leaves from a multitude of plants but ideally of a couple of specific varieties. Then there is the meat. A serious gathering for an important celebration would call for a whole pig, but these days to get a pig in the city will cost a small fortune, so more often pieces of chicken will satisfy as a substitute for the pork.

Once the rocks have reached the right temperature—your guess is as good as mine how that is determined; they are removed from the fire. The embers and ashes are cleared away, the stones returned to the hole and covered with banana leaves. All the prepared meat and vegetables are arranged on top, possibly a sprinkling of salt and maybe a dose of coconut milk. The whole thing is then covered with more banana leaves, more rocks, and then yet more leaves, or maybe even dirt. "Let simmer for many hours. Uncover and serve." The morsels are all spread out on banana leaves, and folks gather round to fill their buckets. Just as I fail to understand how the correct temperature is determined, I am equally uncertain as to the timing for a mumu to be cooked through; but in my experience, they are usually cooked to perfection, although I have tasted the odd bit of underdone pork.

Our first mumu was of the cheating kind: cooked in the oven. This was during our language and cultural orientation. It gives a reasonable representation of the real thing, but without all the labour. Although the food of a mumu might fall into the acquired-taste category, the real blessing of a mumu is not the edibles; it is the relationship. It is the connections and bonds forged between family and friends that drives Papua New Guinea. The time spent preparing the ground, cooking the rocks, waiting for it to be ready are all part of the Melanesian way. "Stap isi tasol"—just wait. Take the time to fellowship, to talk, to appreciate one another. A mumu given in one's honour is possibly the highest form of compliment one can receive. It is the giving of time, the valuing of relationship. It is an indication of the value of a relationship.

As we prepared to leave PNG after many years, our PNG staff, our friends, wanted to have a mumu for us. Relationship being everything, it was the greatest gift to be with these friends as they gave of their time and energy to bless our family. Just being with them, to be a part of this tradition as they worked together to make the mumu, was very cool. As the stones cooked the food, we sat around and "stori-stori"—just chatted. Whoever was running the show determined that the time was ripe, and the mumu was uncovered for us to partake of the banquet. I loaded my plate, and as the fare kissed my tongue, I was surprised to discover that the chicken was moist, the taro and banana were not dry, the kau kau was sweet, and the greens were tasty. I think that day I finally understood that the taste, the flavor, the enjoyment of a mumu is determined not by the cuisine but by the bonds between those that are sharing it, for I have never tasted a better mumu. I think perhaps it is possible to taste love. But no mumu is complete without speeches, and I should have known to expect the unexpected. But when big, tough, quiet Heron stood up with tears in his eyes—ah, Papua New Guinea, *mi laikim yu tru tumas.*

# UNIFORM

## ~Ubaigubi *Is Another Word for "Challenging"*~

*UBAIGUBI.* PRONOUNCED "OO-BY-GOO-BE." One of Jennifer's favourite PNG names. I was going to say "favourite PNG places," except she has never been there; she just thinks the name sounds cool. While Ubaigubi may be a favourite for Jennifer, it would be less so for me. This is not because of the people, for as a very isolated group, they are somewhat shy and quite polite. MAF doesn't land there very often because there is rarely a reason to. Ubaigubi does not produce coffee; it does not have a major school. It is not a local government center. The rationale for my lack of excitement about Ubaigubi is that the runway is difficult. I place it in my top-ten challenging airstrips in Papua New Guinea. Not all of them are scary for a pilot, but they all demand just that little bit extra amount of caution, that little bit extra skill. Narrowing down over three hundred airstrips to just ten is actually not that easy; top twenty might have been easier, but these ten embody the rationale for MAF's rigorous training regime.

In many ways, Ubaigubi is not that hard. Yes the circuit is confined; and yes, the wind blows funny. But it really isn't that short, nor is it that steep. The excitement lies in wait for when the wheels touch down. If there has been any rain at all really, then it becomes rather like a skating rink. The ground has a definite clay quality to it such that the water sort of floats on top, creating a thin layer of

219

mud that prevents solid contact between the tires and the ground. Communication with Ubaigubi is rather poor: the community doesn't have a radio, and cell phone reception is spotty at best. Pilots do their best to estimate the strip condition based on reports from nearby locations, but the position of Ubaigubi in the mountains means that it is subject to its own little weather microcosm. Pilots prefer that Ubaigubi not be the first flight of the day as this allows them to fly by first to see if a landing is possible. Loading the airplane, flying to Ubaigubi then turning around because the runway looks bad is painful for everyone.

Arkosame (ar-ko-sah-me), located in the East Sepik Province, lies in contrast to Ubaigubi. It is a mere 368 meters in length and climbs at a 10 percent slope. Airstrip slope is measured the same as the roof on your house: rise over run. In Papua New Guinea, 2 percent slope is the break point between a one-way and two-way runway. For any slope steeper than 2 percent, aircraft are only permitted to land uphill and take off downhill. When operating in these directions, the slope dramatically increases aircraft performance; it also dramatically increases the difficulty for the pilot. Standing at the bottom of Arkosame and looking up the runway gives the impression of being quite a climb, which it is. I first flew into Arkosame during my first year flying in Papua New Guinea. It is a small community with limited connection to the outside world. There is a road not too far away, which is a good thing as the runway is slowly disappearing. On landing, about halfway up, there is a significant wash out that has crept little by little towards the center of the runway. After transitioned out of the Cessna 206 onto the Twin Otter, I continued to fly into Arkosame for many years, but these days the runway is closed as the gulley has made the strip just too narrow for safe operations. The problem is that the ground drops away on that side of the hill, and without serious mechanical equipment and civil engineering assistance, there was just no way to stop the rot.

Mukili (moo-key-lee), like Arkosame, has been closed for a few years now. I think for the Mukili community, it just became too hard to maintain the runway for the limited use they got from it, which is rather sad, for it must have been a tremendous effort for their predecessors to construct this runway, which climbs an incredible 40 meters over just 359 meters of length. Mukili makes the top ten because of its bump. The first sixty meters of the runway is steeper than the rest, and the slope transition is rather marked. The aim is to plant the wheels on the runway before the bump, but this is way harder than sounds, given that for a Twin Otter, sixty meters is just three body lengths. It is sort of like parallel parking: get it right, and you look brilliant; misjudge it, and you are suddenly in a big mess.

Due to its lack of length, a pilot cannot afford to just avoid that first sixty meters. Were a pilot to give away that first bit, then by the time the wheels touch, the airplane has maybe 250 meters in which to come to a complete stop. So the pilot must aim for the first bit of grass before the slope changes. I propose that Murphy's law was written at Mukili. If the approach to land goes ever so slightly wrong, almost inevitably the aircraft lands on the bump. Second best to landing right at the start would be landing after the bump, yet almost every pilot I know that has landed at Mukili and missed the first sixty meters reports hitting the bump. It might be an interesting project for an engineering student to calculate what happens with the energy when an aircraft strikes the bump compared to landing on a steady slope, but practical experience declares that the aircraft gets ejected, propelled, launched, rocketed back into the air, but at a speed where flying is not really sustainable. The aircraft gobbles through precious meters of runway before slamming onto the ground a second time. Probably a good thing that the passengers are blind to the pilot's eyes, for by now they are certainly saucer size as the pilot works like a madman to bring the beast back under control in the limited runway remaining. I don't personally know anyone that has actually gone off the end, but I know a few that have guzzled copious quantities of adrenaline at Mukili.

The other variation on the theme of short and steep with a bump is when the bump is inverted: when the first few meters of the runway slope down before the runway bends upwards with normal climbing slope for touchdown. Dinangat (di-nun-gut) is found hidden in the Finisterre Mountains of the Morobe Province on PNG's northshore between Madang and Lae. Much closer to Lae as the crow flies, Dinangat is quite difficult to get to. Arriving overhead is relatively straightforward, but the aircraft will be several thousand feet above the tiny village as Dinangat hugs the backside of the range. In bad weather, just getting to Dinangat is its own story. The pilot may need to fly out towards the Pacific to find a good view of the ground before descending and assessing the viability and safety of a crawl up the valley back to Dinangat. This exercise is complicated by the fact that down low, the runway is invisible, so the pilot had better know the terrain like the proverbial back of his hand. Assuming that the pilot finds the runway and gets established on approach, then the effort becomes very much like Ubaigubi or Mukili: getting the wheels properly on the ground. Whereas at Mukili the first sixty meters of runway is steeper upslope than the rest, at Dinangat, the first sixty meters is downslope. As the pilot is trying to get the plane to land, the ground just keeps running away!

Years ago, when the kids were young, we had the chance to visit Disneyland. Nate was approaching his fifth birthday. Remember that we had whisked him off to PNG when he was just a newborn, and the visit to Disneyland was just his second visit back to North America. Well, we decided to take in a 3D movie. I have no idea what the movie was, but near the end, it featured Mickey Mouse. Being in 3D, it was like the cartoon character was right there with us, reaching out his hand to shake yours. Fascinating for a young lad, Nate was up on his seat in an instant, reaching out to touch Mickey. Of course, Nate's hand passed right through Mickey's, which was totally confusing to poor Nate. He dropped the 3D glasses down his nose, saw that Mickey went to 2D, then slid the glasses back into place, and tried the handshake a second time, with equally frustrating results. The glasses went up and down a couple times as Nate sought to resolve the dilemma. Landing at Dinangat is like trying to shake hands with a 3D Mickey: the ground just keeps sliding away from you as you try your hardest to make a connection.

Magleri (ma-gleer-ee) forms the complete antithesis to the Mukilis and Dinangats: it is flat as a pancake. I have no idea how pilots found Magleri in the old days before GPS. Concealed in the Sepik plane, Magleri's runway is just a miniscule scar in the vast expanse of green jungle whose monotony is broken only by the occasional river. There are no landmarks within twenty kilometers of Magleri, and aircraft below two thousand feet could fly within a couple kilometers and never see the place. Surrounded by trees on all sides landing at Magleri is flying into a ditch. Once below the height of the jungle canopy, claustrophobia is an automatic reaction. But it is the takeoff that requires nerves of steel. I would taxi to the start of the runway, line up for the takeoff, complete the checks, then pause. Looking down the far end of the runway, all there is nothing but trees. I knew that I had calculated properly, and I knew that we would take off just fine, as we always did; yet I knew, I just knew, that in a few seconds, I would be getting a good look at those trees and second-guessing myself. I knew, I just knew, that I would be sorely tempted to cheat and pull back on the control column before it was time.

For the takeoff, the aircraft gets off the ground, then needs to fly close to the ground to build up speed to fly for real. Pulling away from the ground too early is bad news. Close to the ground, the aircraft operates a bit like a hovercraft, floating on a cushion of air under the wings. At low speed, the aircraft needs this cushion to stay in the air, so the pilot must harden his resolve and stare down the approaching foliage. The windshield fills with trees, but at the right speed, a slight tug on the control column sends the aircraft soaring skyward like a homesick angel.

Whereas Magleri is invisible due to lack of clues, Gubil (goo-bill) is invisible due to mountains. I would bestow on Gubil the title of worst approach ever. Gubil is located at the confluence of the insignificant Hak, San, and Uk Rivers. The runway envelops almost the entirety of the little piece of clear ground at the junction of the streams. There is absolutely no freedom to manoeuvre for a standard circuit. Pilots must enter the valley either to the west from the Sepik River or from the east, flying along the ever narrowing valley from Miyanmin. In either case, pilots then turn overhead the field to position their aircraft tight against the southern mountain ridges. Within three kilometers, an even smaller spur valley makes its appearance to the left. The pilot has to continue hugging the ridge, diving into the tight space. Evaluating the right moment, the pilot wheels his plane hard right, reversing his course. Even then, the only thing to see is the steep slope on the opposite side of the Hak River.

Again, relying on judgement borne of experience, the pilot picks his moment for another hard right turn to head back towards the Gubil airstrip. The runway remains elusive, the pilot following the route he was taught and has flown before. The aircraft must be configured for landing long before the runway bursts into sight slightly to the right of the aircraft's nose. A few quick silent questions: On profile? Configured correctly? Correct speed? Yes, yes, and yes, and the pilot commits to the landing. If the answer to any of those queries is no, then it is max power, flaps to ten degrees, and raise the nose to go around. But the confined area remains a concern. A small left turn will put the aircraft against the hills again, a vital manoeuvre to position the aircraft for one of just two options. Preferably the valley towards Miyanmin will be clear for a ninety-degree turn in that direction and plenty of room to continue the climb. Should the valley be shrouded in cloud, then the more complicated option is all that remains: a steeply banked 180-degree reversal in tight quarters to fly back out the way the aircraft just came.

It is not just terrain that causes a pilot to cringe. Terrain doesn't move. If you can see the mountains, you can avoid them. Wind, however, moves. Wind is the invisible hand that flicks the plane around. Wind is the fickle factor that can be your friend one moment then, in an instant, turn on you like a rabid dog. That is the character of Aibai (eye-by), at the time a relatively new strip in the Eastern Highlands just a hop and a skip from Goroka in the Wahgi Valley. Because it is newly built, the surface is certainly nothing to write home about to mom. Yet another runway in the short and steep category, it is the capricious wind that makes each and every arrival one for the books. Aibai is built near the top of the ridge line that guards the southern boundary of the Wahgi Valley. The runway sits perpendicular to the valley, and the wind rolls over the top of the ridge line, plunging down the other side, clinging to the runway as it continues its flight towards the valley floor. That would be bad enough, except out in the valley, where the aircraft is initially positioned for the landing, the wind is in the opposite direction.

Lined up for landing, the aircraft receives a constant push, forcing the pilot to reduce power and push forward on the control column in the struggle to force the aircraft to descend.

Partway down the final approach, about the point that the pilot is committed to land, the wind switches direction. It doesn't do so gently. It doesn't do so with warning. It flicks around like an ice hockey player jumping from skating forwards to skating backwards, like a policeman doing a handbrake turn in his cruiser. It is instant, and it is nasty. Pilots politely call it wind shear. When it happens, there is no time for names. The wind that was providing a push now throws up a hand, and the aircraft slows like it flew into Jell-O. Any delay in adding power, and the plane will not make the runway. Failure to correctly adjust the aircraft's altitude will result in a really big mess. Flying into Aibai, a pilot knows this will happen. It always happens, and yet it is still surprising. It is unexpected yet expected.

Any list of PNG's airstrips would be incomplete without Aziana. As Papua New Guinea's shortest and steepest airstrip, Aziana carries a mystique. It is a place that everyone has heard of. A name that every pilot wants to record in their logbook. The airstrip is nestled in the floor of the Imani Valley of the Eastern Highlands, parallel to the river that winds its way from Wonenara in the east out towards the Pacific Ocean many miles to the west. But Aziana is near the end of the valley, where it narrows down, forcing the Aziana circuit to be longer and narrower than standard. Pilots need to hug the ridge, with the trees really close. The final approach ends up being extended, but once established, the rest of the approach is really rather a yawn. The runway is anything but dull. It measures a paltry 320 meters, one-third of a kilometer; depending on the city, only two or three blocks.

Next time you are in a city with multi-storey buildings, stop and look up. Pick a building two or three blocks away and count up from the ground floor: one, two, three, five, ten, fifteen stories. That's Aziana—14.3 percent slope. As the wheels kiss the grass, the parking bay sits fifteen storeys up. Energy management is the term we use. After landing, one would expect the pilot to reduce the power till the engines are just idling. Try that at Aziana, and a pilot will need to do some very fast talking to explain how he managed to put the aircraft on its tail. A lot of power is necessary to climb that mountain, and the inevitable result of loss of momentum is the aircraft tipping over backwards to sit down on its tail.

The thing about Aziana, however, is that the majority of the runway is actually constructed at a 20 percent gradient. By comparison, the maximum permissible highway gradient in the Canadian province of Ontario is just 12 percent. One can't stay in Aziana forever; a takeoff is the natural follow on from a landing. Surprisingly perhaps, the most challenging thing about Aziana is the manoeuvering for takeoff. I have never been on an aircraft carrier ship, but turning the aircraft at Aziana makes me think it must be a similar experience. The entire area for turning is maybe twenty meters by forty meters: one wingspan by two wingspans. On one side is the steep runway. On two more sides are vertical drop-offs. On side four is a vertical incline taller than the airplane wing. Wheels need to clutch at the edges of the clear area to maximize the turning area. By the time the aircraft is aligned with runway, a mere 303 meters remain between the nose of the aircraft and the row of bushes that mark the opposite end of the runway. Once the brakes are released, there is no option to stop safely, for the aircraft immediately tips over the hill and begins its wild ride to lift off, which predictably consumes the entire available runway.

Sometimes it's not the runway that creates the challenge, nor the wind that disrupts the pilot's plans. Sometimes it's the surrounding terrain that plays havoc with a pilot's perceptions. I think that is the reason why for me Golgubip (gol-guh-bip) is the hardest airstrip in PNG. Golgubip hides in the shadow of the Hindenburg Wall at the north extremity of PNG's Western Province. The runway is pretty average at 470 meters and 8.1 percent slope, but it sits in the middle of a wide bowl that is thoroughly deceptive. The entire basin slopes upward from the Wok Wanik River to the base of the towering escarpment known as the Hindenburg Wall. Most flights to Golgubip originate at the mining town of Tabubil just a handful of flying minutes to the west.

Aircraft departing Tabubil for Golgubip try to stay low for the short journey. A slight left turn places the aircraft in the "chute," an area of lower terrain trapped between the Wall and Mount Kuru. Tabubil sits at 1,600 feet above sea level with Golgubip at 4,600 feet above sea level, so the aircraft climbs the whole way, aiming to be at 5,400 feet at Golgubip. That is where it gets really weird, for if the plane is at 5,400 feet a couple miles from Golgubip, it appears to be way too high. If the weather is not so good and the climb is stopped at 4,500 feet because of cloud, then looking towards Golgubip, the pilot is absolutely and completely convinced that he is at the right height, despite being at an altitude lower than the runway!

The problem is that, that start of the Golgubip bowl is at maybe 1,500 feet above sea level, then gently rising up to the 4,600 feet for the runway. Our peripheral vision takes in the ground a long way below us; our mind overlays that on our perception of the runway and decides that the aircraft is higher than the strip. But that is oh so wrong. The pilot cannot fly according to those visual perceptions; he must fly the aircraft instruments, trusting them implicitly, doing rapid mental calculations of forward speed versus distance to the runway, against current altitude and altitude yet to descend, factoring in rate of descent. And it all happens in a couple of short minutes. Every time I went there, I tried to mentally prepare for this expected illusion, and yet somehow, invariably, I would get to Golgubip and end up double-checking the data for the altitude because it just did not look right.

And then there is Selbang (sell-bang). I think if I were to take everything I have written about the previous nine airstrips and roll them all into one, it would give an accurate assessment of Selbang. It is short, steep, slippery due to algae, with two Mukili-like transitions, and lots of visual illusions. Selbang has been the scene of more than one "oops," so it must be treated with the utmost respect. Borne out of sweat, tears, and even some blood, MAF PNG's training regimen is intense. For some newcomers, it seems over the top; but for those who have been around long enough to scare themselves, the training requirements are judged fully justified. There is an old saying, "Learn from the mistakes of others as you won't be around long enough to make them all yourself." Quoted in a myriad of ways and attributed to a wide variety of people from Eleanor Roosevelt to Groucho Marx, it could easily be the unspoken mantra of MAF instructors.

In Papua New Guinea, the foundation of airstrip familiarization is that a pilot may not operate at any airstrip to which he has not been trained. Initially, this means flying there with an instructor pilot multiple times. Over time, as the pilot gains experience, the training may shift to the point where a ground briefing is sufficient. But for places like Selbang, landings and takeoffs with an instructor pilot are always required. It is just that unforgiving. I was fortunate in never having an airplane incident at Selbang or any other airstrip, perhaps that was because at Selbang, in particular, I always flew there expecting the unexpected.

# VICTOR

-*Forging Our Family in* Vanimo~

WHILE WEWAK WAS our first home in PNG, Vanimo was where our family found its identity. Nate had but a handful of weeks under his age belt when we left Canada to commence our missionary story. Our little tribe spent three months in Australia undergoing some training and orientation. Details of our escapades in the training center at Ballarat must wait for another time. Matt celebrated his third birthday there, and Sam reached her fifth, but Nate was not even six months when we moved from there, through Far North Queensland, Australia, and into Papua New Guinea. In our Wewak home, Sam turned six, and Matt turned four, but Nate was not yet two before we moved from what had been his fourth home. Being so young, Nate remembers little of Wewak, so it is Vanimo that as a family captures our earliest memories. It was our time in Vanimo that defined who we are. For our first three years there, we were the only missionary family in the small town. In fact, for a good part of that time, Jennifer was the only "white" lady; and for all three years, our children were the only "white" kids. And so it was we spent lots of time together, both in quantity and quality.

Vanimo, nestled in the top left corner of PNG, is the capital of Sandaun Province. It is only reachable by air or sea, alternatively jungle trek. The only road leads a few miles west to the Indonesian border. Our house, our home, was probably the best we will ever live in. It was situated on top of a hill, on a small peninsula that jutted out into the Pacific Ocean. Due north of our house, there was nothing but water until Yokohama, Japan. The house was a preindependence structure, one of a number built as Australian army officers' housing. It was an elevated bungalow with four bedrooms, two living rooms, and a deck that ran the length of the house. Below the house, there was a garage, a second bathroom, laundry, storage, and an expanse of concrete where the kids could play out of the burning equatorial sun. Surrounding the house was a large yard with space to ride bikes and commence the boys' indoctrination into a love of soccer. Water was supplied to the house through three giant tanks that collected the rainfall cascading off our roof. The house did not have central air-conditioning, but each room had its own wall-mounted unit, not that we could afford to run them. To an extent, it was the character of the house that provided the backdrop for some of the events that have passed into family legend.

For many of you, earthquakes are things you see the aftermath of on the nightly news or your Twitter feed or whatever the current source of news might be by the time you read this. For us, earthquakes were a regular occurrence. Where we lived, they were always minor but very strange to experience nevertheless. There was one in Vanimo that we all remember, from the very youngest right up through the family. It was the one that set the water tanks swaying. Our three rain-collection tanks were huge, standing beyond my reach, even on tippy-toes; they each held many thousand liters of water.

Earthquakes manifest in a variety of renditions. There are ones that come with a short, sharp bang, hitting the house without warning and departing with equal speed. Others arrive with a rolling motion that appears to transform the very ground into waves like the sea. The one we all vividly remember was of the undulating style. It came and seemed to stay. We didn't feel any particular fear, but long after the ground had ceased to move, the water tanks continued to sway. Having set the water in the tanks to flowing from one side of the tank to the other, its own momentum continued the wave action within the tank, which actually caused the tanks themselves to move back and forth, several inches in each direction. We stood on that large deck, the five of us, transfixed by the possibility of the tanks bursting at their seams. That day, the galvanized, corrugated behemoths withstood the pressure. But their days were numbered.

In the tropics, even galvanized steel submits to the ravages of time, starting with little pin-prick holes that can be sealed with silicon, but this only delays the inevitable. Sometime later, in the midst of a torrential downpour, as can only be experienced in the tropics, we heard a mighty crash. Racing outside, we discovered that one of our tanks was no more. Having reached capacity in the heavy rain, one of those tiny holes blew up. The metal ripped up the side till it met a joint in the parts that form the tank, and then continued to split itself apart along the intersections until it reached the top, whereupon it blew off the top and sent water in every direction. A pile of iron wood stacked beside the tank was blown across the yard in the dramatic flood. Fortunately, no one was outside; for had one of us been close when it let go, there is no telling the number of bones that would have been broken.

The area under the house, in addition to its other functions, was the repository for all of the "outdoor" toys. There were, of course, balls and bikes, but we had also accumulated a minor construction force of second-hand metal Tonka earthmovers. These rather substantial toys were stored in an old wooden crate we had used to ship some of our belongings to PNG. The story of that crate is one in its own right, but it travelled with us in all our moves until we retired it when we left PNG. One day, when I was off flying, the kids, presumably on recess from home school, began to entreat their mother to come to their assistance. And by that, of course, I mean they were bellowing for their mother as only young children can. As she arrived from the upstairs, the children informed their mother that a spider had taken up residence amidst the Tonka trucks.

Now, unless you have experience in this sort of thing, as you might if you have spent time outside the frozen north, or unless you are and ardent follower of Discovery Channel, you have no idea what Jennifer was about to face. You are perhaps now thinking "tarantula," and you might be close, only the average tarantula pales in comparison to what the kids had discovered. South of the equator, there are bird spiders, so called because they take down birds! The arachnid in the toy box was of sufficient size to move those metal trucks. Not move around them, not through them—actually push them aside.

Under other circumstances, there is no doubt that I would have received a summons to deal with this intruder, especially as Jennifer's fear of spiders matches my fear of snakes. But I was gone, and the spider needed to be. That protective maternal instinct kicked in, and armed with little more than a broom, Jennifer ordered the children to turn over the old crate. The spider exited said box, and Jennifer chased it down, beating it with the broom while emitting a fearsome war cry: "Die, sucker, die!" Should you feel I exaggerate, please indulge me with one more tale. As we recounted this event to former residents of the house, they shared their own story. On entering the toilet one day, a member of that family had witnessed four hairy legs peeking out from the right-hand side of the toilet bowl. The other four legs were seen to be gripping the opposite side. A spider that can reach around a toilet bowl can surely move a mass of Tonka trucks.

In some countries, there are schools that meet the needs of mission kids. With the exception of the capital city and a couple of mission-run schools, this is not really the case in PNG. Certainly in little Vanimo, there was no education for our children, so Sam, Matt, and Nate attended MIS (Marples International School) as the only students. Jennifer was the teacher, and they say I was the principal. The second living room became the schoolroom. Jennifer taught math and science, English, history, and geography.

MIS had a music program and physical ed, even a Christmas pageant! Jennifer started Sam in kindergarten and, in two-year increments, added Matt and Nate. School was generally a structured affair with a start time, recess, and lunch. Several years later, we came across an early school piece written by one of the kids, explaining why it would be advantageous to all to extend recess by an extra five minutes. Jennifer worried plenty those years about whether the kids were getting the educational start they needed. Their transitions to "real" school when we moved to Goroka and the kids attended Numonohi Christian Academy, and then later when they went to university prove that Jennifer's efforts during those years were more than adequate.

The advantage of homeschool was the flexibility it allowed. Although there were but three stores in the town, they were sufficient to meet most of our grocery needs. So there would be the weekly field trip to the shops. For the kids, these still took on the air of adventure as distractions were limited. Each store had security at the door, so the kids could play hide-and-seek on mom without fear of them disappearing; the guards would never have let them out the door. As they scampered through the aisles, the other moms, PNG ladies all, would keep Jennifer well apprised of where they were. But the day they discovered the freezer section was memorable, for hidden within one chest freezer were heads. Pigs' heads. Lots of heads complete with ears and eyes blankly staring up at them as they cracked the lid. Ever after, the kids would race into the store, seeking permission to check out the freezer.

Just like "real" school, homeschool came with school holidays, and even the adherence to the likes of Canada and even Halloween. Now I am certain that some of you are thinking *missionaries?* Halloween? Can this be? When there is little entertainment to be bought, one has to make one's own, and kids always like an excuse to dress up. So yes, we had Halloween. The beauty of the Vanimo house was its abundance of doors. There was of course a front door and a back door. In addition, there was the patio door off the master bedroom. Downstairs, there was the door to the laundry and also the door to the garage. With so many doors, the kids had an entire subdivision to visit. Of course, it would be no fun if mom and dad opened every door, so Jennifer and I dug in the closets for our own costumes, tried on our acting skills, and became the whole street as the merry threesome trotted from door to door.

We did have some regular fun too. It may have been instituted earlier, but certainly it was at Vanimo that "Friday night" became a tradition. Friday night became junk-food and movie and Lego night. Normal rules of decorum were set aside; burping was acceptable on Friday night. The kids quickly learned that mom was completely incapable of emitting an even remotely satisfactory belch. This too became a traditional source of amusement: Jennifer straining to emit the weakest of sounds. There were no pizza parlours or burger joints, no taco stands or chicken places, so as with a good portion of our food, junk food too came from scratch. Pizzas appeared from oven, burgers with homemade buns, and what remains a favourite to this day: homemade nuggets and fries. We would sit in the living room watching a movie, which back then was most likely to be a Disney cartoon like *Mulan* or, under significant protest from the boys, a Barbie adventure. Following on from eating and the movie came Lego.

Over the years, we accumulated an impressive collection of Lego and Mega Bloks, sufficient to make anything the kids requested. Their job was to dream, mine to bring those dreams to fruition, Jennifer's to find that special piece that I needed. We created all sorts of things from simple stables for Sam's collection of horses, to incredible reproductions of all sorts of aircraft. One time, we managed to use practically all the bits in the construction of a magnificent spaceship, complete with a hangar bay that held a rover, and smaller fighter types and mini-freighters. All were to scale, made to fit our rather large assortment of Lego people.

Many times, the kids headed to bed before the projects were complete, so every Saturday morning became like Christmas with the young ones rising early to see if dad had finished while they slept. Sam was old enough to watch her brothers, so on Saturdays when I was not flying, Jennifer and I could sleep in while the kids played with their Lego.

Perhaps the best and the most difficult creations were the result of a find we made dating back to my own childhood. Back in the '60s, the height of cinema graphic art was—puppets! Well, perhaps marionettes. With my early childhood spent in England, there were some "live"-action puppets like Basil Brush, a red fox about whom I remember little except watching on Saturday evenings. There were also "stop"-action puppets as I watched on the young children's trilogy of TV programs: *Trumpton*, *Chigley*, and *Camberwick Green*. But the find we made was a series of video tapes of the original *Thunderbirds* episodes. In their series of adventures to save mankind from ne'er-do-wells, the Thunderbirds travelled in Thunderbird 1, Thunderbird 2, Thunderbird 3, and Thunderbird 4. Each was a unique, sleek machine that my young children were certain I could recreate out of square blocks. Unwilling to disappoint, I picked up the gauntlet, churning out reasonable representations of the four T'birds, complete with all their articulated parts. On our return to Canada after more than seventeen years in PNG, we shipped twenty-two crates of our possessions: one was full of our Lego horde. Up till now, we have refused to divvy up the collection. On the passing of their parents, I suspect there will be greater angst among the three offspring over what constitutes the equitable distribution of the Lego than over whatever may remain of the family fortune.

Living on the ocean, almost literally at the beach, we probably went for a swim every week. There was the town beach, but it was little more than a place for a quick dip. For a real beach experience, we packed up the picnic, loaded the dogs into the dodgy old van that was our means of transportation, and headed twenty minutes down the coast road toward the Indonesian border to our little piece of paradise: Sandfly Beach. Sandfly was a fantastic place. There was a freshwater stream that emptied itself into a small lagoon, which in turn flowed into the ocean. The lagoon and ocean were separated by a great sandbar. With trees overhanging, this was the perfect spot to spend an afternoon with family and friends. The dogs raced about, in, and out of the water until they were totally spent. In flashbacks to my own childhood, I followed the tradition of my own father and built sand vehicles for the kids. Digging into the soft sand, we created both cars and planes for the enjoyment of our children. The lagoon was sufficiently shallow for the kids to stand at the edges and yet deep enough for there to be a challenge for their developing swimming skills.

On the opposing side of the sandbar, the waves of the ocean crashed with vigor. The kids were too small to venture in by themselves, but with the security of dad alongside, they loved to head into the surf to be thrown about by the force of the waves. The ocean and the lagoon only met where the water from the river flowed into the ocean. Except, that is, for one time. There was a day when the breakers were crashing with more-than-normal violence. Matt and I were in the lagoon, together but not side by side, when one of those waves broke right over the sandbar and sent a torrent of saltwater into the freshwater lagoon. Like a mini tsunami, the water grabbed my small son and carried him away, pushing the water back upstream. Fortunately, the stream cascading out of the coastal mountains ran under the road at Sandfly, so Matt's departure was limited. I raced to his rescue as he came spluttering to the surface. Undeterred, he returned to his play, and the escapade became just another yarn from the land of the unexpected.

Our other source for aqua adventure was a waterfall hidden away in the jungle behind a Catholic mission station. This was a spot that waited till Nate was a little older as it required a short but rather obstacle course like hike. There was a small river that flowed behind the station. PNG is filled with these rivers, hidden away beneath the jungle company, unseen to all but those in the know. We followed the river, cutting back and forth across it to find the best route over uncharted terrain. But the reward was certainly worth the mild expenditure of energy, for appearing out of the jungle was an incredible pool. A boulder the size of house formed the backdrop, over and around which fell the water. Around the edges, the pool was calm and serene; against the waterfall, it was turbulent and agitated. The water spilled over the rock face in a curtain effect, but to one side, there was a chute of sorts down which the water surged; and at the bottom, it kicked out in a powerful jet.

The kids lacked the strength to approach the chute side, and even I had to approach at an angle, for so fearsome was the outflow that it was impossible to swim against the current. With a child clinging to my back, I would manoeuvre around the edge of the pond, seeking to find purchase on the few rocks hiding beneath the surface that allowed me and my little one to keep our heads abovewater. Struggling to hold against the tide, we would ready ourselves, then yield to the inevitable and shoot off in a water-propelled ride that would rival any theme-park offering. Around the other side of the pool, where the water curtain emptied into the pond, the boulder actually tucked in underneath, hovering above the surface. Except from the side, this secret room was concealed from view. It was possible to pass under the waterfall and end up in a tiny vault behind the falls. To get inside, the kids would again ride my back, closing eyes and mouth as we slipped though the deluge.

We enjoyed our time in Vanimo and were very sad to leave. If Jennifer and the kids happened to be in town when the plane landed, they would slip over to say hi. With the airport being very small, the children were free to climb around the plane and get rides on the baggage trolleys. It was in Vanimo that the kids really became part of what we were about: the purpose of MAF. Each evening, as we sat around our dining-room table for dinner, I would tell the stories of the day. The kids got to know the names of the places I visited and where they were. We would play the "where did dad go today" game: "I went twenty-seven minutes east from Vanimo." The kids would chorus their replies: "Aitape? Nuku? Lumi?"

For our family, it was not about dad flying and everyone else along for the ride. Visitors at Vanimo were few and far between, so extra people at the table was a novelty for the kids, one that they enjoyed. Early in our time, I received a call from a pilot with SIL Aviation (aviation arm of Wycliffe Bible Translators) who would be spending the night in Vanimo and was looking for a place to lay his head. In the mission community in PNG, especially in the mission aviation community, we always seek to help our brothers and sisters. So even though I had never met the caller, we opened our door. I met him at the airport where he was closing up his Cessna 206, and we went up to the house. The kids were a bit nervous to meet a stranger, but for them, he was about to get stranger still. He emerged from the shower wearing a T-shirt and a lap lap. Now, a lap lap is essentially a piece of material wrapped around the waist like a skirt. "Dad," they whispered, "he's wearing a skirt!" The pilot became a good friend, spending many nights with us over the years even after we moved to Goroka. When talking about him, the kids still say, "Is that the lap-lap man?"

Like Christians the world over, on Sundays we went to church. We tried a couple different ones but settled in a tiny church plant. When we started attending, they were meeting in a government conference room; but before long, they moved into the settlement area, building a small shelter from bush materials and free offcuts from the lumber mill. The floor was sand, there were no seats, the roof was grass thatch, and the walls were open to allow the breeze to flow. Ironically, there was a sound system. The more charismatic-style churches in PNG love their guitars and sing with great passion.

One of the church leaders was a young man named Tovin. We loved Tovin. The kids loved Tovin. The kids loved him because of his energy in leading worship, for when Tovin started to get blessed, the children were rapt. Tovin would start to dance, twirling around and bouncing on one foot. He would grab a banana leaf and start waving it while he danced. The thing was, he held a microphone with a cord. As he twirled around, the cord would wrap around his legs. At the moment the children were certain he would fall, Tovin would reverse direction and unwind the cord.

I don't know how it happened exactly, but Jennifer ended up teaching Sunday school. There was quite a little group of kids, with very little English, so Jennifer spoke in Tok Pisin. We had some material, but she basically made it herself. They started meeting under a tree, but eventually some folks in Canada donated some money for us to build another small shelter, like a mini version of the church building. I also got involved, often preaching twice a month. It was always an enigma to me. Most of the folks that attended had limited education. Some understood English, but many not so much. The PNG guys that spoke invariably read the scripture passage from an English Bible whereas I always read from the Tok Pisin Bible. My Tok Pisin improved significantly over those years, due no doubt in part to all the preaching. Tok Pisin has maybe three thousand words, so I learned how to explain Bible principles and theological ideas without the actual word. In my preaching in that tiny church, I also learned one big difference between PNG church and Western church: in Canada, the pastor had best be dome talking before the people are done listening; in PNG, the people do not quit listening until the pastor is done preaching.

The church, however, went beyond its own feeble walls, sending out two young men as missionaries down the PNG-Indonesian border to a village left behind in time. There are many remote villages in Papua New Guinea; many people live as they always have, as subsistence farmers. But the village where those young men went was beyond that. They returned after a few months to tell the church about their journey. It was rather funny because they were doing their best to explain poverty to those who were themselves rather poor. But in comparison, the settlement folks that attended our church were rich, for they had pots to cook in and clothes to wear. Desperate to make his point that these people needed help, he held up a grass skirt and announced, "This is what the ladies are wearing!" The grass skirt was little more than a strip of grass to tie around the waist with a few strands of grass hanging from it. The threads of grass that made the skirt were at least a couple centimeters apart; the skirt covered nothing and would have provided no warmth or protection whatsoever.

It was in Vanimo that Jennifer and I first encountered what a Christ-transformed Papua New Guinean looks like. While most of the families at our church were dirt poor, Jack and Clare were not. Jack was the head magistrate for Sandaun Province. He went on to become head magistrate for Papua New Guinea. Jack and Clare were so different from others that we met. The status of women in PNG remains a huge issue, with significant separation even between married couples. A husband and wife may rarely be seen together, often in public apparently leading separate lives. Not Jack and Clare. As I drove to the airport each morning, I would often see them out walking together, side by side. As parents, they disciplined rather than punished. As those who have been blessed, they gave from what they had. In his role as magistrate, Jack also worked to bring the principles of Christ into his court. As magistrate, a lot of what he did was dispute resolution, and Jack worked hard to bring about reconciliation rather than apportioning blame.

Having been settled in Wewak, Jennifer and I moved to Vanimo under some protest. But in the land of the unexpected, we found a home. A place that we came to love. There really is only one way to end this chapter. As we sat on the Air Niugini F28 jet airliner, leaving Vanimo for the last time, Matt told his mom that he was sad because "*we* won't get to serve the people of Sandaun anymore."

# WHISKY

## ~Wewak: *Our First Home~*

FOR A MISSION Aviation Fellowship family, their first base holds an unassailable place in their hearts. All families begin their MAF journey with orientation and training in Mount Hagen, but very few remain there for longer than a handful of months. Most families complete their language, cultural, and initial technical orientation then move to another of MAF's operational bases around the country. It is in this first PNG home that we come to grips with life as a mission pilot and as a missionary family. There is a special feeling about that place, for it is there that we come of age. It is there we dig deeper in our cultural understanding. It is there that we make mistakes and either learn or quit. It is there that we really understand the strength of our call. For our little family, Wewak was that place.

Wewak sits right on the Pacific Ocean about 260 kilometers north of Mount Hagen. It is an old town with memories of World War II. It is one of the original bases of MAF in Papua New Guinea. That first house was built to the original MAF floor plan. A slightly raised single-storey ranch-style, that house held the stories of a hundred families. Our time in that home was just a year, but it was a year full of adventure and learning. We learned about PNG culture, how to be a family, how to be self-sufficient when necessary, how to deal with sickness and injury, how to exist alongside cockroaches. Above all, we learned to really trust in God as He cares for even the little things.

Our first PNG friend in Wewak was Daniel. At the time, Daniel was working as a traffic officer at Wewak base with aspirations to be an aircraft engineer. Daniel was also "ten toea"—single. Daniel is now married with children and, through MAF, realized his dream of becoming a licensed aircraft maintenance engineer. He lived on the same housing compound as our family, and through him, we were able to get some early insights into PNG culture. Knowing that Canada would be quite foreign to Daniel, we shared some photos with him when he was visiting in our house one day. What I assumed would be a simple exercise of "this is our house" turned into a cross-cultural expedition. I don't recall how the conversation transitioned, but the question arose about who built the house. I replied that we had bought it. Daniel looked quizzical and asked, "Who owns the land?" My response that we did seemed to confuse him. He rephrased, "What happens to your house if the owner wants the land back?" Now it was my turn to be perplexed. "They can't have it back," I countered. "It is ours." This had rapidly turned into bewilderment ping-pong.

Daniel, likely convinced I was short on brain power, and I, equally assured that his grasp of English was worse than my hold on Tok Pisin, the query came, "Who is the papa of the ground?". It was apparent that I was now on foreign ground in my understanding of the concept of land title. I am fairly certain we ended that discussion at an impasse, but with a determination on my part to investigate the notion of "papa ground." In time, I discovered that there is a reverse appreciation of land ownership between Canada and Papua New Guinea. In Canada, the majority of land would be crown land; when in doubt, it probably belongs to the government. In PNG, every hill, every stream, every tree, every blade of grass has a traditional and rightful owner: the papa graun. More than that, everyone knows the lineage to the extent that I can land at an isolated community, point to a ridge in the distance, and have my question of ownership answered clearly. In that light, land is rarely sold. Only within the town line is property bought and sold in what Westerners would consider a normal transaction. Elsewhere, a purchase is really only a lease and a flexible arrangement at that. Should I build a house on the land, it can be suggested that I have improved the land, therefore increased its value, consequently the lease assessment; and as a result, I should pay more for the land lease! As they say in PNG, "het i pen yeh"—it gives me a headache.

It was also through Daniel that I received another lesson in the power of the PNG bush knife. We had an early introduction to the place of the bush knife in PNG society during our orientation in Dusin, but I really saw this tool in action one afternoon after a torrential rainstorm. There was a beautiful, fragrant frangipani tree in the center of our housing compound. The frangipani is a tropical tree that tends to grow wide even as it climbs higher. Unlikely to reach significant stature, the frangipani is noted for its five-petaled flower of brilliant white that transitions to luminous yellow towards the center of the blossom. The tree must have grown too large to support itself, for during the rain, half of the tree separated itself, dropping a huge limb with its many branches onto the driveway. I ventured forth with my handsaw as the only option at my disposal. Headway was slow and tortuous, until Daniel arrived with his bush knife. Where my saw had struggled, binding on the soft wood of the frangipani, Daniel's machete rapidly reduced the lost bough to kindling. Three strikes were all that was required to sever a branch the size of a forearm; smaller limbs were dispatched with one well-placed swing.

It was on the former site of that frangipani that I thought I would experience my first death in PNG. Night and the cover of darkness bring out the undesirable elements of any culture, and PNG is no different. To combat these "raskols" (thieves), we employed a night watchman. Of course, being an equatorial country. the length of night varies very little with sunrise and sunset. varying by scarcely an hour throughout the year. So even with our young family and the necessity of decent bedtimes, any visit to friends for supper would see us back at the compound after dark. Our guard would usually sit where the frangipani had been as this provided an almost unimpeded view of all corners of the fence line and also placed him face on to the gate.

Pulling our vehicle up to the fence one night, the guard failed to stir. Even as the headlights played over his face, there was no motion. The night really not being that old, there was no cause to keep our young ones quiet. Our kids being kids, it was unlikely that we could have kept them quiet anyway. *Slam! Bang!* went the sliding door on the van. Chatter between Sam and Matt conducted at full volume; Nate was not much more than one year old. Yet even with all the commotion, the guard stirred not. I said to Jennifer, "I think he's dead. You better take the kids inside." I walked cautiously over to him, in part afraid that he was dead and in part anxious that he wasn't and might jump to life and commence swinging at the white apparition emerging out of the shadows. With trepidation, I approached. Thankfully, the drowsy watchman awakened peacefully. This was not to be our sole encounter with sluggish night guards. Just another facet of cross-cultural life where we were obliged to adjust our expectations.

It was in Wewak that we instigated our family Friday-evening ritual, a custom that we maintain to his day, albeit in a form that has evolved over the years to match our current family status. Friday night is junk-food night. We also suspend normal rules of proper behavior, allowing certain latitude in what is considered acceptable. In Papua New Guinea, there were no restaurants as found in Canada at the time. No McDonalds. No DQ. No Pizza Hut. Whatever junk food we were to partake of was going to be from scratch. Hamburgers made from ground beef and buns from manually kneaded dough. Pizza, likewise, with a base mixed, raised, and spread on the pans by us. Fries began as potatoes purchased at the market in Mount Hagen. Maybe it was the investment of effort that made it a once-a-week special event. As the kids grew, building of Lego became part of the routine, as did watching a movie. In time, the imaginations of our little ones grew to the extent that Lego construction bled over to Saturday mornings.

There were less exciting ways to spend time not involved in flying. Self-sufficiency is a necessity on many foreign mission fields, especially in developing countries. Wewak did not have a town water supply, so our needs were met through collecting rainwater off the roof. The sound of rain hitting the corrugated metal roof became something of a comfort for our children, a sound that even now as adults they long for. The water would stream down the roof, into the gutters, then down into the large tanks to be delivered back into the house through an on-demand electrically powered pressure pump. Additionally, our house was equipped with a two-hundred-liter roof-mounted header tank to supply water pressure in the event of the all-too-frequent power blackouts that rendered the water pump useless. Another sound to which we became accustomed was the reverberation of a tree frog arriving on our water tank every suppertime. The small bright-jade-green frogs spent their days sleeping in the moist rain gutters, rousing themselves at dark to venture out. It was one of these intriguing creatures that met his end in our header tank.

Our dog Nugget was displaying signs of poor health, the source of which was something of a mystery. It is not uncommon for thieves to attempt to defeat guard dogs by feeding them batteries. We eliminated this as likely prospect and then narrowed the investigation to the water source. Nugget's water bowl was filled from a tap that ran directly from the header tank, and it did not smell right. As a pilot, many folks are surprised to learn that I have a fear of heights. More accurately, I have a fear of the sudden stop that follows a fall from a roof. Having no choice but to swallow my apprehension, I ventured onto the roof. Raising the lid of the header tank, I was assaulted by a smell so foul that in stepping back, I all but lost my footing.

Doing my best to limit breathing through my nose, I dared another peek into the water barrel: a ghostlike being floated just below the surface. Translucent white, it was patently the remains of a frog. As much as I detest heights, smells are possibly worse. I have an overly sensitive gag reflex that would repeatedly drive me back from the front line of this battle. An attempt to scoop the dead amphibian in one go was a miserable failure, serving only to raise the power of the stench. I was forced to make multiple trips from the tank to the edge of the roof, draining the tank one jug at a time. There was little Jennifer could do except send words of encouragement as I battled the combined acrophobia and nausea-inducing odour. Safety from falling lay back by the tank, but that put me in range of the rotting carcass. Retreat from the stench put me close the edge of the roof. In the end, we took the day cleansing the tank with a bleach solution before sealing the lid well and truly as a repeat of the incident was to be avoided.

While only the poor dog felt the result of the dead frog, other maladies assaulted the family. The question that needs to be answered by all tropics dwellers is that of malaria prophylaxis. They say the only way to not contract malaria is to not get bitten. The only way to avoid the female anopheles mosquito that carries and transmits malaria is to be safely inside at dusk, barricaded behind flywire or mosquito nets. Some say that malaria is perhaps inevitable when living in the lowlands, so it makes sense to treat the illness rather than attempt to prevent. Some say that antimalaria medicine is the best. Others select natural methods: tea made from papaya seeds.

With young children, we decided that we should go with traditional antimalarial medicine. With a baby, this is all but impossible however. Our regimen was chloroquin weekly and Paludrine daily—the double medicine since some strains of malaria are chloroquin resistant. We tried to use liquid chloroquin for Nate, but he just wouldn't take it; so in the end, we gave up and started on the pills at a very young age. Of course, a full-strength pill is not appropriate for children, and child doses are not available, so we had to cut the pills to size. Chloroquin pills are coated, which is good because they are terribly bitter in taste, but cutting the pill defeats this barrier and exposes the bitterness. We would give the kids their pill, make sure they had water, then tell them to pop the pill. Nate, however, had a tendency to grab the pill and throw it on his tongue before he had water available, exposing his taste buds to the full force of the nasty flavor. Before we could get that sorted, and before Nate reached his second birthday, he contracted malaria.

Malaria diagnosis is a bit of a black art. The pharmacy in Wewak could conduct the simple blood test: prick a finger and squeeze a drop of blood onto the test strip. The package shows three possible results, but the pharmacy had their own poster indicating in the order of twenty possible outcomes. It is my recollection that a positive test was the only reliable result, negative results not necessarily meaning freedom from malaria. Even knowing whether to get tested can be a predicament as the symptoms are random. It was clear that our little baby was in strife, and as a toddler, it was very difficult to get any sense from him about what he was feeling or to get medicine into him. He went down very rapidly, unable to even keep water down. Fortunately, we knew a missionary couple with a registered nurse. It appeared that we were going to need to bring out the big guns and so arranged for our friend to give Nate a shot of quinine. The one shot had a miraculous effect, with Nate recovering very quickly with no residual side effects.

That wasn't Nate's only medical adventure during our year in Wewak, nor was it our only chance to witness the recuperative powers of young children. The "shub" was a foreign beast to us when we moved to the southern hemisphere. Quite common in the houses we lived in, a shower tub, or shub, has the footprint of a stand-alone shower but the depth of a bathtub. Perfect as a bath for young children, not so much for those of larger stature. The thinner rim of the shub, in comparison to a bathtub, made us nervous for our newborn as he learned to crawl. In our nightmares, we pictured young Nate endeavouring to pull himself upright on the edge of the shub but then overbalancing on the narrow edge and face-planting into the tub. In light of this, we dictated a parental order to Sam and Matt that the bathroom door remain closed at all times, Nate was a slippery little fellow and fast on all fours when properly motivated.

Playing with his older siblings one day, he made a break for the bathroom door, which had been left ajar. Mindful of the parental decree and full of motherly parental instinct, Sam bolted for the door to close the offending hatch before Nate could come to irreparable harm. While Sam won the race to the gate, regrettably, it was a close-run thing to the extent that as the portal slammed shut, Nate's little pinky intercepted the doorjamb.

Prior to that, in spite of Nate being our third child, I had been unaware that an infant's finger was sufficiently pliable to be able to go flat as a pancake. Now I am really bad with the sight of blood on TV, but I handle the real thing without any trouble. I wasn't so good with prenatal videos but took the real births in stride. Jennifer is perhaps the other way round in that I was actually the emergency medical technician of the family. I was already at work when Nate's finger was squished, but Jennifer was still rather pale when I arrived home in response to the 911 sent my way. In Papua New Guinea, 911 doesn't exist. Ambulances barely exist. But in Wewak, there was a hospital. Not a hospital that you select given the choice, but at least a hospital. A hospital with a real doctor.

Not really knowing what the long-term implications of a crushed finger were, we elected to head for the hospital. Now, that might seem like an obvious choice, except the hospital is built on a swamp, and merely driving by increases one's exposure to the potential of contracting malaria. We managed to find the doctor, a rather crusty lady of Australian descent. She had clearly engaged with life in PNG, for she presented herself in bare feet. She was, however, very competent, knowledgeable, and caring. She had no doubt that Nate's finger would be just fine in no time at all. The Band-Aid she placed on it was, I am sure, a Band-Aid solely for the parents' benefit. It remained on the finger almost until we got back to our house. And the doctor was right, for by the next day, the finger had reinflated without even a scar as a war trophy.

With that experience in the background, we were slightly better prepared when Matt ran at full gallop into the post for the clothesline. The clothesline was actually one of those trees with one central post and four arms that stretch to the compass points, connected by rows of plastic-covered wire for the suspension of clothes to dry in the breeze. This specimen was a stout fellow, able to be raised and lowered in height above the ground through a system of hidden pulleys actuated by handle encased in a knuckle partway up the main trunk. This handle was conveniently placed for an average-height adult to apply the necessary leverage. Convenient for the adult, inconvenient for Matt's head, for the handle resided in line with Matt's eyebrow. Our two oldest children were playing outside in the tropical sunshine, some game that involved running and chasing. In a bid to escape his older sister, Matt made tracks for the end of the house.

Sam, in hot pursuit, could see that Matt's trajectory would involve a meeting with the immoveable clothes tree. Casting a rearward glance over his shoulder to try and make sense of her desperate warnings, Matt grasped the meaning of Sam's word and flung his glance back in the direction of travel in time to catch the grip of the handle just to the left and slightly above his right eye. I had heard that head wounds bleed. Personal experience had also left me with the impression that they hurt. Matt proved both of those hypotheses as he explained in unintelligible fits of screaming that he was indeed injured. Seeing as how he was bleeding somewhat profusely, a mere kiss on the head accompanied by a generous hug was just not going to do.

A trip to the hospital was judged to be potentially more dangerous than being fixed up by doctor dad. We rummaged through our first aid kit, which we had fortuitously well stocked with items we actually knew very little about. I also rummaged through my memory banks for something, anything, of relevance I might have subconsciously acquired in various first aid courses over the years. With Matt sufficiently calmed for me to be able to conduct some triage, I was fairly sure that stitches would normally be called for by any self-respecting medical professional. Distinctly lacking in medical qualifications yet convinced that I did not want to submit my son to the probable post-operative infection likely to result from a visit to the swamp hospital, I delved again into the first aid kit. While lacking in qualifications I did discover that we were not lacking in self-adhesive butterfly sutures. Deciding that a cool scar was the worst that could result from my activities, and since a scar on a boy's head is more socially acceptable than for a girl, I went ahead and closed the gash with a couple of my trusty sutures. Kids being what they are, Matt was off and running in no time, perhaps now more concerned with getting away from the hack surgeon than with garnering possible gifts of sympathy from his mother. There is a scar, a very small one, that you would miss if you didn't know to look for it.

In some ways, all of these adventures were minor in comparison to other things associated with lowlands living. There were the roaches. When we first moved into our Wewak home, we discovered we had cockroaches. It didn't seem like a massive infestation, but there were sufficient critters to make us want to deal with them, especially with Nate crawling around at the same level. We went on a search mission for cockroach motels, but unexpectedly to us, we could find none in the Wewak shops. In MAF PNG, if you can't find something where you are, one should always ask around because it might be available elsewhere. We started with our very helpful stores department in Mount Hagen and soon had a supply of baits with which to combat our unwanted guests. We set them up in the usual dark corners, mostly in the kitchen and in the cupboards. Next morning, we conducted a mass burial for the fourteen pests that had succumbed to the Mortein motels. Perhaps our house was harbouring a greater number of fugitives than we knew! The decontamination, however, was not powerful enough for all.

Once the sun had gone down and the children were asleep, our house was rather quiet, there generally being little disturbance on the outside road. Jennifer and I were quietly reading one evening when we became conscious of a strange sound emanating from the kitchen. The noise was similar to the sound of sandpaper on wood, only very light and gentle, like doing a finish sanding with fine grit paper on hard wood. Now, our house was the standard layout. Picture a square box with a divider splitting it in half, side to side, but extending through perhaps just two thirds of the square. On one side of the wall is the kitchen; on the opposing side is the living room with the remainder given over to the dining room. The kitchen and dining room were separated only by a countertop. From our seats in the living room, we could not quite see through to that part of the kitchen counter.

Initially, I ignored the random noise, attributing it to imagination. But when Jennifer had the same imagining, it was clearly time to investigate. I am not sure why, but we did move to the kitchen with stealth. We had barely rounded the corner of that dividing wall when we spied the source of the smooth, rhythmic scratching. We had left some stale bread on the counter edge to dry out to be turned into breadcrumbs, and perched atop that little pile was the largest roach I have ever seen. From across the room, I could see its mouth parts working the bread. Its legs were so long that light was visible beneath its body. Some people—my children—suggest that I am prone to exaggeration when it comes to animal stories.

They say I employ copious amounts of hyperbole (exaggeration for effect). I deny all allegations in that regard and in this instance maintain that if you can hear it eat, it is one major cockroach.

Cockroaches were not the worst that we had to contend with. Mould was the worst. I suspect when you think of mould, you conjure up images of the multicoloured growth of cheese gone bad, or possibly the furry aspect of a long-forgotten container of last month's dinner hiding in the back of the fridge. Tropical lowlands mould is more insidious, more invasive, and certainly not confined to the fridge. Our walls would quite literally grow. People may wonder why missionaries employ house help, but keeping the mould at bay in our Wewak home was practically a full-time occupation. The wall at the corner of our dining room was our test board. Our haus meri (house lady) could clean that wall to a sparkle. Give it just a single day, and that wall would lose its shine, transitioning through satin to a distinctly flat finish.

As we sat at dinner on day 3, tiny dots would have made an appearance. By day five, the wall colour had definitely shifted; and by the end of the week, the kids were drawing pictures in the stuff that was springing from the paint. About that time, the haus meri had completed cleaning the rest of the walls and was back at the beginning for the start of another lap. For a family new to the tropics, new to mission life, new to a lifestyle where all meals were made from scratch, and with a very young family, the constant battle against the invasion of the spores was quite demoralizing. But it was during that year that Jennifer came across Leviticus chapters 13 and 14.

I would hazard a guess that not many people are familiar with Leviticus. Sermons based on the third book of the Pentateuch are as rare as hen's teeth and Bible studies on the minutiae of Jewish law as exceptional as pink unicorns. So how exactly Jennifer stumbled into Leviticus, let alone making it through to chapter 13, is as miraculous as the raising of Lazarus. The second half of Leviticus chapter 14 goes into explicit detail about the cleansing of a house from mold. This was a revelation: God cares about mould? As a couple of kids having grown up in Christian families with the benefit of years of Sunday school and sermons and Bible college degrees, one would have thought we would have known this. I mean, I even took an entire course on the first five books of the Bible, being forced to read them through five times each, and still I had missed this nugget. I probably didn't care about mould in Bible college, but in Wewak, PNG, it was an unexpected revelation, a shock to discover that some five thousand years earlier, God had discussed mould in a way that would bring encouragement to a couple of newbie missionaries fighting culture shock, malaria, and mould.

Our little family in Wewak during our first year in PNG.

Delivering water containers for the transport of
clean water during a typhoid outbreak.

Villagers greet the plane during relief flights following cyclone Guba.

A couple of young cassowaries at Kopiago, Southern Highlands province.

# X-RAY

## ~ X-ray machines *and Tractors* ~

FROM CROCODILES TO goats, school books to bandages, water tanks to bridges if you can think of it, I have probably had it in the aircraft. Aside from the complete house we moved from Sendeni to Menyamya, and pipes for the hydro project in Marawaka, the most complex cargo would have to be the x-ray machines and the tractor.

I think whenever I mention having flown a tractor in the plane, people picture one of those cute little ride-on lawn mowers that look like a kid's go-kart with a hand mower slung underneath. On the other end of the spectrum, if you are a wheat farmer in Canada's prairies then your tractor is bigger than my plane. The entrance to the passenger cabin of a Twin Otter is comprised of two doors. The front door is the passenger entrance. The rear part is opened when the passenger cabin is transformed in whole or in part to cargo configuration. Together the two doors open up to create a cavity 1.25 meters high and 1.4 meters wide. While you couldn't drive your car through it, the portal is large enough for most items that we want to carry.

Traditional building methods in Papua New Guinea involve a bush knife and an axe as the primary and potentially only tools. When building a house this can be ok but constructing a school classroom calls for a little more finesse. There is lumber aplenty in the jungle, but in its raw form: a tree standing tall. An axe may see it to the ground, but cutting into planks requires something more industrial, like a portable sawmill. For the plane, walk-about sawmills are a squeeze. To my mind deceptively named, there is nothing either "walking" or "portable" about these machines. In major logging operations the tree goes to the mill, but for smaller projects in PNG, and even some larger ones, it is far easier to take the mill to the tree. Well, easier and cheaper for the customer. The Otter will carry sawn lumber effortlessly, but if the project calls for several loads it is far more efficient to take the mill to the trees. There are two relatively light aluminum rails that are usually a stretch for the internal length of an Otter. Though not large in diameter, due to their length the rails often need to go through the rear cargo doors at a tight angle, through the doorway that separates the cockpit from the cabin, into the cockpit to clear the rear entryway, before sliding back to the rear of the cabin. That is the easy bit. The engine is situated on a frame. Once erected, the frame slides back and forth along the two previously mentioned rails to compose a saw that can cut planks from full-length trunks. This frame with its engine is not just the heavy bit it is also the awkward bit. First off, the weight is not evenly distributed, one end being way heavier than the other. While the cargo doors can swallow the saw frame, the aircraft is not wide enough for the machine to enter straight in, so it has to be maneuvered, on an angle through the door, and then wiggled through a ninety-degree turn to settle into place inside the plane. Since the engine hangs below the frame, the skeleton rides on wheels. Unfortunately, to make it through the door the wheels need to come off. So once in the aircraft, there is considerable agitation among those involved in the process: those men supporting the ungainly device heartily encouraging others to "get the wheels on!"

In comparison with the tractor, those sawmills are a snap. The request came from our partners at New Tribes Mission to fly the tractor, front-end bucket loader, grass slasher and trailer from the coastal port of Wewak to Malamaunda hidden just inside the central range. There is neither road nor river to Malamaunda. If it were a military operation they would use an aircraft with a rear cargo ramp and parachute the tractor in. That option not being available to us, we sent the Otter. We were assured it would fit through the door, so off we went to Wewak. On arrival, we observed a small dump truck parked just off the ramp – the name for the area where an aircraft parks. Sitting upon said truck was a full-size tractor. The missionaries had thought this through: it is not possible to drive the tractor up a ramp into the aircraft, and pushing it with manpower was equally unlikely. I think they had figured it out by themselves that we would be stretched to get it through the door, such that the best chance of success would be to push the tractor straight off the truck and into the plane; the deck height of the truck being equal to the floor of the plane. We had allowed a significant amount of time to load the plane, guessing that this would be a puzzle only defeated with lots of talk and lots of sweat.

It isn't enough to get the items physically in the aircraft. They have to be balanced. Imagine trying to balance a pencil on your finger. Place a paper clip on one end and the pencil hits the floor. Place an identical paper clip on each end and the pencil remains on your finger. Try a bigger one and the clip cannot be at the end it must be closer to the point where the pencil rests on your finger. And that is the challenge in loading the plane; putting everything in with the aircraft on the ground, then attempting to fly it. Everything has to be positioned just so: too much weight forward and the plane will never get off the ground; too much weight aft and the plane will lift off and go vertical, then tailslide to an ignominious end.

As I recall we got the bucket in first and then went for the main event. With the dump truck backed up as close to the plane as space and nerve allowed we pondered the reality of maneuvering the tractor through the door. Although the tires were deflated, it made little difference; the tires were so new that releasing the air made them shrink only a smidge. With the nose through it was then rather obvious that the steering wheel was now a hindrance, so off it came. Now steering by pushing the front wheels the tractor slid through the door frame with bare millimeters of clearance. With the rest of the parts stowed in and around the tractor, we set to the task of securing the load. A runaway tractor is bad at the best of times, but in an airplane, it is rather more problematic than most scenarios. Fortunately, the weather held for our arrival into Malamaunda thirty minutes or so after departure. Then began the act two: the removal of said tractor, without the aid of a dump truck. With some onsite labour, we were able to remove everything stowed around the tractor. A couple of lengths of timber materialized from somewhere to function as wheel ramps. We ran a tie down strap around the front axle and out the emergency exit opposite the cargo door and installed willing helpers as an anchor. With great caution, and much trepidation, the tractor was steered, without the wheel remember, around the corner of the cabin, out the door and onto the makeshift ramps. With a second contingent of willing hands guiding it on its way the beast was soon back on terra firma. The uninformed would have thought we did this every day; why all the fuss? Things always seem to go out of the plane a lot more easily than they go in.

I think sometimes it is rather easy to take for granted the blessings we enjoy living in the west. We assume the availability of many things that most of the world has, at best, restricted access to. At some point in the midst of his childhood development, Nate went through a phase when he was seemingly always "broken". There was the time he ripped open his ankle right down to the bone, calling for three layers of stitches. He may have broken a finger two or three times; I lost count. Then there was the ankle again; a greater possibility of a break at that time. The school used to run a sort of fair on or around September sixteenth, Papua New Guinea Independence Day. Each grade would be responsible for providing two or three activities for the mission community, and the local PNG community to have fun with. Nate was maybe eleven, and in his super competitive stage, and there was a timed obstacle course. Perhaps I need say no more? One of the obstacles was a pile of six barrels; empty 200-liter aviation fuel drums set on their sides; three on the bottom, then two, then one on top. The racer was supposed to climb up and over the stack. The first few racers carefully climbed up one side and then climbed down the other. As the course times decreased it became clear to all that one way to shave a few seconds was to jump from the top of the stack of barrels rather than climbing down. The pinnacle would have been around five to six feet high. Nate ran the course on multiple occasions endeavouring to hold down the top spot for the fastest time. Unbeknown to us, on one attempt he had landed poorly as he flung himself from the peak of the mountain, sustaining damage to his ankle. Being tough, and motivated, he continued to run the course, injured as he was. Each successive touchdown following the flight from the crest resulted in further damage to the weakened hinge. Eventually, someone sought us out and informed us that Nate "seemed to have hurt his leg". By the time we tracked him down he was all but lame, and I finished the Independence Day celebrations carrying Nate around on my back.

In the midst of these adventures, young Nate had required a number of x-rays to determine the extent of his self-inflicted injuries. In Goroka, the medical clinic of New Tribes Mission was very gracious to attend to our health complaints, including two Achilles tendon ruptures sustained by Nate's father – me – while playing soccer. In the early days, the clinic did not possess an x-ray machine, so Jennifer had to be brave and take Nate to the local hospital for his x-ray. I wish I could find the words to describe the adventure of going to the hospital. I have been there a couple times, once following the passing of one of our PNG workmen. It is hard to describe the difference of that hospital from the one I know you are picturing in your mind. When I was a child I sustained a skull fracture relating to my inability to properly negotiate a slide. That was back at the dawn of the seventies. If you are able to picture a hospital from that long ago, then you are perhaps Forty percent of the way to envisioning the Goroka Hospital. The condition was as much about funding as anything. Nevertheless we were happy to have access to an x-ray machine. For most of Papua New Guineans, this is a luxury they are denied.

Some sixty kilometers northwest of Mount Hagen, capital of the Western Highlands Province, lies a hidden valley. It cradles a tiny offshoot of the Sau River, a waterway that is named on the pilots' charts, but practically indistinguishable from the air. The dead-end valley holds the community of Kompiam. As insignificant as it appears on the map, it is even more so in the view from the plane. And yet, it is the district administrative center. More importantly to the peoples of Yenkis, Pyarulama, Megau, Mengamanau, Labalama and more, it is the location of their hospital. Established in years long before my time, the Baptist Mission hospital is the only place of refuge for the sick and injured for miles around. MAF planes are regularly called upon to conduct medevacs and patient transfers to and from this bastion of care. It is actually possible to drive from Mount Hagen to Kompiam if you are stalwart and brave. The journey begins traveling west from Mount Hagen to a little junction call Togoba. The vehicle then picks up the road northwest to Wapenamanda. It meanders fifty plus kilometers on and around various mountain slopes, through Balk and Kamaga, up and over the Tomba Gap, before descending into Wapenamanda. The road continues northwest for another thirty-five kilometers to the Kompiam turnoff, just before reaching Wabag. I urge you to think more "poorly maintained back-country road" than major highway. And that is before the turn-off. From that point on the remaining twenty-five kilometers are more akin to a cow path than something recognizable as safe passage for a vehicle. Perhaps that is why MAF was asked to fly in not one, but two x-ray machines for the hospital.

The instruments had begun their journey 15,000 kilometers from their eventual destination. Initially traveling by sea, the x-ray machines had originated in Spain making land at the Port of Lae on the North Coast of PNG. From there the few kilometers of road inland to Nadzab airport that serves the city of Lae is fairly reasonable. For sensitive equipment that is about as far as you would want to venture by truck, especially as the manufacturer had marked that the contents of the packing crates were "muy fragile". The Highlands Highway, which isn't a highway as you and I might define it does reach from Lae to Mt Hagen. The first couple hundred kilometers race across the floor of the Ramu River Valley, the flat road coming to an abrupt termination at "the Kassam". The Kassam Pass is where the highway makes its way from the Ramu up into the highlands. Fifteen or so kilometers of switchbacks and gradients transitions the road from sea level to 5000 feet above sea level. Going up is a chore for the driver and a trial for the cooling system of the vehicle. Coming down is a test of both nerves and brakes.

We flew the Otter the thirty-five minutes from Goroka to Nadzab to carefully load the expensive cargo. We did our very best to execute the smoothest of takeoffs; working hard to find the quietest air on the 420 kilometers run to Kompiam. All our efforts could have been for naught however for at the end of the journey we were still faced with the airstrip at Kompiam. While at 700 meters in the length the runway is plenty for an Otter, and the slope is insignificant in PNG terms at three percent, the dry gravel and grass mix of the surface is not designed for smooth landings of aircraft transporting sensitive medical equipment. In addition, the circuit at Kompiam is best described as "non-standard ". The pilot conducts a little of what is known as "contour flying": driving the aircraft close to the terrain that infringes on the normal operating area to gain the space needed to set up the aircraft for landing. Tracking on an oblique angle to the runway, the pilot aims at the bedroom window of a tiny house on a mountain slope that blocks what constitutes a normal final approach to the runway. Seemingly at the last moment, the pilot banks the aircraft hard to the right, rolls wings level and a handful of seconds later the aircraft is over the runway settling for touchdown. For any other aircraft the touchdown would quite possibly scramble the electronic brains of the x-ray machines, but this is a de Havilland Canada (now Viking Canada) Twin Otter, and this is the kind of mission at which the *TwOtter* excels.

Over the threshold at a target speed of about sixty-eight knots for a maximum performance STOL (Short TakeOff and Landing) landing; a gentle pull on the control column to raise the nose. Feel the sink towards the ground. Roll the right wrist forward on the power lever grips in anticipation of the wheels touching the gravel. With the nose pointing skyward the over-size main wheel tires skim the grass as I hold off the touchdown, bleeding speed in a concentrated effort to have the vertical speed reach zero as the tires compress onto the runway. Then a twist of the grips and a slight backward pull on the power lever to slip the propellers into beta range, pre-cursor of reverse thrust. Holding the nose wheel off the ground as long as possible; grudgingly permitting it to alight onto the stone runway. And that is how we do a soft landing on a gravel runway, safely delivering x-ray machines into a hospital in the middle of nowhere serving isolated people that have been forgotten by all but God and his people. I have zero recollection of how we got the large crates out of the aircraft and onto the back of the truck. My part in the delivery was complete, and as near as we could judge a success. The last kilometer of the journey from the airstrip to the hospital was, thankfully someone else's concern.

# YANKEE

## ~Yawa *and My Hero Friedemann~*

"DR. LIVINGSTONE, I presume?"—the fabled and perhaps fanciful greeting attributed to Henry Stanley on finding Dr. Livingstone in 1871 on the shores of Lake Tanganyika in present-day Tanzania. The event conjures up images of missionaries dressed in lightweight tropical suits and pith helmets, or dresses stretching from neck to ankle, even in the heat of sub-Saharan Africa. Associated in my mind with those images are the same people partaking of afternoon tea. There are reports from the early days of mission aviation of pilots being met by missionaries in the remotest of locations with tea and cake. For me, these stories fell into the class of legend or even myth:—until I landed at Agali during the very early days of my flight training in Papua New Guinea.

There is little to recommend Agali as a destination of choice. It is a tiny village isolated on a plateau above the Strickland River. The runway is not overly challenging, but the approach can be fun when the wind is rattling around the mountain peaks that guard the tableland. Training for pilots with MAF in PNG begins with observer flying. Travelling around with an experienced pilot for a few days allows a new pilot to see how all the bits of the puzzle fit together so he has a good understanding of the ultimate objective of his training. It was all rather overwhelming at the start. There was so much to learn.

The day began with early-morning departure from Mount Hagen for the high altitude forty-five-minute run across the Kandep basin into Tari. From there, it was along the Kopiago Valley to the west before curling around into Agali. Memories fade with time, and I am sure there must have been a couple more landings in there before we landed at Agali. However, the memory that is as vibrant as the day it happened was the reception we received. The missionary couple came to greet us and placed a tray on the tail plane of the aircraft. On the tray, Coke in glasses, with ice! Life is full of surprises, but for me, that was the very definition of unexpected. To receive anything was unanticipated. For it to be Coke in a glass was startling. For there to be ice was astonishing. There is no electricity in Agali, so the ice would have been made in a kerosene freezer. There are no shops in Agali. Any store-bought goods are like gold, so a gift of Coke was an incredible sacrifice. Perhaps also an indication of the esteem granted to mission pilots by the missionaries we are privileged to serve. A visit of an aircraft is a welcome interruption to the isolation in which missionaries often serve in developing countries, so we take a moment to say hi, exchange inbound and outbound mail, and sometimes just lend an ear. These are the people that are my heroes: the missionary families that minister at the ends of the earth.

Bu'u (boo-oo) is easily at the extreme edge of the far end of remote. It is a very difficult airstrip: short, steep, undulating, and ridiculously slippery. The only reason MAF ever flies to Bu'u is to serve the ministry of missionaries Ray and Cheryl; and with limited reason to go there, it is a challenge to train new pilots for this runway. Ray and Cheryl's house is located halfway up the strip with the parking bay at the very top. Preferred aircraft parking is beside the house due to the problems of carrying cargo down the steep incline.

Following one landing during which we blew right by the house, I turned around to taxi back down the hill to park beside the house. Probably not my best decision. The Twin Otter is pretty good going downhill so long as undertaken with great care, but that day, the strip was so slick that any attempt to turn put the plane into a sideways drift. It took every ounce of my experience, which by that time was quite significant, to bring the plane to a stop in the desired spot. Fear that the plane was headed over the edge was clearly etched on the faces of the spectators. When our family moved to Goroka, Tim was my training captain for learning the ill-mannered and unpredictable temperament of Bu'u. Visits to Bu'u from outsiders were few and far between, and Ray and Cheryl invited us in for morning tea. The weather at Bu'u on our training day was unexpectedly fine and clearly going to remain that way, so we were thrilled to be able to accept their invitation. It was a privilege to share with this amazing couple. That wasn't my only opportunity to partake of Ray and Cheryl's hospitality.

Whether due aircraft breakdown or foul weather, some of my pilot colleagues seemed to get stranded "out bush" on a regular basis. During our time in Papua New Guinea, I was fortunate to get stuck just once. Weather at Bu'u is most predictable in the early morning, so all flights there are planned to occur first in the day and as early as possible. The weather at Bu'u would best be described as putrid. The strip at Bu'u is concealed in a tight little valley on the edge of the Staniforth Range in the shadow of White Slip Mountain, far from the MAF Goroka base. There is little to no room to manoeuvre at the strip, but when the weather is uncooperative, it is more often the takeoff after an eventful approach that creates the difficulty. After takeoff, the pilot must guide the aircraft into a right turn to follow the valley out to the lowland to the south. Prior to takeoff, seeing around this corner is all but impossible in conditions of rain and low cloud.

Having negotiated several layer of cloud, we got the Twin Otter onto the ground with no real drama. But as soon as the engines were stopped, the heavens opened, and the cloud descended like a cold wet blanket. Ray and Cheryl once again invited us into their home. We ventured forth several times throughout the long day, always with optimism, but never with reward. The valley remained filled with an impenetrable gloom that persisted till the sun set. The following morning, the weather was not awesome, but at least sufficient for us to safely depart. On reflection, I was happy to have spent those twenty-four hours with Ray and Cheryl, for it permitted a window into their world of ministry and, from my perspective, sacrifice.

The Marawaka Valley is full of villages and runways: Andakombe, Boikoa, Asinuwe, Ande, Usarumpia, Marawak, and Sendeni. Sendeni is the place from which we moved a complete house. It is the place that we had an aircraft come to grief caught in a massive wind downdraft. It was also the home of Andrew and Cathy. Missionaries with New Tribes Mission, their boys were friends of our boys at school in Goroka. The communities of the Marawaka Valley produce many tonnes of high-grade coffee beans, and with no roads, the only route to market is the plane. With the Twin Otter capable of lifting eight hundred kilograms at one gulp, it still takes multiple trips to clear out a season's harvest, so we visit Sendeni many times. Andrew and Cathy's home is adjacent to the runway, so when they are in Sendeni, they often pop out to say hi, sometimes providing a coffee when we have a couple minutes to spare. Homeschooled at the start, once their kids entered the high school years, they were off to boarding school for eight weeks at a stretch. In the early years, the only communication available was HF radio, which does not allow for private chats as anyone with that frequency on their radio can listen in.

As time passed, e-mail over HF became an option, but it was very slow and unable to handle anything more than short text. Eventually, cell phone coverage extended into the Marawaka Valley and, with it, better e-mail connection. Of course, the cell phone tower only worked as long as there was sun to charge the batteries through the solar panels, or fuel in the tank for the backup generator when cloud cover obscured the sun. Of course, if the cloud persisted, then the fuel supply would be expended, and helicopters would not be able to make replenishment flights, and the cell phone tower would die. With our kids in the same school as Andrew and Cathy's, I would be able to pass on first-hand accounts of goings-on at the school, reports of sports games and other social events. Jennifer and I decided early on that our family members were not good candidates for boarding school, mom and dad included. Many mission families undertake this route as a necessity for remaining on the mission field, some surviving and some even thriving, but it wasn't for us. I have high regard for those that figured out how to make it work to the advantage of their children.

For airplane fanatics, 17 December 1903 is an historic date. Most believe that on that day, powered, controlled flight by a machine heavier than air was accomplished for the first time. Real die-hard aviation buffs will know that there remains some minor controversy around this claim. Of course, most people don't care about this debate, and the same majority are equally unconcerned with the rapid progress in aircraft design over the next forty-five years. By the end of World War II on 2 September 1945, airplanes had matured into machines with practical value. Christian pilots who had flown in battle were convinced that the airplane could be used for more than destruction, so Mission Aviation Fellowship was birthed in the aftermath of six years of devastation. These pilots knew that in countries now developing, the plane would be a great tool in the missionary endeavour. MAF embarked on a journey to make the plane the feet of the Gospel. From those early days of only flying missionaries, Mission Aviation Fellowship has developed into a team that multiplies the effectiveness of thousands of partners. Among those is my dear friend, Pastor Kimin.

Long before our family moved to live in the highlands town of Goroka, Dave and Carol left their hometown and country to minister to the people of Karimui District through church planting and pastoral training. As PNG goes, Karimui airstrip is "easy as pie." For the Twin Otter, it is a straightforward eighteen-minute flight from Goroka. In decent weather, aircraft departing Goroka head for the Kawkaw Gap (pronounced the same as the noise a crow makes). Hopping this low point in the range that guards the western edge of the Goroka valley, pilots either continue their climb to cross the nine-thousand-foot Elimbari Ridge, or deke left to pass overhead the disused airstrip at Nambaiyufa on the eastern slope of Elimbari. Looking ahead, there is the Waghi River, with the unofficially named Nomane ridge on the opposite side. Tagged with this title by pilots because of the Nomane community and airstrip lodged on its slope, it is the same piece of terrain that holds the runway at Aibai. In good weather and minimal wind, the most direct route is straight over the ridge, but it only adds a couple minutes to the flight to bear slightly left and follow the Tua River Valley all the way to the Karimui basin.

In rotten weather, this is the only course available, and even then poses a couple of gates that must be negotiated.

The valley at the junction of the Waghi and Tua Rivers narrows dramatically and takes an S-turn that is a magnet for rain and its associated reduced visibility. Pilots navigating this path must fly so as to be able to peer around the corner before committing to the passage while leaving themselves sufficient room to reverse their course. In such conditions, pilots select "poor weather configuration," slowing down and extending the wing flaps that permit safe flight at slower speeds; slower speed resulting in a smaller turning radius, which is a necessity to avoid an unscheduled encounter with an unyielding mountainside. The valley widens slightly for the next few kilometers before the final chicane. In the space of eleven kilometers, the valley shrinks in width and turns 90 degrees right, followed by a bend 135 degrees left then an immediate final curve about 70 degrees right again. Even at "poor weather configuration," it is all over in less than four minutes. At its tightest and in the worst weather, the valley constricts to little more than a kilometer. Thankfully, the conditions are rarely that poor; and in the Twin Otter, we would just climb to an altitude that clears the mountains and punch through the clouds.

MAF pilots based in Goroka have flown that route back and forth thousands of times over the years in support of the development of the community as a whole and Dave and Carol as missionaries. Pastor Kimin is one of those who was mentored by Dave and Carol during their long years of service. The student has become the teacher as Pastor Kimin now travels within a fifty-kilometer radius of Karimui, reaching out to other communities like Bomai, Negabo, and Pinero. Fifty kilometers may not seem far, but without roads and a vehicle, it is all on foot, except for when he can fly with MAF. The way MAF partners with Kimin is quite different than our relationship with Dave and Carol, but the connection is no less vital.

The account of the skirmish at Karimui that resulted in the utilization of my poor first aid skills has a second chapter. As the rabble-rousers worked their disturbance, some of the passengers attempted to rescue their belongings while others tried to remonstrate with the troublemakers. In the midst of the chaos, one of the original three angry men raised his bush knife above his head and prepared to strike an innocent person from behind. It reminded me of one of those movies with knights in armour. Our family has visited the Tower of London in England and saw a great display of medieval weapons, including giant two-handed swords. The scene replays in my mind, and it plays out like one of those knights of old wielding one of those massive blades. I am certain the machete was nothing in comparison to that sword of old, but there is no doubt it was the longest blade I ever saw in PNG. And with the man poised to strike with all his might and anger channeled through the steel, I was certain I was about to witness a man being cleaved in two from head to toe. It was another of those slow-motion moments where I knew there was nothing I could do. I could not possibly reach the area in time; I didn't even know what to do. Then out of nowhere, unexpected, a small figure appeared and wrapped that would-be murderer and his "sword" in a bear hug the likes of which you have never seen. With all the action that was taking place, I am certain this little scene was observed by just a few.

In a split second, the action passed by; but in that instant, that moment of time, I had witnessed the saving of a life, probably several lives. Pastor Kimin, with no regard for his own life, had jumped in to save another. MAF is about transforming in the name of Christ, and transformation is seen when people put aside their normal assumptions of right and wrong, go against their culture when necessary, to present Christ. Pastor Kimin saved several lives that day, one physically and actually, and several more due to the PNG culture of retribution known as "payback." PNG culture says if you kill one of mine, then I will kill one of yours. Then because I killed one of yours, you will need to kill one of mine. It never ends. By stopping that one murder, Pastor Kimin avoided a narrative of violence that would likely have continued for generations.

They say that Christianity in PNG is a mile wide and an inch deep. I think that could be said of many countries, including my own. In PNG, this statement is reflective of the history of missions. Over the years since World War II, PNG has received thousands of missionaries. Today the towns have many churches that operate with no restrictions. While there are still remote villages that have never received the Gospel, many have but remain in dire need of discipleship. There are stories of isolated communities where the pastor can't even read. There are also many villages where the government is not yet able to sustain health and education. It is to these many communities that churches now reach out to preach, teach, and heal the sick through training programs, schools, and health clinics. These men and women of Papua New Guinea are also in my book of heroes. I may be privileged to fly them out to the jungle and bring them back, but in the interval between those events, those Christians hike the rainforest and cross swollen rivers on what are called bridges but do not resemble any bridge you have ever walked on. They reach out to their own, for that is their calling.

While our family was living in Wewak, I made many flights in support of Pacific Island Ministries in Ambunti. PIM works in a variety of areas: medical orderly training and provision of medical supplies, literacy and schooling, provision of potable water, pastoral training. Doug and Leah lived there, along with Friedemann and Elfrieda and their three young boys. Friedemann was a second-generation missionary to PNG. His dad had "built" a number of airstrips in the East Sepik while Friedemann was still a child himself. Ambunti was the center of the PIM ministry that reaches out to multiple communities. It was a Thursday when I flew the Cessna 206 into Ambunti to pick up Friedemann to fly him to Yawa. To be honest, as I left Yawa that day, I was glad I wasn't staying. When I returned a week later and heard what Friedemann had been up to, I was really glad I hadn't stayed.

I had actually flown Friedemann to Yawa 1. He was going to walk to Yawa 4 to see how things were progressing with construction of their airstrip. Yawa 1 and 4 are only six miles apart, but there isn't even a bush road to connect them. It takes eight hours to cover the six miles of steaming jungle and murky rivers. The swamps are chest deep, full of slimy bloodsuckers and plenty of malaria-transmitting mosquitoes. On our fairly frequent flights together, I came to understand that Friedemann invariably contracted malaria on his village trips, coming down with the symptoms a week after he returned home. Untreated malaria can be deadly. Treated, it can be a cruel experience with symptoms similar to flu, only far more debilitating. Because malaria is actually a blood-dwelling parasite, the symptoms will only abate if the parasites are dealt with. Combinations of treatments are necessary to fully eradicate the little bugs. Unless the medicine targets the liver where the parasites originally lodge, a recurrence is almost certain. Knowing that he would almost certainly be ill in the week after his trip, I always found it incredible that he would still go out.

Having survived the outbound trek, Friedemann spent his days inspecting the airstrip work site and communicating with the people what they needed to do to complete the construction. Evening hours were invested in Bible study; the community gathered round the fire discussing things of God. Spending time visiting in a jungle village is far from a fun camping trip. Digestive systems unaccustomed to local cuisine rebel in unpleasant ways. Beds are present in name only. Unusual scents assault the nasal passages. At the end of a week, the body is beyond worn. The thoughts of having to hike back through the swamp must have been demoralizing. With no means of communication, all I could do was arrive at Yawa 1 at the agreed upon time and hope that Friedemann had made it back. Freidemann was visible even from one thousand feet overhead the runway. When I landed the aircraft to take him home, Friedemann's smile was broad, tired but broad. I pulled the mixture lever to starve the engine of fuel, turned off the ignition, flicked the electrical master switch, and cracked open the door. Sliding out of the seat and ducking as I stepped out from under the wing, Friedmann greeted me, "I'm so glad to see you. I was afraid that you wouldn't be able to come."

The official motto of the United States Coast Guard is Semper Paratus ("Always Ready"). I think perhaps the unofficial mission statement, first uttered by Patrick Etheridge in 1954, would be, "You have to go out, you don't have to come back." I think this applies to my mission heroes: they know they have to go out, but do so with no guarantees of how or if they will come back. I am just glad to have helped a few of these heroes go and come back.

# ZULU

## -Zebras *and Other Things*
## *I Don't Understand-*

No, THERE ARE no zebras in Papua New Guinea! But I still wonder, are zebras black with white stripes, or white with black stripes? I know for certain if I asked my daughter, having studied animal science at university, she would have an answer. It would entail large scientific words far beyond the comprehension of a simple pilot. There would be words like *chromosome* and *pigment* thrown in. Some say that because the hair on the bellies is white, the zebras are certainly white with black stripes. The opposition cries that because beneath the hair, zebra skin is black, then they are assuredly black with white stripes. The scientists join in with their words heavy with Latin etymology, and I am lost. There are many other things that I do not understand: Why did God create mosquitos? Why are people afraid of flying? Why are other peoples' customs so strange?

Culture shock. If you have had the privilege of visiting a country other than your own and stepped outside the established tourist zones, then you know what I am talking about. It is that feeling one gets upon realizing that you are no longer at home. It is a disquiet, a comprehension that you do not understand the rules of the society in which you are standing. It is the alarming recognition that you are as helpless as a newborn baby. The language is foreign, the food is unfamiliar, the currency is alien. Culture shock is best absorbed by preparation, mental and emotional. Expectation is both friend and enemy. Anticipation of culture shock may lessen the harsh blows. Presumption of knowledge and preparedness are potential knockout thumps.

Jennifer and I experienced our most potent culture shock not upon entering Papua New Guinea but during our orientation process in Australia. We expected that PNG would be so far removed from our experience as to be unimaginable, and we were not disappointed in that. By contrast, I think we never imagined that Australia could be uncomfortable; after all, it is a country of the Commonwealth, uttering at least a vague representation of the queen's English. Money is accounted in dollars and cents. Driving may be on the wrong side of the road, but there are traffic lights and stop signs that people obey. Could we have been more wrong? No disrespect to all my Australian friends, but at first blush, this was one bizarre country. I mean, all I wanted was a coffee, but the board offered me the choice between a "short black" and a "flat white." How could a man with red hair be called "blue"? My son was sick and needed to see a doctor; look for one that advertises "bulk billing," I was told. We were invited to a "barbie" for New Years. I am a grown man, and married at that. I thought, why would we want to attend an event apparently in honour of a girl's plastic doll? Is this some strange cult? Fortunately, before we embarrassed ourselves totally, we learned that a "barbie" is a "barbeque." As if that wasn't enough, we then made the acquaintance of some New Zealanders and made the internal assumption that those from NZ and Aus are approximately equal. If you are from NZ, please forgive me for this most egregious sin.

Our family was attending MAF orientation along with some other families, two of which were from New Zealand. The first family had a son whose birthday was within days of our son Matt's third birthday. As they were the same age and we were all separated from family and friends, the moms decided that a joint celebration was in order. Liam's mom suggested cheerios and tomato sauce as appropriate party fare. Jennifer covered her confusion with the assertion that we would provide mini pizzas. The postplanning conversation in our house went something like this: "Oat cereal and tomato puree? We better tell the kids to keep their comments to themselves." Turns out that in NZ, English cheerios are cocktail sausages and tomato sauce is ketchup.

The other family, who became good friends that we crossed paths with over the years, really set me back on my heels. It was Kate who covered me in confusion. Funnily enough, the four adults were engaged in a conversation about differences between our two home countries when Kate asked me, "Do you wear skivvies all year long?" I was speechless, dumbfounded, gobsmacked—I learned that one from the Aussies. *That's rather personal,* I thought to myself. *I mean, I don't think we know each other well enough to be discussing my choice in appropriate undergarments for summer versus winter.* Some carefully worded question of clarification yielded the information that in NZ, a "skivvy" is a mock turtleneck.

There were, of course, many instances of culture shock and confusion over customs in PNG. I remember one such event on one of my very first observer flights. Training for new pilots with MAF PNG starts with simply watching. A new pilot is paired with an experienced pilot to observe. The newbie has no responsibilities for the flight. All he has to do is watch how the pilot flies, see how he does the paperwork, witness how he interacts with the people at the airstrips. We had landed the aircraft at Eleme, just past the Yuat Gap where the Yuat River breaks out of the highlands into the Sepik plain. I recall little about that day, except for the distraught wife with the stone. She was, in fact, wife number two, or maybe number one; it is so hard to know unless you are told. The husband was one passenger, travelling with his other wife to the "big city" of Mount Hagen. The left-behind wife was not amused, and failing in her first attempts to drag him from the aircraft, she then proposed to disrupt his travels by damaging the aircraft. Others in the community managed to disarm the lady, laughing most of the time, perceiving her threats to be idle. Questions swirled in my mind: *Why was this funny? Why did he need two wives? Why would he want two wives? Why did he not seem to care for this wife whom he had married?* Questions for which there are no answers.

Throughout my stories, I have shared of the priority of relationship. My understanding is that this is borne out of generations of tribal allegiance. In a country where survival is historically dependent on cooperation, family comes first. The extended family must function as a unit to build houses, plant gardens, and protect one another from hostile intruders. Offences cannot go uncountered, for to extend mercy, grace, and forgiveness would be to invite further invasion. And eye for eye is not enough; payback must raise the stakes. I think that perhaps this is human nature, but the shock is that in Western culture, we don't kill because we fear prison; we conceal our desire for retaliation under a veneer of civility. But as I learned by living within this society, I couldn't help but wish for a little of the wantok system.

A "wantok" is anyone who speaks the same language, who has "one talk" in common with you. These are brothers and sisters for whom a Papua New Guinean must and will give everything. Traditionally, there is no need for social assistance or retirement funds. No reason for there to be a food bank or adoption service. I desire in our Canadian towns a little more of care for our neighbor, a little less selfish ambition.

I try to understand how all of these customs play out in real life, but some of it just does not compute. My definition of common sense is absent. My description of rational behavior is not applicable. Democratic elections in developing countries are often a challenge. During our time in Papua New Guinea, this was certainly true. Like most cross-cultural observations, outsiders need to be cautious about passing judgments as there is much to be understood. In PNG, where the primary responsibility is traditionally to the family, then voting is often along the lines of family allegiance rather than political party and ideology. With a population below seven million yet over 800 languages and a parliament that comprises just 111 seats, there is potential for disagreement. The simple math suggests that if each language group represents a tribe, and each tribe wants to elect a member of their family to represent them in government, then at least seven people will run for each seat. It is actually more like nine because twenty-two seats are taken up by the governors of the twenty-two provinces. So for governor, there could be thirty-six candidates for each seat.

There is much at stake in national elections as to win means access to government funds for the next five years. There are usually allegations of corruption, with counter-accusations of vote buying, and counter-counter claims of ballot fraud. In elections, these battles can often boil over into actual street fights, resulting in closure of roads, hospitals, airports, and other services. Just when it seems that civil war will break out, there will be the announcement of a meeting, of an agreement, and the next day people will be back at work, the streets will be calm, and everyone will be acting like nothing happened. From my Canadian perspective, I don't understand the uncontained violence, and neither do I comprehend how it all returns to normal so quickly. Yet from the PNG perspective, it all makes sense. I won't begin to try and explain it to you.

Perhaps one of the customs that people from Western countries understand least and that gets them upset is the tradition of "bride price." In countries where there is significant social pressure for gender equality, I fear that the assumption for Westerners is that any people group who do not strive for this, who do not make it happen are backward and ignorant. I think that this point of view is based on a lack of knowledge of customs and the very real cultural groaning that is happening in these countries. In chapter "India," I introduced Immanuel Jude, who is my age but was born in the stone age. We would do well to remember from whence we have come. The "wantok system" in its original form has distinct advantages, especially in a lifestyle that is based on subsistence farming. And so it is with "bride price."

The custom of bride price is actually found in the Bible, in the Old Testament story of Isaac. When sent by Abraham to find a wife for his son Isaac, Abraham's servant "gave costly gifts to [Rebekah's] brother and to her mother" (Genesis 24:53, NIV). The custom was repeated when Jacob married Leah and Rachel, working for seven years for each them for their father, Laban (Genesis 29:20, 27). In Papua New Guinea, a man must pay the family of the lady he wants to marry. The price is negotiated and is based in part on what the loss of the daughter means to the community. Additionally, the would-be husband is probably not in a position to pay the amount as the bride price can be a combination of several pigs, cassowaries, as well as cash and miscellaneous household items and food. A single pig can cost in excess of a month's wages. It is then the man's family that, in the tradition of wantok, will come together to meet the obligation. But this is not a simple financial transaction, for the transfer of the wealth occurs at a party. Paying of bride price is a celebration, in fact, quite possibly a series of celebrations as it can take years to complete the full payment. And lest you believe this is still the selling of a woman, if the husband mistreats the wife, it is quite within the realm of possibility that the lady's family will seek revenge, in true PNG style.

No doubt this sill seems strange to many, yet traditionally marriage would occur within the tribe, so bride price was a way of redistributing wealth within the extended family. In turn, this would keep everyone on equal financial footing, so reducing the chances of thievery and infighting within the tribe. And suddenly bride price starts to make some sense. Have you ever wondered why ladies receive engagement rings, why men do not? There is a lot of sociology in the answer, but one part of the puzzle is that the engagement ring replaced the tradition of bride price!

Imagine now that you are trying to explain Jesus to someone whose understanding of laws and courts is limited, perhaps nonexistent. How does one begin to put in plain words that we are all evil people, in need of a Savior to *pay the price* for our sins. And yet the explanation is already there. The Bible tells us that Christ gave Himself for the church, as his wife (Ephesians 5:23–25). No man has paid a greater price for his bride. The church is the bride of Christ, and the bride price is paid. In our culture, this makes no sense to us. Unexpectedly to me, bride price makes the Bible real to some of the other people that Jesus came to save.

# EPILOGUE

WHEN I RECOUNT the tale of how our family ended up in Papua New Guinea with Mission Aviation Fellowship, I begin just as I began this narrative of our family's adventures in PNG: "It streaked across the night sky. It was more felt than seen. As if sprinting away from its own noise, attempting to capture its own silence." I then reveal how, one evening, at a little church campground, God spoke to me and asked me to fly for Him. I follow up with this: if I knew then what I know now, I would have raced away! Only, that isn't true. Not even a little bit, for I wouldn't trade any of it. Jennifer would no more surrender those memories than yield up our children. Samantha, Matthew, and Nathaniel wouldn't trade fires and beaches and swimming holes for all the movies and fast-food restaurants that Canada has to offer. Their returns to Canada, their passport country but yet to be home, were rocky and emotional. But they will tell you that the price was worth it. I know because I have asked them.

From my first training flight in Papua New Guinea on 10 June 1999, through to my final ride on 20 May 2016, I recorded in my pilot logbooks 9,594.3 hours of flying; 18,661 takeoffs and 18,661 landings. In flying, it is a good thing for those two numbers to match. My last day, my final duty was to do a check flight with Brad, to certify him as an MAF Twin Otter captain. We took off in the morning under clear skies headed for Ande and then Wonenara. We returned to Goroka and then went southwest to Negabo and Appa. The final run took us from Goroka to Guwasa, followed by Maimafu and one final return to our home in Goroka. The day had been sweet with good weather and everything going more smoothly than we could expect. As I lined up on runway 35 left for that last landing, I spied the airport fire trucks parked astride the taxiway entrance to the

277

MAF parking bay. As I cleared the runway, the fire engines lit up their water cannon to generate an arch beneath which I drove the airplane. In aviation, the liquid frame is offered in recognition of achievement. The water cascaded all over the aircraft, and I had to turn on the windshield wipers so I could see where we were going. As I turned the corner, we were greeted by the sight of my best copilot—my Jennifer—and a group of well-wishers, organized by my coworkers. My base guys were in the forefront, bearing a sign: "RTM, you are a champion." Not a champion, I thought, for I have given nothing and received everything. I am just an average guy, a pilot fortunate enough to be able to do what he loves in the service of the Lord, in the Land of the Unexpected.

As I reflect on those times, it seems just yesterday that we landed in Port Moresby with our suitcases and three little children, and then I look up that baby boy, now a man, and realize it was a lifetime ago. I returned to PNG a year later to conduct some instructor pilot training on the Otter. I expected the greetings from my friends and coworkers. But as I stepped out from a store, and man with a big buai-stained grin greeted me with, "Richard, welcome back." Then I was in another store, and the cashier spoke to me, "Richard, is that you?" Try as I might, I have no recollection of meeting these people, and yet there it was. I tell folks that we invested our kids' childhood in missions, often unaware of the impact we were having on those around us. With each new welcome, I was reminded that we simply went where God led, doing what we could to see isolated people physically and spiritually transformed in Christ's name. To realize that our family was responsible for transformation was, well, Unexpected!

# ABOUT THE AUTHOR

RICHARD ALWAYS WANTED to fly, but he could never have imagined where that dream would take him.

Born in England, Richard's family emigrated to Canada when he was in junior high. It was at a summer camp during high school that he felt the call to be a missionary pilot. Richard met his wife, Jennifer, at Bible college; and following the birth of their last child, the family departed for Papua New Guinea to serve with Mission Aviation Fellowship.

Seventeen years later, having raised their three children through high school graduation and with a bucket full of near-unbelievable tales, Richard and Jennifer returned to Canada.

Richard and Jennifer continue to serve with Mission Aviation Fellowship, training up future generations of mission aviation families at Prairie College in Three Hills, Alberta, Canada.

CPSIA information can be obtained
at www.ICGtesting.com
Printed in the USA
LVHW031935030519
616625LV00002B/10